The Dynamics of Foreign-Policy Decisionmaking in China

The Dynamics of Foreign-Policy Decisionmaking in China

Lu Ning

WestviewPress
A Division of HarperCollinsPublishers

All rights reserved. Printed in the United States of America. No part of this publication may be reproduced or transmitted in any form or by any means, electronic or mechanical, including photocopy, recording, or any information storage and retrieval system, without permission in writing from the publisher.

Copyright © 1997 by Lu Ning

Published in 1997 in the United States of America by Westview Press, 5500 Central Avenue, Boulder, Colorado 80301-2877, and in the United Kingdom by Westview Press, 12 Hid's Copse Road, Cumnor Hill, Oxford OX2 9JJ

A CIP catalog record for this book is available from the Library of Congress.
ISBN 0-8133-3315-6

The paper used in this publication meets the requirements of the American National Standard for Permanence of Paper for Printed Library Materials Z39.48-1984.

10   9   8   7   6   5   4   3   2   1

Contents

Introduction: An Emerging Giant? ... 1
Notes, 5

1   The Foreign Affairs Structure ... 7

   An Overview of the Political Power Structure, 7
   The Foreign-Policy Decisionmaking Structure, 8
   Notes, 17

2   The Organization of a Bureaucracy and Sectoral
    Mechanism and Processes ... 20

   The Anatomy of a Bureaucracy: The MFA, 20
   Policy Initiation, Coordination, and Subversion, 33
   Notes, 35

3   The Case of the MFA—Its History, Cadres' Corps,
    and Political Culture ... 40

   Its History and Cadres' Corps, 40
   The Political Culture, 54
   Notes, 66

4   Main Actors—The Central Leadership ... 76

   In the Mao Era, 77
   In the Deng Era, 87
   Notes, 95

5   Main Actors—Institutions and Individuals ... 106

   Foreign Affairs Institutions, 106
   Individual Bureaucrats and Researchers, 136
   Notes, 143

6 Changing Dynamics in Foreign-Policy Decisionmaking   150

   Foreign-Policy Decisionmaking in the Era of Mao, 150
   Foreign-Policy Decisionmaking in the Deng Era, 156
   Notes, 166

7 Western Theories and Chinese Practices   171

   The Classical School, 171
   The Institutional School, 175
   Theory and Practice: A Summary, 176
   Notes, 180

Appendix I: Foreign-Policy Decisionmaking Structure   185
Appendix II: The Foreign Affairs Office
   of the State Council   187
Appendix III: The Ministry of Foreign Affairs   189
Appendix IV: The Ministry of Foreign Trade
   and Economic Cooperation (MOFTEC)   191
Appendix V: The Hong Kong and Macau Affairs Office
   of the State Council (HMAO)   195
Appendix VI: The Taiwan Affairs Office of the
   State Council (TAO)   197
Appendix VII: The Overseas Chinese Affairs Office
   of the State Council (OCAO)   199
Appendix VIII: Xinhua News Agency   203
Bibliography   205
About the Book and Author   211
Index   213

Introduction:
An Emerging Giant?

The end of the Cold War has dramatically shifted the focus of international relations to trade and economy. Nowhere is the quest for economic growth pursued with such single-mindedness than in the Asia-Pacific region where its success is rapidly transforming this vast and diverse region from Ulan Bator to Jakarta, from Urumchi to Tokyo. Increasingly countries in the region view their national security in terms of sustained economic growth. The economies of the Asia-Pacific region (excluding the United States and Canada) now account for 34 percent of world output. Their share is expected to reach more than 40 percent. Trade between the United States and the Asia-Pacific region is 40 percent larger than U.S.-West European trade.

The most noticeable is the recent rise of China. In the past 18 years since China embarked on a course of economic reform, China's real Gross National Product growth has registered an average rate of more than nine percent a year. Measured in terms of purchasing power, China's economy now ranks third, behind only that of the United States and Japan.[1] If it maintains the current rate of growth, which the World Bank says is likely to happen, in about 15 years, China would have surpassed the United States and become the world's biggest economy.[2]

The implications of this transformation for the rest of the world have not been fully assessed. Already we are witnessing some of its impact on international relations:

- China's continued trade in missile and nuclear technologies is causing serious tensions between China and the United States, which in the past two years has twice imposed sanctions against the former;
- China's military modernization program—its post-Cold War arms purchases and shift of its military doctrine to "fighting local wars"—together with its continuing territorial disputes in the South China Sea have caused anxieties among its Southeast Asian neighbors;
- China's growing trade surplus with the United States and Western Europe has become a major point of friction between China and those countries;

- Partly because of the dynamic growth in China, East and Southeast Asian economies, which in the past had been dependent on the markets in industrialized countries and thus vulnerable to their economic downturns, have been able to maintain their economic growth through the last economic recession in the West. The growing economic integration of South China, Hong Kong and Taiwan may soon emerge as a new engine of growth for the region;
- China's high economic growth rate is outstripping the growth of its domestic energy supply. Since the second half of 1993, China has, perhaps irreversibly, become a net oil importer. Most of its future oil imports will have to come from the Middle East, particularly the Gulf region, via the South China Sea.[3]

If the current trends continue, China will become a much more significant player in world affairs in a decade. However, as its economy is rapidly being integrated into the world economy, China maintains a communist system of political control by a single party. Under this political system, major decisions, particularly political and foreign policy decisions, are made with little transparency. This is in sharp contrast to the significant impact these decisions are likely to have on the rest of the world, and hence likely to produce great uncertainties that may have serious implications for future international relations and maintenance of world peace.

In the meantime, foreign policy decisionmaking in China is undergoing a period of transition. In the early years of the People's Republic of China, Mao Zedong allowed a limited degree of top leadership participation in some of the key foreign policy discussions and debates, as in the early decision to enter into strategic alliance with the Soviet Union, known as "leaning to one side" in the new regime's foreign policy orientation, and most importantly the decision to intervene in the Korean conflict in 1950.

However this limited involvement on the part of the top communist leadership would soon come to an end when Mao assumed an increasing totalitarian role after stifling dissent first in society (the 1957 Anti-Rightist Campaign) and later within the Communist Party (the 1959 Lushan Conference). By the end of the first decade of the communist victory, a strong-man model emerged in China's foreign policy decisionmaking. Together with high level appointments and military affairs, foreign policy decisionmaking became one of the three most centralized areas in China's political system. Mao, as Chairman of the Communist Party and its Military Commission, dominated foreign policy decisionmaking until his death in 1976.

Since the death of Mao, China under Deng Xiaoping has undertaken a program of reform and opening to the outside world. The political system as a result is evolving from a totalitarian to an authoritarian model.[4] China's foreign policy decisionmaking has also been in a process of transformation from a "strong-man" model to one more characterized by bureaucratic, sectorial and regional competition.

As the Long March generation passes from the scene, the new generation of political leaders lacks both authority and charisma to dominate foreign policy decisionmaking. Foreign affairs bureaucracies have become increasingly influential. At the same time, in the process of decentralization and opening to the outside world, new actors like the defense industry, the People's Liberation Army (PLA), and provincial authorities, which had previously played little role in foreign policy decisionmaking, have now gained a stronger voice in foreign affairs. Already overseas arms sales by the defense industry and the PLA, and pirating of intellectual properties, textile quota evasion and aggressive marketing of prison-labor products, some with tacit approval by provincial authorities, have become major points of contention between China and the West.

What are the implications of this transformation in China's foreign policy decisionmaking? Will China emerge in the next century as a superpower, playing a hegemonic role in world affairs like the former Soviet Union, or is it going to follow the Japanese model content with a status of an economic giant? Or is the new model of bureaucratic, sectorial and provincial competition going to end up in a fractionalization of foreign policy decisionmaking (a clear possibility if the failure of the "market-Leninist" approach leads to the country's disintegration as predicted in a 1994 Pentagon commissioned study[5]) in that country of 1.2 billion people armed with nuclear weapons?

Because of the excessive secrecy with which China has guarded its foreign policy decisionmaking, its structure, mechanism and processes have always been more or less an enigma to Western sinologists and policy analysts. Although there have been a wealth of Western literature on China's foreign policy since 1949, few have dealt directly with foreign policy decisionmaking. Of the few studies that focus on the issue, besides unveiling the *formal* structure of China's foreign policy establishment, they generally fall short of explaining the internal mechanism and dynamics of the policy making process, thus are inadequate as a guide to understanding China's foreign policy decisionmaking.

Since 1978, especially since the late 1980s, a flood of information detailing some key foreign policy decisions has become available through the publication, mostly in Chinese, of memoirs of important political figures and senior diplomats who either participated in or witnessed some of the decisions made in the past, and of historical research on past events like the Korean War conducted by Chinese scholars with access to official archives. The availability of some information from Russian archives greatly complements the Chinese materials. This study relies heavily on eyewitness accounts, research products of those with access to archival materials and personal experience.

This is a study that centers on only one particular aspect of decisionmaking in the People's Republic of China. It is neither a comprehensive survey of decisionmaking in China nor an attempt to cover all aspects of foreign policy decisionmaking. This is because decisionmaking in terms of structures, processes, mechanisms and dynamics varies greatly in different fields and on different levels. It is therefore well worth it to take note of the following points to avoid undue expectations—and disappointments:

- The scope of this study is deliberately restricted to the area of politico-military decisionmaking with a focus on the top leadership and its chief foreign policy bureaucracy—the Ministry of Foreign Affairs. As it is noted earlier, this is one of the most centralized areas in decisionmaking. Thus it is perilous to generalize the findings in this study.
- A disproportionate length is devoted to the examination of the role or interest of the PLA and the defense industries in the foreign policy process not because they have acquired preponderant or independent foreign policy roles, as often the conventional wisdom assumes, but to clarify issues that are of great interest in the West.
- On the other hand, the making of foreign economic decisions both at the center and local levels, though becoming increasingly central to China relations with the rest of the world, is dealt with only very briefly. The reason for this is that foreign economic decision making is such a complex and dynamic area of inquiry following a decade and a half of reforms and decentralization that it is necessary to deal with the subject in a separate study.
- Similarly local foreign affairs authorities are not examined in this study as they play no policy role in politico-military decisions.
- Most cases studied took place before 1990 because they are the ones that can be documented by the author. While a trend of decentralization continues in the 1990s and Chinese foreign policy has to cope with dramatic changes in the post-Tiananmen and post-Cold War environment, the basic structure, processes, mechanisms and dynamics in the making of China's foreign politico-military policy decisions have not changed substantially. The findings of this study thus remain relevant.

The author wishes to emphasize that this study is not intended to fit into any of the pigeonholes of existing paradigms with some of their ideological connotations; nor is it aimed at establishing an original comprehensive theoretical framework of its own. Rather it attempts to examine the changing dynamics of decisionmaking through a series of case studies against some of the existing Western theories on decisionmaking and on Chinese foreign policy as they are understood and found relevant by the author. One of its main purposes is to provoke discussions and debates, that, hopefully, may lead to a renewed quest by more competent scholars for a meaningful theoretical framework of foreign policy decisionmaking in China based on a better understanding of its structure, processes, mechanisms and dynamics.

Ironically 20 years after the Vietnam War in which the U.S. intervened to stop the now proven fallacious "Chinese communist expansion," Beijing again has to defend itself against an alleged "China threat" stemming largely from ideological grounds but also from a lack of transparency on the part of Beijing. This study hopes to shed some light on the main actors, the structure, the processes, the mechanisms and dynamics of making foreign politico-military decisions in the belief that as China integrates into the world economy and emerges as a world power, it is ultimately in its own interest to promote greater transparency in its decisionmaking process, not only in the field of economy and trade, but also in foreign policy. Excessive secrecy breeds misunderstanding and suspicion and is ultimately detrimental to Beijing's own interest.

Notes

1. Steven Greenhouse, "New Tally of World's Economies Catapults China into Third Place," *The New York Times,* May 20, 1993.

2. Jim Rohwer, "China: The Titan Stirs," *The Economist,* November 28, 1992. The combined economies of China, Hong Kong and Taiwan will overtake that of the United States in less than a decade. Greenhouse, op. cit.

3. According to Mr. David Fridley of East-West Center, by the year 2000, China's crude oil import will reach 1.1 million b/d, of which 950,000 b/d will come from the Middle East. Personal communication, April 1993.

Marcus W. Brauchli, "China's Oil Needs Outstrip Its Supply: Booming Nation Turns to Imports, Foreigners for Help," *The Wall Street Journal,* September 14, 1993.

4. Nicholas D. Kristof, "China Sees 'Market-Leninism' as Way to Future," *The New York Times,* September 6, 1993.

5. *China in the Near Term,* Under Secretary of Defense (Policy) 1994 Summer Study Organized by the Director, Net Assessment, Newport, Rhode Island, August 1–10, 1994.

1

The Foreign Affairs Structure

**An Overview of the
Political Power Structure**

In order to understand fully the foreign policy establishment and its structure, it is necessary first of all to briefly examine the general power structure of the People's Republic of China. The governing regime of the PRC consists of three major vertical systems (*xitong*): the Communist Party, the Government, and the Military.[1] At the apex of these systems is the Political Bureau of the Chinese Communist Party, which is often further crystallized in the form of a leadership core (*lingdao hexin*), as after "June 4" and Deng Xiaoping's formal retirement in 1989, or, of a single person—like Mao Zedong, as during the Mao era.

The three major systems operate on five levels: (1) central (*zhongyang*), (2) provincial (for the party and government) / army (for the military)—*sheng/jün*, (3) prefectural (civil) / division (military)—*di/shi*, (4) county (civil) / regiment (military)—*xian/tuan*, and (5) township (civil) / battalion (military)—*xiang/ying*.[2]

Horizontally, on each level there exists a set of seven standard institutions: (1) the Communist Party (CP) Committee, (2) the CP Advisory Committee,[3] (3) the CP Discipline Inspection Committee of the Party system; (4) the People's Congress, (5) the Government, (6) the People's Political Consultative Conference of the government system and (7) the Military.[4]

For the purpose of efficiently controlling and running the whole political system, this system is divided into six major functional sectors (*xitong* or *kou* for short) that cut across the three major systems of the party, government and the military. Each sector is supervised by a member of the Standing Committee of the Political Bureau of the Communist Party of China (CPC). The six sectors are as follows:

1. Military Affairs;
2. Legal Affairs which includes legislative, judiciary and law enforcement affairs;
3. Administrative Affairs which includes industrial and agricultural production, finance and commerce, foreign affairs, health, education, science, sports, etc.;
4. Propaganda Affairs which include media and cultural affairs;
5. United Front Affairs which include non-communist political parties, religion, minority, Taiwan and Hongkong and Macao affairs;
6. Mass Organization Affairs which include union, youth, women organizations and associations.

Under each one of the six major sectors there are also a number of sub-sectors, such as the foreign affairs, which is often supervised directly by an important member of the Politburo through an institutionalized or non-standing organ like leading small group (LSG) (*lingdao xiaozu*).

This system of sectoral division for management known as *guikou guanli* is an informal one in the sense that it does not appear on any of the formal organizational charts of the Party, Government and Military.[5] The purpose is for the CPC Politburo Standing Committee to exercise centralized control of the whole political system and its processes.

The Foreign Policy Decisionmaking Structure

The Apex

One of the characteristics of the Chinese political system is the high concentration of political power in the CPC. Within the party, power is further concentrated in the hands of one or a few leaders. Foreign affairs, together with the military affairs, and party organizational (high ranking personnel) affairs, have long been considered one of the most sensitive areas that demand an even higher concentration of decisionmaking power.

The Paramount Leader and Leadership Nuclear Circle   On May 31, 1989, on the eve of "June 4" crackdown, Deng Xiaoping in his talks with CPC Politburo Standing Committee members Li Peng and Yao Yilin said: the leadership nucleus (lingdao hexin) of the CPC's first generation is Mao Zedong, that of the second generation leadership is Deng Xiaoping, and that of the third is going to be Jiang Zemin.[6] Although the speech was meant to admonish the two to submit to the leadership of the newly nominated Jiang Zemin, it reveals that in the Chinese political system the ultimate power rests in the hands of a single paramount political leader.

Foreign affairs has always been one of the key areas where the ultimate decisionmaking power is retained by the paramount leader. This paramount leader may or may not be the Chairman or General Secretary of the Party or State President, but most often he controls the military as the Chairman of the Central Military Commission (CMC).[7]

On his side, the paramount leader creates an informal nuclear circle consisting of one or two members personally designated by himself. In the Mao era, this nuclear circle included Liü Shaoqi and Zhou Enlai in 1949–1966, Lin Biao in 1966–1971, Zhou Enlai in 1971–1974, Deng Xiaoping in 1975, Hua Guofeng in 1976. In the Deng era, there were Chen Yün, and before 1986 Hu Yaobang, before 1989 Zhao Ziyang, after 1989 Jiang Zemin, and after 1990 Yang Shangkun. Up to late 1992 the circle consisted of Deng, Chen, Yang and Jiang.[8] Since then, Yang retired in late 1992, and Chen died in April 1995. Deng in declining health is no longer involved in decisionmaking.[9] Jiang and Li Peng form the new nuclear circle. The paramount leader and the leadership nuclear circle wield the ultimate foreign policy decisionmaking power in China as they can veto or ratify decisions made by the Politburo.

The Politburo and Its Standing Committee The Politburo is the most important institution of political power in China. It stands at the apex of the formal foreign policy structure under the informal personalized arrangement of supreme political power of the leading nucleus and nuclear circle. However the Politburo consists of members from provinces and other cities than Beijing and its size is comparatively large. These two factors make it too cumbersome to decide on foreign policy issues that often demand immediate attention or direction. Therefore real foreign policy decisionmaking power rests with its Standing Committee. However most important foreign policy decisions such as war and peace and a major shift in foreign policy orientation are often still subject to deliberations by the Politburo for legitimization.

In more recent years, the Politburo is often used as a training ground for future senior political leaders.[10] Except for its members that oversee specific foreign affairs functional departments in the government and the party, and for its Standing Committee members, most of the Politburo members are marginally involved in the making of foreign policy decisions.

The highest foreign policy decisionmaking institution is the Standing Committee of the Politburo. Normally the Standing Committee includes the Chairman of the CPC, the Chairman of the CMC, the State President, the Chairman of the Standing Committee of the National People's Congress, and the Chairman of the Chinese People's Consultative Conference.

The party constitution adopted at the 12th Party Congress stipulates that the General Secretary, the Director of the Central Advisory Commission, the First Secretary of the Central Disciplinary Commission and the Chairman of the CMC must be members of the Standing Committee. At the time these posts were held respectively by Hu Yaobang, Chen Yün and Deng Xiaoping. The three other members were State President Li Xiannian, NPC Standing Committee Chairman Ye Jianying, and the Premier of the State Council Zhao Ziyang.

Members of the Standing Committee of the 13th Party Congress were Party Secretary Zhao Ziyang, Premier Li Peng of the State Council, Hu Qili, Yao Yilin, and Qiao Shi. Both Zhao Ziyang and Hu Qili were forced out of office after "June 4" in 1989 and were replaced by Jiang Zemin and Li Ruihuan.

Since 1992, the Politburo Standing Committee of the 14th Party Congress consists of CPC General Secretary Jiang Zemin, Premier of the State Council Li Peng, Chairman of the Standing Committee of the NPC Qiao Shi, Chairman of the People's Consultative Conference Li Ruihuan, Vice Premier Zhu Rongji, Vice Chairman of the CMC Liü Huaqing and Hu Jintao.

Within the Standing Committee, one member, usually one with more experience in the field, takes charge of the foreign affairs sector—*waishi kou*—as the Head of the CPC Central Foreign Affairs Leading Small Group—*Zhongyang Waishi Lingdao Xiaozu*. From 1977 to 1987, it was Li Xiannian. Since 1987 it has been Li Peng.

The Secretariat In the official power structure, immediately under the Politburo there is the CPC Secretariat. Its role however has been ill-defined and changed from time to time. From the late 1940s up to 1956, the Secretariat was the supreme decisionmaking body within the CPC, serving as the present-day Standing Committee of the Politburo.[11] In the party organizational restructuring on the 8th Party Congress of 1956, the Secretariat as we know it today was created in subordination to the Politburo to carry out day-to-day operations. It was abolished during the Cultural Revolution, but re-established at the 5th Plenum of the 11th Party Congress in 1980 by Deng Xiaoping to circumvent his political rival, Party Chairman Hua Guofeng and the conservative dominated Politburo.

In June 1958, the CPC Central Committee and the State Council issued a joint circular entitled *Circular concerning the Establishment of Financial and Economic, Political and Legal, Foreign Affairs, Science, and Cultural and Education Small Groups,* in which it stipulates: "The decisionmaking power concerning major policy orientations and principles and guidelines rests with the Politburo. The Secretariat is responsible for making detailed plans and overseeing (their implementation).... The actual implementation and decisionmaking authority regarding implementing details belong to government agencies and their party groups."[12] According to the 1982 Party Constitution, the Secretariat is the executive body (*banshi jigou*) of the Party Center to handle the day-to-day work (*chuli dangzhongyang richang gongzuo*). Therefore officially the Secretariat is not a decisionmaking body. Rather as the executive body of the Politburo, it plans and supervises the implementation of decisions made by the Politburo.

Of the three major systems, the Secretariat has always exercised direct leadership over the party bureaucracies, but its control of the government and particularly the military has not been consistent. When it was first recreated in 1956 under Deng Xiaoping, it managed all the three systems with the Secretary General of the CMC, who was in charge of the day-to-day work of the military, a permanent member of the Secretariat. When it was revived in 1980 after its abolishment during the Cultural Revolution, it continued its past tradition of a broader role that encompassed the military.

Its power reached a new height at the 12th Party Congress with a total of 12 members. But with the downfall of its General Secretary Hu Yaobang in 1987, its influence declined. At the 13th Party Congress, to further weaken the power of Hu's associates who remained in the Secretariat, the Secretariat's role was limited to running party affairs. Senior government and military officials were withdrawn from its rank. Its size was reduced to six. This was done under the pretext of separating the party from government. After "June 4," four members of the Secretariat were dismissed. Of the four members of the new Secretariat, three are members of the Politburo Standing Committee. Thus the Secretariat existed only in name. For a time after CMC Secretary General Yang Baibing joined the body at the 5th Plenum of 13th Party Congress in late 1989, it looked that the Secretariat was to regain some of its lost power. However the subsequent 14th Party Congress in 1992 confirmed that the role of the Secretariat is restricted to only managing the party affairs.

Although in reality, the Secretariat has been at times involved in some of the major decisions, it has *never* played a decisionmaking role in foreign affairs, which before the Cultural Revolution was overseen personally by Premier Zhou Enlai in conjunction with the Politburo with Mao making the ultimate calls. During the Deng era, all the major foreign policy decisions were made by the Standing Committee of the Politburo and Deng with his nuclear circle.

The CPC Central (Committee) Foreign Affairs Leading Small Group

The body that takes overall charge of foreign affairs is the CPC Central Foreign Affairs Leading Small Group. Headed by a member of the Standing Committee of the Politburo, the Foreign Affairs LSG supervises policy implementation and coordination of the foreign affairs sector known as *waishi kou*. First established in 1958, the LSG consists of key members of the Politburo Standing Committee and the top bureaucrats of government and party foreign affairs agencies. More recently it also includes a senior member of the military.

However this body is NOT a standing *institution* and has no permanent staff. It instead relies on the Foreign Affairs Office of the State Council for staff work and to exercise overall sectoral coordination. The Foreign Affairs Office of the State Council, as the executive body of the Central Foreign Affairs Leading Small Group, therefore, serves as the central processing unit (CPU) between the decisionmakers and implementing organs in the party, government and military systems.[13] Similarly all decisions which are beyond the mandates of bureaucracies must be submitted to the decisionmakers at the Center through this CPU, regardless of from which of the three major systems it originates. From here all foreign affairs activities of the PRC are coordinated and this concept is called *guikou* and the Foreign Affairs Office of the State Council is the general entrance/exit for decisions in the foreign affairs sector.

At the time of their creation in 1958, the functions of the LSGs were not very well defined. The circular only emphasizes that the LSGs "are directly subordinate to the CPC Politburo and Secretariat and report directly to the two bodies."[14] At the 2nd plenum of the CPC Politburo held on December 16, 1987, a reform package was adopted for the CPC Central Committee institutions. Under this reform package, the functions of the organs of the Party Central Committee are redefined in three categories according to the roles they play: (1) decisionmaking consulting bodies—*juece zixün jigou*, (2) executive bodies—*banshi jigou*, (3) service institutions—*shiye jigou*. All leading small groups fall under the first category. They are composed of leading members of the relevant government, party and military ministerial ranking agencies, and in most cases have no permanent office or staff. They convene regular meetings to discuss issues, exchange ideas and put forward proposals as policy alternatives for the Politburo and its Standing Committee to make decisions.[15] However as the LSG provides a forum for the top decisionmakers and top professional bureaucrats to meet face to face, the policy preferences and recommendations by the LSGs are likely to have an important impact on the outcome of the final decision. Therefore the Foreign Affairs LSG in fact plays a pivotal role in the decisionmaking process.

The foreign affairs sector is further divided into a number of subsectors. When the Central Foreign Affairs LSG was created in 1958, the sector was further divided into six subsectors with six different lead party, government or military institutions identified as their respective subsectoral CPU or entrance/exit:[16]

1. The Ministry of Foreign Affairs for all political, legislative (including NPC), judicial, humanitarian interactions with foreign countries.

2. The Ministry of Foreign Trade for all commercial, economic, business and financial interactions.
3. The Commission for External Cultural Liaison for all cultural, art, education, information, mass media, health interactions.
4. The State Science Commission for all scientific and technological interactions.
5. The Ministry of Defense for all defense-related interactions.[17]
6. The Commission for Overseas Chinese Affairs for overseas Chinese affairs management.

In the 1987 reorganization of the Central Foreign Affairs LSG, it was further consolidated into five subsectors: government, party, military, economic and trade, and propaganda.[18]

In order to better handle issues that cut across vertical government, party and military systems, some CPC central leading small groups have been abolished and additional LSGs set up. For example, before 1988, there existed a CPC Central External Propaganda Small Group headed by Zhu Muzhi with the CPC Propaganda Department as the lead institution. However at the 2nd plenum of the 13th Politburo held on December 16, 1987, it was decided to disband the group due to the confusion over its line of authority and to its ineffectiveness.[19] The management of overseas propaganda is apparently placed under the jurisdiction of the Foreign Affairs Office of the State Council, which handles it in conjunction with the Information Office of the State Council. (See Appendix II).

In 1987 before the death of Jiang Jingguo (Chiang Ching-kuo) in Taiwan, a CPC Taiwanese Affairs Leading Small Group was created to strengthen the Taiwanese affairs. It was headed by the then Politburo member and Executive Vice Chairman of the CMC Yang Shangkun and its members included Liao Hui, Director of the State Council's Overseas Chinese Affairs Office, Yang Side, Director of the State Council's Taiwanese Affairs Office, and Yan Mingfu, Director of the CPC Central United Front Department.[20] Now the LSG is said to be headed by Vice Premier and Foreign Minister Qian Qichen.

On September 26, 1989, an additional LSG regarding military sales abroad was created under the title of the Military Products Export Leading Small Group, with the CMC as the lead body.[21]

The Central Bureaucracies

Beneath the structure at the apex of political power, there are a number of institutions which operate independently in foreign affairs. Most of them are of provincial/army rank. In the government system, they are chiefly the Ministry of Foreign Affairs, the Ministry of Foreign Trade and Economic Cooperation and Xinhua News Agency. In the party system, there is the CPC Central (Committee) International Liaison Department. In the military system, there is the PLA General Staff Department. The Commission of Science, Technology and Industry for National Defense (COSTIND) which oversees China's defense research and development (R&D) and defense industry straddles the government and the military systems.[22]

In addition to restricting the decisionmaking power of central bureaucracies and their party groups to implementing details, the 1958 CPC Central Committee and State Council joint circular further stipulates: "With regard to major policy orientation, principles and guidelines, and to implementation planning and supervision, government organs and their party groups have the power to make recommendations. But the decisionmaking power belongs to the Party Center."[23] This rule is still in effect today.

The leadership structure within a government ministry or party department at the central level was until recently almost a miniature of the central party structure and mechanism described above.

Officially the system at the ministerial level was called *dangwei lingdao xia de xingzheng shouzhang fuzezhi*—the system of administrative chief executive responsibility under the leadership of the party committee or party group.[24] The ministerial Party Group—*dangzu*, like the Politburo, was the highest decisionmaking body in the bureaucracy before the 13th Congress of the CPC. It consisted of most of the ministers including vice and assistant ministers. Within the Party Group there were also a very few—often only one or two—who were identified as key or nuclear members—*dangzu hexin chengyüan*, equivalent to the Standing Committee members of the Politburo.

However at the 13th Party Congress, the Party constitution was revised to abolish the party group in the leadership structure of government bureaucracies, which conflicted with the minister-responsibility system introduced in the PRC Constitution.[25] This change is part of the political reform package introduced at the 13th Party Congress in an attempt to separate the party from the government so as to reduce party interference in the running of government affairs. In its place, the minister is designated as the chief executive under the administrative chief executive responsibility system—*xingzheng shouzhang fuzezhi*. A system of administrative conference—*xingzhen huiyi*—has been instituted to replace the Party Group meetings as the chief venue for collective decisionmaking.[26]

The chief executive—the minister, takes overall responsibility for running the bureaucracy. Under him, there is a division of labor among vice ministers and assistant ministers with each taking charge of a number of regional and/or functional departments—*si*, or bureaux—*jü*, in an arrangement similar to the practice of sectoral control of the Politburo Standing Committee.

Each regional or functional department or bureau has one chief officer in charge of the overall work of the department and also the work of one or two divisions—*chu*. He is assisted by two deputy chiefs who respectively take charge of a number of divisions. There is a fourth departmental ranking officer who oversees *zhengzhi gongzuo*—the political work of the department in the role of a political commissar in the military, only with much less power.

Further down the echelon, a division chief is assisted by two deputy chiefs with each in charge of a particular aspect of the division's responsibility. In a number of bureaucracies there is another layer in the power structure called *ke*—section.[27]

Between 1982 and 1984, a major reform of China's government and party bureaucracies took place. As a result, a post responsibility system known as *gangwei zeren zhi* has been established, under which the task, power and responsibility associated with each bureaucratic post are clearly defined and the size and composition of each unit are quantitatively set after an exercise called *dingbian dingyüan* (see Appendixes).[28] This was followed by a reform of the Chinese wage system in 1985.[29] A bureaucrat is now paid according to the bureaucratic post he holds instead of his ranking in the cadre system as in the past.[30]

As a result of these reform measures, the responsibilities and decisionmaking powers of each bureaucratic post is explicitly defined in the form of internal regulations. For all policy matters in foreign affairs, the decisionmaking power rests with the ministerial leaders and above. Departmental officials have the power to oversee the day-to-day operations that fall under their respective jurisdiction under established rules. Even for these kinds of decisions with clearly established rules and precedents, a proposed course of action is often referred to the responsible ministerial leader for ratification. For matters that have no rules or precedents to follow, it is usually up to the ministerial leadership and above to make the final call.

In the whole political system in China, the high level of concentration of decisionmaking power in foreign affairs, as noted earlier, is only matched by the high level personnel affairs and the military affairs.

The Local Foreign Affairs Structure

Foreign affairs offices exist in all provincial governments and governments of major municipalities that are open to foreigners. Provincial foreign affairs offices and foreign affairs offices of municipalities with provincial rank are normally of bureau/division (military) rank, while those of prefectural ranking municipalities are of county/regimental rank. A provincial or municipal party secretary or vice governor/mayor is usually designated to take charge of foreign affairs. Local foreign affairs LSGs also exist in provincial and major municipal governments.

Corresponding offices of foreign economic relations and trade, overseas Chinese affairs, Taiwanese affairs, etc. also exist in most of the provincial and municipal governments. These offices come under the dual jurisdiction of the relevant ministry in the central government and of the local government, with the former providing professional guidance while the latter is responsible for its day-to-day operations.

Few local offices also boast of their own research institutions. Notably the Shanghai Institute of International Relations under the Foreign Affairs Office of the Shanghai Municipal Government. However they are the exceptions rather than the rule. Most of the provincial and municipal offices rely on the cooperation of academies and universities situated within their boundaries to provide support and conduct research and analyses for the local authorities.

Decisionmaking Methodology

Finally, it is important to understand the methodology used in making decisions. Formally, the CPC adheres to a system called democratic centralism under which the majority rules. However, the higher the level, the more importance is attached to unanimity. Officially, the Standing Committee of the Politburo makes decisions on the basis of *consensus*. If deadlocked over an issue, the session is often recessed and followed by another round of informal consultations among its members and with the paramount leader or members of the nuclear circle. When repeated consultations fail to resolve the difference, it is often up to the paramount leader to make the final call known in Chinese as *paiban*.[31] Below this level, decisions are made by the chief executives of government, party and military institutions in consultation with their respective aides under the chief executive responsibility system. If necessary, an executive meeting known as *xingzhen huiyi* that involves the ministerial leadership is the forum to make decisions collectively.

In practice, decisions are seldom put to an actual vote although each member's opinion is made known by way of statements made during the meetings. The decisionmaking bodies at the Center and in a bureaucracy are not made up of members of equal standing as they are officially supposed to be. Rather they are often constructed in an informal hierarchical structure with each member deriving his place in this structure not only from the office he holds, but also from certain intangible factors such as seniority, experience, expertise, personal access etc. The authority of each member is in fact unequal.[32] When the recognized most authoritative person makes his opinion known, the rest of the members tend to concur.

Senior members sometimes may be able to persuade him if or when his opinion is not out of a firm conviction. Depending on their respective relationship with him, junior members generally would refrain from voicing a different opinion once the opinion of the most authoritative person is known. During the Mao era, all decisionmaking bodies were reduced to rubber stamps. The recent trend however points to more equality among members of the decisionmaking bodies at the Center. The emphasis on unanimity and consensus building at this level will probably not change.

Notes

1. Yan Huai, "*Zhongguo Dalu Zhengzhi Tizhi Qianlun* (Understanding the Political System of Contemporary China)," *Papers of the Center for Modern China*, No. 10, August 1991, p.#2.

2. Ibid.

3. The Advisory Committee in fact exists only at the Central and Provincial levels and in major cities where there has been a high concentration of revolutionary veterans. As it has often been used as a vehicle to ease their transition to retirement, there is ample reason to believe that its existence is only of a transitional nature.

4. The military consists of institutional and operational components at similar levels as the civilian system. On the institutional side, there are the seven military regions (Shenyang, Beijing, Lanzhou, Nanjing, Guangzhou, Jinan, and Chengdu), provincial military districts, prefectural level military subdistricts, and country and township departments of military affairs.

5. Yan, p.#6.

6. *Zhonggong Nianbao 1990* (CPC Yearbook 1990) (Taipei: Institute for the Study of Chinese Communist Problems, 1990).

7. In 1959 after the disastrous Great Leap Forward, Mao relinquished his State President title. From then on till his death in 1976, Mao remained the Chairman of the CPC and Chairman of the CMC. In 1976 Hua Guofeng succeeded Mao as the Chairman of the CMC. Although in reality he lost his power as the paramount leader to Deng Xiaoping at the 3rd Plenum of the 11th Party Congress at the end of 1978, he would remain in that post till 1982. This is usually considered an aberration. Deng after his rehabilitation in 1977 assumed the post of the Chairman of the CMC in 1982. In 1989 he relinquished this last official post and formally retired. He, however, remains the paramount leader in China.

8. Yan, pp.#20–21.

9. Personal communication with a MFA source, January 1995. Testimony of John Deutch, Director of the Central Intelligence Agency, before the US Senate Select Committee on Intelligence, February 22, 1996.

10. Yan.

11. At the 7th Party Congress, the following five people were elected *secretaries* of the Party Secretariat: Mao Zedong, Zhu De, Liü Shaoqi, Zhou Enlai, and Ren Bishi. Ren later fell seriously ill. In June 1950, Chen Yün became acting secretary

and formally replaced Ren in October that year when the latter died. The five were later known as the Big Five Secretaries (*wu da shuji*) of the Party. Qiü De et al (eds), *Zhonghua Renmin Gongheguo Shilu* (A Chronological Record of the People's Republic of China), Vol V, *Wenxian yü Yanjiü* (Documents and Research) (Changchun: Jilin Renmin Chubanshe, 1994), p.#1.

12. Zheng Qian, Pang Song, Han Gang and Zhang Zhanbin, *Dangdai Zhongguo Zhengzhi Tizhi Fazhan Gaiyao* (An Outline of the Evolution of the Contemporary Chinese Political System) (Beijing: Zhonggong Dangshi Ziliao Chubanshe, 1988), p.#89.

13. Like many similar cases in the Chinese power structure, the Central Foreign Affairs Leading Small Group and the Foreign Affairs Office of the State Council are one institution, one team of staffers, but with two name plates (*yiban renma, liangkuai paizi*).

14. Zheng Qian et al, p.#91.

15. Jiang Weiwen, "*Zhonggong Gaoceng Jigou Gaige Fangan Da Pilu: Zhonggong Gaoceng Renshi Da Tiaozheng* (A Big Exposé of the Reform Plan for the High-level CPC Institutions: A Big Reshuffle of the High-ranking CPC Officials)," *Guangjiaojing* (Wide Angle), no. 184, January 16, 1988, pp.#6–7. The second category includes such Central Committee institutions as the Central General Affairs Office, the Central Organization Department, the Central United Front Department and the Central International Liaison Department. They are responsible for handling the day-to-day work of the CPC under the leadership of the Politburo and its Standing Committee. The third category includes the party newspaper *Renmin Ribao* (People's Daily), the Central Party School and the Party History Research Office.

16. According to the 1958 Joint Circular of the CPC Central Committee and the State Council regarding the establishment of the CPC Central Foreign Affairs Small Group and the Foreign Affairs Office of the State Council. *Zhonghua Renmin Gongheguo Jingji Guanli Dashiji* (Chronicle of the Economic Management of the People's Republic of China) (Beijing: China Economics Publishers, 1986), p.#106.

17. As in the case of the State Council Foreign Affairs Office, the Foreign Affairs Bureau of the PLA General Staff Department, also known as the Foreign Affairs Bureau of the Ministry of Defense, serves as the executive body of the CMC Foreign Affairs Office in the one office, one team of staff and, in this case, three name plates arrangement.

18. Jiang Weiwen, p.#8.

19. Ibid., p.#7.

20. Ge Ai, "*Zhongguo Duitai Gongzuo Xinbushu* (CPC's New Arrangement for its Taiwanese Work)," *Guangjiaojing* (Wide Angle), December 1988, p.#12.

21. The LSG, headed by CMC Vice Chairman Liü Huaqing and Vice Premier Zou Jiahua, consists of vice ministerial officials of the defense industry and the MFA. Yan Kong, "China's Arms Trade Bureaucracy," *Jane's Intelligence Review*, February 1994, p.#80.

22. COSTIND was created on May 10, 1982 by merging the Defence Science and Technology Commission, the National Defence Industry Office, and the CMC's Science, Technology and Equipment Commission. Representing the inter-

est of the defense industry, COSTIND is under the dual leadership of the CMC and State Council. Ibid.

23. Zheng Qian et al, p.#91.

24. Pang Song and Han Gang, "*Dang he Guojia Lingdao Tizhi de Lishi Kaocha yü Gaige Zhanwang* (A Historical Review and Reform Outlook of the Party and State Leadership Systems)," *Zhongguo Shehui Kexiie* (China Social Sciences), No. 6, November 10, 1987, p.#5.

25. Ibid., p.#16.

26. Ibid., p.#20.

27. The exact number of vice ministers, assistant ministers, deputy directors of departments and deputy division chiefs may vary with different bureaucracies.

28. Lee, Hong Yung, *From Revolutionary Cadres to Party Technocrats in Socialist China* (Berkeley: University of California Press, 1991), Chapter 11.

29. On June 8, 1985, CPC Central Committee and the State Council jointly issued *Guojia Jiguan he Shiye Danwei Gongzuo Renyüan Gongzi Biaozhun* (Standard Pay Scale for Personnel of State and Government Organs and Institutions), which was officially implemented in July 1985.

30. Between 1956 and 1985, a 25 grade cadre system was in place. According to this scale, cadres of grades 1 to 6 were senior leaders of the country, 7 to 13 were high ranking cadres, 14 to 17 were middle ranking cadres and 18 and under were ordinary cadres. All Chinese bureaucrats were paid according to their respective ranking in this system and not the actual post they held. For instance, Zhou Enlai was paid as a 2nd grade cadre instead of his premiership, and Jiang Qing, Mao's wife, was paid as a 9th grade cadre. See Li Zhisui, *Mao Zedong Siren Yisheng Huiyilu* (The Private Life of Chairman Mao) (Taipei: China Times Publishing Company, 1994) p.#333, and Quan Yanchi, *Zouxia Shengtan de Zhou Enlai* (Zhou Enlai Desanctified) (Beijing: Zhonggong Zhongyang Dangxiao Chubanshe, 1993), p.#220. This system was replaced by a 12 grade pay scale linked to the bureaucrat's post in the bureaucracy in 1985. See Yan, p.#23.

31. Hu Qiaomu, former CPC Politburo member and secretary to Mao Zedong, Washington, DC, May 1989. This process is best illustrated by the initial paralysis and indecision of the Politburo Standing Committee caused by Zhao Ziyang's dissent during the political crisis in May and June 1989, as described in Yang Shangkun's speeches at the May 22, 1989 meeting of party, government and military cadres in Beijing, at the enlarged CMC emergency meeting on May 25, 1989, and Zhao Ziyang's speech at the 4th Central Committee Plenum of the 13th Party Congress in June 1989, *Xinbao* (Hong Kong), June 4, 1994, p.#9.

32. It is perhaps helpful to think of these bodies in terms of a Chinese family with a patriarch, the senior son and his brothers and their wives and children arranged in a hierarchy in accordance with Confucian teachings. It is no accident that in private Yang Shangkun would refer to Deng as *laoyezi*—grand patriarch. Xü Jiatun, *Xü Jiatun Xianggang Huiyilu II* (Xü Jiatun Hong Kong Memoirs II) (Hong Kong: H.K. Lianhebao Youxian Gongsi, 1993), p.#373.

2

The Organization of a Bureaucracy and Sectoral Mechanism and Processes

The central foreign affairs bureaucracy is mainly represented by the Ministry of Foreign Affairs (MFA), the Ministry of Foreign Trade and Economic Cooperation (MOFTEC) under the State Council, the International Liaison Department of the CPC Central Committee, and the General Staff Department (GSD) under the CMC. Each represents the CPU for a subsector. In the current power structure, these bureaucracies are of equal ranking and except for the GSD, organized in a similar way. Even though they perform different functions within the foreign affairs establishment, they follow some standardized or well-established procedures and processes. Instead of going through each one of the bureaucracies, this chapter will focus mainly on one of them—the MFA, which has a reputation of being the most professional among its bureaucratic equals thanks to years of direct supervision by one of the chief architects of contemporary Chinese diplomacy—Zhou Enlai.

The Anatomy of a Bureaucracy: The MFA

The Ministry of Foreign Affairs (MFA), *waijiao bu*, is administratively a subordinate ministerial organ under the State Council, *guowuyüan*. Professionally though, the MFA reports directly to the Standing Committee of the Political Bureau through the Group Leader of the (CPC) Central (Committee) Foreign Affairs Leading Small Group (LSG), who is often a member of the Politburo Standing Committee designated to take charge of the foreign affairs sector, *waishi kou*.[1]

The MFA is easily one of the largest central bureaucracies with its officially approved staff size fixed at 2660 people in 1990. Its actual size that year was 3201. In comparison, The Ministry of Machine Building and Electronics Industries—its closest rival in the central government system—had a staff size of only 1654.[2]

The Organization of the Bureaucracy

The MFA formal structure currently consists of the General Office, plus 18 *external* affairs departments and offices of departmental rank, and five *internal* affairs departments (see Appendix III).[3]

The General Office, *bangong ting*, though of departmental ranking, is a first-among-equal department. It supervises such vital units as the Confidential Communications Bureau, *jiyao jü*,[4] and controls the Confidential Traffic Division, *jiyao jiaotong chu*, and the powerful Secretariat, *mishu chu*.[5] The Confidential Communications Bureau is itself a department that manages China's diplomatic communications, mainly with China's diplomatic representations abroad. The Confidential Traffic Division is in fact a confidential document delivery and exchange service.[6] The Secretariat consists of two groups of people, with one group manning the 24-hour Situation Room, formally known as *bangong ting zhiban shi* or *banzhi* for short, and the other consisting of personal secretaries to the ministers. According to regulations, the Foreign Minister has two secretaries, and each Vice and Assistant Minister has one.[7] The General Office also serves as a liaison between the MFA and provincial Foreign Affairs Offices through its Office of Local Foreign Affairs, *difang waishi bangongshi*.[8]

The 18 *external* affairs departments and offices are further categorized into two types: one group called regional departments, *diqü si*, the other group functional departments, *yewu si*. There are currently seven regional departments—Africa, *feizhou si*, Asia, *yazhou si*, West Asia and North Africa (Middle East), *xiya beifei* (or *yafei* for short) *si*, Eastern Europe and Central Asia, *dong'ou zhongya* (*ouya*) *si*, Western Europe, *xi'ou si*, North America and Oceania, *beimei dayangzhou* (or *meida* for short) *si*, Latin America, *lamei si*, and two regional offices: Hongkong Macao Affairs Office, *gang'ao ban* and Taiwan Affairs Office, *tai ban*. The nine *external* functional departments and offices include: International Organizations and Conferences—*guoji si*, Treaty and Law—*tiaoyüe falü* (*tiaofa*) *si*, Information—*xinwen si*, Protocol—*libin si*, Consular—*lingshi si*, departments, and Office of Policy Research—*zhengce yanjiü shi* (or *zhengyan shi*), Office of Translation and Interpretation—*fanyi shi*, Office for the Compilation and Editing of Diplomatic History—*waijiaoshi bianji shi* and Diplomatic Couriers' Team—*xinshi dui*.[9]

Of the numerous *internal affairs* departments only the Confidential Communications Bureau—*jiyao jü*, and the Personnel Department—

ganbu si, have some relevance to the foreign policy process, particularly the Personnel Department.[10]

As a typical regional department, the Department of North American and Oceanian Affairs consists of three divisions, or *chu:* the First and Second U.S. Divisions, *meiguo chu,* and the Canadian and Oceanian Affairs, *jia ao xin chu.* The First U.S. Division is in charge of daily operations handling casework, *ban'an,* while the Second is research, *diaoyan* (short for *diaocha yanjiü*). The whole department has a body of roughly 50 professionals with the First U.S. and the Canadian Oceania boasting of 20 respectively and the Second American around 10.

The Information Department is a relatively small functional department when compared to the Consular and Protocol Departments. With roughly 60 people it was divided into four divisions in the 1980s. The First Division with about 20 people managed foreign correspondents both based in China and on temporary assignments.[11] The Second Division with fewer than 10 people oversaw the supply of propaganda literature and films to Chinese missions abroad and organized internal briefings for the domestic press. The Third Division had around 20 people. It conducted research and provided daily briefing to the ministerial leadership on developments around the world. The Fourth Division with fewer than 10 people managed the bi-weekly MFA public news briefings to foreign and Chinese journalists.[12]

The Ministry maintains some 159 diplomatic and consular missions abroad (by the end of 1994). In overseas missions, most of the people employed by the MFA come under the jurisdiction of two offices: the office of research and investigation, *diaoyan shi,* and the general office, *bangong shi.*[13] Most professionals work in the office of research and investigation except for the protocol and consular sections which come under the jurisdiction of the general office. In larger missions, separate offices are set up to manage the press, consular affairs, etc. In the mission to the United States, there is also a congressional affairs group, *guohui zu,* consisting of five people under the research and investigation office.[14]

MFA Subsidiary and Associated Institutions

In addition to the departments in the formal structure of the MFA, the Ministry has under its jurisdiction a number of other institutions. The degree of its control varies.

Guoji guanxi yanjiü suo—the Institute of International Studies—is treated as part of the Ministry sharing the same pool of human resources. Its personnel matters are handled by the MFA's Personnel Department. The World Affairs Publishing House, *shijie zhishi chuban she,* which publishes chiefly a weekly popular international affairs magazine called *Shijie*

Zhishi (World Affairs), and the Foreign Affair College, *waijiao xüeyüan*, which officially is a college, operate more independently nowadays as a publisher and a college, although the MFA provides professional guidance and appoints its senior officials.

Although officially they come under the jurisdiction of the MFA, the Diplomatic Service Bureau, *waijiao renyüan fuwu jü*, which provides logistic support to the diplomatic corps in Beijing, and the Angler's Terrace State Guest House, *diaoyütai guobin guan*, by and large operate independently. Their senior officials are appointed by the Ministry but they operate their own personnel systems.

In a system of reward, the MFA often provides opportunities for people in the above institutions to work in Chinese missions abroad. For instance the Chinese Consul-General in New York, Mei Ping, was a Vice President of the Foreign Affairs College.

The two other institutions over which MFA has jurisdiction are the Chinese People's Institute of Foreign Affairs (CPIFA), *waijiao xüehui*, which interacts with leading foreign political, business, social and academic figures, and the Chinese People's Association for Friendship with Foreign Countries (CPAFFC), *duiwai youxie*, which is China's principal instrument for people's diplomacy. The two organizations are often treated as part of the MFA with the CPIFA still sharing human resources with the MFA. However, the Friendship Association since the mid-1980s has only maintained a close professional relationship with the MFA.[15]

Finally, the MFA also takes charge—*daiguan*—of the Red Cross Society and Soong Ching Ling (Madam Sun Yatsen) Foundation on behalf of the State Council. In reality the two organizations act more or less independently. The MFA only serves as a conduit for their official instruction requests and reports to higher authorities.

The Information Flow

Sources of information for decisionmakers in the MFA come both from internal and external channels. There are mainly three channels for inhouse information generation: (1) cable communications from Chinese missions abroad, (2) foreign media, mainly wire services of Associated Press, Agence France Presse, United Press International and the Reuters, as well as CNN, and (3) daily bulletins on diplomatic activities. The Fourth Division of the Information Department (ID4D) is the chief body for the inhouse generation of information based on foreign sources. The General Office is responsible for inhouse generation of information based on MFA sources and for information from other party, government and military bureaucracies. It is the MFA's window both for the inflow and outflow of information.

The ID Fourth Division. ID4D consists of around 20 officers with one division chief and two deputies. At least 6 officers under the direct supervision of a deputy division chief are responsible for "news watch" and daily briefing. The rest of the officers are responsible for analysis under the direct supervision of the other deputy division chief. ID4D itself does not generate any "raw" information. It instead is a generator of processed information mainly from foreign sources. Its work is twofold: providing the ministerial leadership with the most up-to-date information on major developments in the world on a 24-hour basis, and publishing an analysis on new developments, be it political, economic or military.

Daily Briefing. When Wu Xüeqian became Foreign Minister (FM) in 1982, he instituted a practice called *jiti bangong*—collective office session. Every morning at 8:30—half an hour after the official work day started, all ministers and at least one departmental ranking official from every department would gather for a session in which a briefing was provided by two officers of the ID4D who had been on overnight duty. The session provided a forum for the ministers to meet face to face together with their chief aides from various departments to discuss matters that had come up overnight or needed attention. If possible, a course of action would be decided on, to be implemented by departmental officials after the session.

ID4D news watch team is divided into three pairs that rotate to be on night watch and to do morning briefing. While one pair is on night watch, the other two pairs take turns in day watch in an operation similar to a news organization in the West.

Most of the work falls on the night watch since most of the major developments in Europe, North America, Africa and Latin America take place during the night because of the time difference. Typically the night watch starts at 7:00 p.m. The two officers on duty will keep a close eye on the stories from the four wire services, the Voice of America broadcasts[16] and on CNN news received via satellite through the American Armed Forces Radio and TV Network.[17] In the meantime they will read through *Cankao Ziliao* (Reference Material) published by Xinhua News Agency to catch up with what has happened during the day.[18]

Barring major crises, the officers on duty will read and sort news stories and make a determination as to what is important that warrants a report next morning. As normally 6–8 items are selected for each briefing, the two officers will make a division of labor with each tracking two or three stories. If a major crisis or an event that demands immediate attention occurs, the officers on duty must first report, often through telephone, to the 24-hour Situation Room of the General Office's Secretariat and then inform the relevant department.[19] The officers on duty in the

Situation Room will in turn inform the relevant minister(s) and if necessary central leadership.

After midnight, ID4D officers will pick up the latest edition of *Reference Material* together with major newspaper and periodical news analyses and commentaries in original English provided on a daily basis by Xinhua News Agency.[20] About four or five in the morning, the officers begin to assemble all the information on hand and write a synthesis of each item preferably with a very brief analysis or comment. At the same time, they will monitor VOA broadcasts and review CNN news roundup and tape one or two TV news items that are determined to be most relevant or simply for their visual effect.

Before 8:00 a.m. preparations for the briefing materials are completed. The officer who is going to make the presentation will go through all the items carefully, seeking clarifications from his partner if, when and where necessary, before handing it over to the deputy division chief for review. The chief on duty that day will arrive at 7:30—30 minutes earlier than the normal office hour—and go through overnight diplomatic cable traffic from overseas missions if available and make subsequent additions or other revisions to the briefing material if necessary. At 8:30 the briefing starts and it normally lasts around 30 minutes.[21]

During the session one of the officers would take careful notes on the comments made and questions raised by the ministerial leadership. After the briefing, the officers and the divisional chief on duty that day who also attended the briefing would update the rest of the division on the subjects that have been discussed at the briefing session, the questions raised and instructions received. These would serve as a guide for the next briefing team and those responsible for research and analysis as to what issues and developments need special attention.

The daily briefing sessions were cancelled after the departure of Wu Xüeqian in 1988. Instead the ID4D officers on duty are required to submit their daily briefing items in written form to the ministerial leadership. Otherwise the process is not significantly altered.[22]

Xin Qingkuang *(New Development)* and Xin Qingkuang (Jianbao) [*New Development (Brief)*]. The most important task for ID4D is the responsibility to publish *Xin Qingkuang* and *Xin Qingkuang (Jianbao)*. To most of the rest of the MFA, ID4D is better known for its publication than its official name. It is often referred to as New Development Division. Despite the similarity of the names of its two publications, the latter is not an abbreviated version of the former. They are two completely different publications.

Jianbao as it is known in the ID is a publication that provides a brief background and a concise analysis on current issues and new developments.

Based on the principle of *yishi yiyi* (one issue deals with only one subject), it does not have fixed dates of publication but averages one issue every two or three days. Depending on the subject, most issues are classified as "strictly secret." Occasionally there are issues classified as "top secret."[23]

It mainly caters to the top leadership but also provides a useful though somewhat simplified framework for high ranking officials at ministerial and provincial levels to view through "correct" lenses current international developments. Thus its circulation is restricted to ministerial leadership of central bureaucracies and provincial/army officials. Provincial foreign office chiefs also have access to the publication.

Because of its tighter restriction, there is a lot of emphasis on brevity and timeliness as central leaders have little time to read a long piece. Most issues are no more than two pages long, printed double-sided on a single sheet of paper. Under no circumstance will it exceed five pages. In order to avoid political pitfalls, it is officially an analysis according to the foreign press which serves as a convenient cover for the views of the ID4D analyst. With few exceptions, most of the issues are written and edited by ID4D.

Xin Qingkuang on the other hand is an inhouse analysis of the MFA on major recent international development, one that is more substantial, in-depth and systematic. It is mainly intended for senior officials of the central bureaucracies and provincial authorities, and for leaders of academic research institutions. It is therefore generally less restricted in its circulation.

Because of the nature of this publication, it is often substantially longer in length ranging on average from five to ten pages. Although ID4D writes some pieces, most issues are written by regional departments which either contribute on their own initiative or are solicited by ID4D. ID4D is responsible for the editing of all pieces irrespective of their origins. A recurring problem with most pieces is that often they are too long. The longer the piece the less likely that central leaders will read it. Therefore one of the chief tasks in editing is to find ways to shorten the pieces, sometimes over some strong objections from their authors.

Since 1983, encouraged by Deng's "emancipation of the mind" campaign which ushered in foreign policy readjustment, ID4D began to open up *Xin Qingkuang* for individual contribution. A few among the normally conservative cadre corps have ventured to take up the challenge. Most of them have been foreign policy suggestions that are "non-traditional" or "unconventional" in their approaches. Thus the publication also provides a forum for some unofficial but lively discussions of foreign policy issues. A few have caught the attention of top leaders who later initiated policy changes based on the suggestions.

ID4D officers responsible for the two publications are divided into two teams with one responsible for the "east front" and the other the "west front." The "east front" team is responsible for all developments in Asia, Africa, Russia and Eastern Europe while the "west front" focuses on Western Europe, North and Latin America, and Oceania. Each team comes under the supervision of one divisional chief. A division of labor is made for each individual officer to keep track of developments in a general geographical region or country. Once a particular issue is identified, one or two officers will be chosen on an *ad hoc* basis to follow the issue more closely and ultimately produce a piece on it. For major topics, staff meetings are held to discuss and debate the issue before the actual writing is initiated.[24]

ID4D through its daily briefings and the two publications is the main body within the MFA that provides *dongtai diaoyan* (research on current developments) material for the ministerial and central leadership. It in a significant way influences the perception of the decisionmakers in the ministerial and central leadership.[25]

The General Office. The General Office itself does not produce any reports and research papers. It oversees MFA's internal generation and the inflow and outflow of information by controlling the distribution of such information.

In addition to ID4D's briefings and the two publications, the MFA generates three forms of information: diplomatic cables, *Waijiaobu Jianbao* (Foreign Ministry Bulletin), and *Waijiaobu Wenjian* (Foreign Ministry Document).[26]

Diplomatic Cables. The telecommunication between the MFA headquarters and its overseas missions is mainly conducted in three ways: by radio communications with its overseas missions that have such facilities, through international telegraph or telex services. Telephone and facsimile are used more often for communications over routine or urgent matters that are not confidential. There have been attempts to encode confidential facsimile communications. It is not clear if they have been successful or regarded as reliable.

Diplomatic cables are written by foreign service professionals in various departments and missions. The encoding and deciphering are handled by the Confidential Communications Bureau technicians in the MFA and its overseas missions. For those missions with their own radio operations, cables are transmitted and received via *waijiao zongtai* (the General Diplomatic Radio Communications Station), a PLA operation.

There are two delivery cycles for incoming diplomatic cables. An a.m. cycle for which cables from overseas missions are delivered around 8:00 a.m. and a p.m. cycle around 1:00 p.m. Very urgent cables are delivered as soon as they are deciphered. For outgoing cables, the communication time varies with each mission. For instance telex communications can be done on a 24-hour basis, while for radio communication a specific time needs to be worked out between the mission and the headquarters.

While the author of a cable will determine its secrecy classification and urgency, the General Office determines the scope of distribution of incoming cables.[27] Because of its nature, circulation of incoming diplomatic cables are normally highly restricted and compartmentalized. For case cables, an MFA department receives a copy of a cable only when it is deemed relevant to the department's work. Research report cables are more widely distributed. Junior officers below section ranking rarely see any cable. Country desk officers can only have access to those concerning the specific country.

Diplomatic cables are generally of two types. One type concerns specific cases and is often shorter. The other type are research reports prepared by the research sections of overseas missions. Despite repeated efforts to crack down on abuses of the cable traffic system, the MFA has had little success in persuading chiefs of overseas missions to use diplomatic couriers instead for transmitting less urgent research reports to Beijing. The reason for the failure is due to the fact that only diplomatic cables are guaranteed to reach the desks of ministerial leaders and a better chance to reach central leaders. For an obscure small country post, documents through couriers can hardly be expected to reach the desk of a division chief.

Waijiaobu Jianbao. The Foreign Ministry Bulletin is a publication that reports to the central leadership on important and substantive issues that have come up in diplomatic exchanges, representations or conversations the previous day. It focuses on activities in China, mostly in Beijing. There is a great deal of emphasis on timeliness. As the requirement is for the top leadership to be informed the next morning of what has happened the previous day, most come out overnight. This is also a highly restricted publication. Except for those classified as top secret, the MFA departmental chiefs have access to most of the Bulletins so as to stay in touch with what is happening in other regions. The distribution of Bulletins that are classified as top secret is highly compartmentalized. For highly sensitive matters only the minister and the vice or assistant minister in charge have those issues.

Waijiaobu Wenjian. The Foreign Ministry Documents are usually used to publish the full text of the transcripts of important high level diplomatic talks, exchanges, representations. The time requirement is usually less stringent than for the Bulletin on which some abbreviated versions of the transcript may have already been published. In order to avoid political problems, all transcripts concerning talks between a top leader and foreigners must be submitted for his personal review and clearance before going to print. Ironically, top Chinese leaders from Mao to Deng have had a habit of using such occasions to convey important messages for domestic audiences. In such cases, the Foreign Ministry Document is changed into an issue of CPC Central Committee or joint CPC Central Committee and State Council and possibly the CMC document to be widely distributed to the leaders of central government, military and party organs and provincial leaders.

Sources of Information from Other Bureaucracies. The MFA ministerial leadership has access to a variety of information in both original and processed forms from other government, party and military bureaucracies. The most relevant among them are Reference Material by the Xinhua News Agency, *Jünqing (Jianbao)* [Military Situation (Brief)] and *Jünqing* by the Second Directorate of the PLA General Staff Department, *Qingbao* (Intelligence) by the Ministry of State Security. Those publications by the military and intelligence organs are considered processed information. The MFA leadership relies mostly on internally generated information. For external sources of information, it attaches far greater importance to Reference Material for which daily reading is imperative. As for research products by such academic institutions as the Academy of Social Sciences, they are often ignored as mostly irrelevant.

There is only one cycle for the internal collection of documents. They are collected in *wenshu chu*—Documents Division of the General Office at 8:00 a.m. by the secretaries of various MFA departments. The outgoing documents will be delivered every morning by the Confidential Traffic Division to the document exchange center located in the Confidential Communications Bureau of the CPC Central (Committee) General Office west of Zhongnanhai, where incoming documents are picked up and taken back to the MFA.[28]

Information Selection and Processing. On departmental level, information, both processed and unprocessed, received by the department is only categorized into different files for the departmental leadership. No attempt is made at pre-selection for the departmental leadership. It is up to the individuals of the departmental leadership to make a determination as to what to read and what not. As a rule, diplomatic cables receive priority attention, as do the documents produced by the MFA. The departmental leadership will also decide on the selective availability of these documents to its subordinates.

On the ministerial level and above, the story is different. The main reason for the control of information flow on this level is the overwhelming nature of documented information in the Chinese bureaucracy.[29] The control mechanism over the availability of information for the ministerial leadership lies in the hands of their each individual secretaries.

Each morning at 7:30—half an hour before the arrival of the minister, his secretary starts his day by collecting all printed documents from the Document Division of the General Office and all overnight diplomatic cables from overseas missions and sometimes, though rarely, from provincial/municipal governments from the Situation Room of the General Office. He immediately starts to go over very quickly all the cables and documents and makes a determination as to what are relevant. Once the selection is completed, the cables, documents and the outstanding cases will be put into different files and presented to the minister who arrives around 8:00. Unless there is something that demands immediate attention, the minister usually goes over all the cables and documents first before going to the ID4D daily briefing, and begins handling cases upon return. The selection process is repeated for the p.m. cable traffic around 1:00 p.m. Thus by controlling the information that reaches the desks of ministerial policy decisionmakers, their secretaries play a crucial role in helping shape the perceptions of the ministerial leadership.[30]

The Situation Room of the Secretariat normally has the most complete set of information available to the MFA. Documents from other bureaucracies made available to the MFA with a single copy are retained in the Situation Room. Some of them are highly sensitive, for instance, information on the testing of some strategic weapons or weapon systems, information on foreign spy satellite overflights, military operations such as those along the Sino-Vietnamese border in the 1980s. The officers on duty are also responsible for keeping a record of their telephone communications with other bureaucracies or senior officials. For some of the most sensitive issues that have come out of the foreign press such as alleged Chinese arms sales to sensitive regions, alleged Chinese spy activities, or defections, Xinhua News Agency would print a top secret, highly restricted edition of *Reference Material* called *Cankao Ziliao* (*Qingyang*)—*Reference Material* (*Proof Copy*). It is the responsibility of the on-duty officers of the Situation Room to make a judgement as to which minister(s) should the information be made available to. All members of the Secretariat have access to all the information available in the Situation Room. Therefore to some extent, the secretaries are better informed than their superiors.

Communication Within and Without the Bureaucracy

As examined in Chapter 1 of this book, the Chinese political power is divided into three major systems: government, party and military. The foreign affairs bureaucracies of the three systems *officially* do not communicate with each other under the ministerial level. This does not mean that they do not talk to each other. Informal telephone and to a less extent fax communications have been most active at divisional and departmental levels. However as far as official proposals, reports and requests for instructions are concerned, they invariably take the form of ministerial level case documents.

Communications Within the MFA   In the MFA, work under regional departments is divided into two general types: case processing—*ban'an*, and research—*diaoyan*. For instance, the American Affairs Division consists of two separate divisions, with one responsible for processing cases and the other for research. For smaller country desks manned by two people, one would be responsible for case processing and the other for research. For a division that supervises mostly small countries that need only one desk officer for each country, the officer is normally responsible for case processing and the research is often done by the research sections of its overseas missions and a number of people within the division that are designated to carry out research collectively for these countries of the region.

There are two general types of case documents generated by various bureaucracies: action memoranda—requests for instructions (RFI) for a particular course of action, and reports on actions already taken. Policy proposals are often made in conjunction with either an instruction request or a report. Although an office-automation office was set up in the mid-1980s which began to equip on an experimental basis several departments with computers and computer operators, up to the late 1980s most of the drafting of documents was still done by hand.[31] Within the MFA, *official* communication takes place only on departmental level.

Typically, an RFI document is drafted by the desk officer after a discussion with his or her divisional chief that sets out the guidelines. If the proposed course of action would require cooperation or acknowledgement of any other department within the MFA, a telephone discussion with the relevant division of the department concerned is often initiated to obtain general endorsement. If the relevant division decides that the matter is serious enough, it will obtain orally the approval of its departmental leadership. When there is reservation or disagreement, an interdepartmental meeting will be convened to resolved the differences. Only when the differences cannot be resolved at departmental level that the relevant ministers will be involved. The ministers may take the matter to the FM if an ultimate judgement by the FM is warranted.

When a course of action is agreed upon, the RFI document will be drafted by the desk officer in the name of the lead department. After the signature of its departmental chief, it is sent to the relevant department(s) through the department secretaries who will register, deliver and acknowledge receipt of the document.[32] The relevant division will examine the document first before submitting it to the departmental chief for co-signing the document. It will then return to the lead department to be checked for any revision before being submitted to the minister in charge of that department for official approval. The minister will routinely refer it to the minister in charge of the co-signing department for co-endorsement. Most of the decisions on this level are routine, within the scope of well-established guidelines for country or regional policy.

Communications with Other Bureaucracies Researchers in various central bureaucracies almost never communicate with each other. Researches are almost always done independently within each bureaucracy, unless a specific research project is mandated by the top leadership to be a joint research project. Only in case processing do bureaucracies communicate with each other, particularly in cases that need cooperation or coordination of more than one bureaucracy, and thus the approval of the top leadership.

Within the foreign affairs sector—*waishi kou*, government, party and military bureaucracies communicate *officially* only on the ministerial level. Most communications take place within a limited number of bureaucracies: between the MFA and the Ministry of Foreign Trade and Economic Cooperation over foreign trade and foreign aid, between the MFA and the CPC Central International Liaison Department over relations with communist countries, between the MFA and Commission of Science, Technology and Industry for National Defense (COSTIND) over overseas arms sales, and between the MFA and the General Staff Department of the PLA and the CMC Foreign Affairs Bureau over military relations with other countries, arms purchases and sales and other military related issues.

The communication process between bureaucracies is similar to the communication process within the MFA. A lead ministry is first identified. The desk officer will draft the RFI document, but instead of in the name of the department, it will be in the name of the ministry/ministries. When the internal process is completed, the divisional chief will discuss it with the relevant division of the co-signing ministry/ministries. Much of the bargaining take place at this or the departmental level if disagreement appears. Much of the communication is done by telephone. If the case is deemed sensitive, discussions are done over secured telephones.[33] Facsimile machines have been introduced in the central bureaucracies in the late 1980s. However its use is strictly limited and heavily guarded not because of possible reception of overseas "subversive" material but out of a fear of leaking secret documents to outside the MFA.[34]

If and when the differences cannot be resolved at the division or department level, the responsible minister of the lead ministry will discuss directly with his counterpart(s) of the co-signing ministry/ministries. If they are still unable to resolve the differences, either an inter-ministerial conference is called or the co-signing ministry can attach its opinion to the original document or submit its opinion separately to the CPC Central Foreign Affairs Leading Small Group (LSG) for decision by the top leadership.

In most cases, case documents are delivered by the Confidential Traffic Division of the General Office. However in the case of very urgent documents, a desk officer, often the most junior, will hand deliver the document and wait for co-signature before taking it back to the MFA, a process known in the Chinese bureaucracy as *paoqian* (running for signature).

Policy Initiation, Coordination, and Subversion

Foreign Policy Initiation

The highly centralized decisionmaking power has created much inertia in the bureaucratic foreign affairs establishment toward taking initiatives in the formulation of major foreign policies. During the Mao era, the initiation of major foreign policies became almost exclusively the prerogative of Mao and Zhou. In the Deng era, although Deng is no long the only initiator within the leading nuclear circle of major foreign policies, the basic dynamics have not substantially altered. Most major foreign policy initiatives have originated from the top.

Political leaders of the Politburo Standing Committee seldom communicate directly with each other over the phone or see each other except on official occasions. In fact during the last years of Mao when he did not even participate in any official functions, no one, not even his wife or Zhou Enlai, was able to see him. Communications with him had to be conducted through his designated liaison officers. Even during the Deng era, official communication among top leaders is often handled by their respective secretaries in the name of their respective offices.

Most political leaders in the past had no or little knowledge of foreign languages. They relied mostly on the processed information provided by the foreign affairs establishment for international development.[35] On this level, there has not been a systematic effort to brief them directly by any of the foreign affairs bureaucracies on a daily basis. Most of them rely on their secretaries to pre-select information available to their respective offices before they either read them or listen to an oral presentation by their secretaries.[36]

Major foreign policy initiatives on this level often originate from written instructions or comments by members of the leading nuclear circle on diplomatic cables, foreign affairs reports, documents etc. pre-selected for them by their secretaries. Depending on the nature of the issue involved, the written comment or instruction is transmitted to the relevant bureaucracy via the

Foreign Affairs Office (FAO) of the State Council for followup actions. Or when warranted, a meeting of the Foreign Affairs LSG, the Standing Committee of the Politburo or the Politburo is convened to discuss the matter.

For initiatives concerning the implementing details of established foreign policies, the process is often the reverse with the relevant bureaucracy taking the lead in drafting an RFI with a proposition for a specific course of action to be submitted to the FAO—the staff office of the Foreign Affairs LSG—for approval by the central leadership. Depending on the significance of the issue, the Head of the Foreign Affairs LSG could either approve it himself and/or submit it to other members of the Politburo Standing Committee for ratification or approval. If and when any of them believe the issue is very significant or contentious, he can suggest to members of the leading nuclear circle to call for a meeting of the Standing Committee or the whole Politburo.

There are of course always exceptions to the general dynamics as outlined above. Major foreign policy initiatives can also originate from below. However the critical condition for its success is access. Too often such bold initiatives are lost in the long, strictly structured bureaucratic process. The initiator therefore must have direct access to the top leadership to be effective. This is often achieved outside the proper channel through personal connections with the people who have direct access to the top leaders—the back door as it is known in the system.

Foreign Policy Coordination

The Chinese political system is known for its heavy reliance on meetings and official documents to build policy consensus and to ensure policy coordination. When serious differences occur between two bureaucracies that cannot be resolved between them, the dissenting bureaucracy can either co-sign the RFI with its reservation attached before it is submitted to the central leadership, or submit its own opinion separately. If the central leadership does not have a consensus or strong opinion, a meeting is convened to resolve the differences. Once a resolution is reached, a document is drafted to establish a rule to regulate or coordinate activities in the relevant field. Depending on its intended scope, the document can be a State Council document to govern activities in the government system, a joint CPC Central Committee and State Council document to govern activities of the party and government systems, or a joint CPC Central Committee, State Council and CMC document covering all party, government and military systems.

The central leadership is not a policy coordinating body. Policy coordination is conducted through the FAO in the name of the Foreign Affairs

LSG. Or more often when an issue is too technical, a bureaucracy is identified in the document as the lead coordinator and the interpreter of the rule(s) established in the document. Related matters therefore must be cleared by the lead coordinator first before its submission for central approval.

Subversion of Established Policies

Official rules of the CPC dictate that once a policy is established, subordinate units must carry it out faithfully. Openly flouting the rules of established policies by bureaucracies that have lost out in the formulation process is as uncommon as their whole-hearted implementation.

Subversion of an existing policy starts with creative interpretation of such a policy. In the formulation process, the dissenting bureaucracies will try to make the language ambiguous so as to leave enough room for future interpretation. Bureaucracies also lobby for a favorable interpretation of the rules.[37]

Another way of subverting the existing policy is to exaggerate the harmful effect of the policy in its implementation. It can be done in formal reports to the central leadership or through informal channels via personal connections with the top leaders. The purpose is to create exceptions or reopen the whole issue for policy revisions.

In conclusion, during the Mao era, the foreign affairs bureaucracies played little role in foreign policy decisionmaking. They were used mainly as instruments for information collection and processing, and for policy implementation. Subversion of existing policies was non-existent. During the Deng era, the role of the foreign affairs bureaucracies in decisionmaking begins to increase as China greatly expands its interaction with the rest of the world and management of foreign relations becomes more complex. The current generation of leadership is dominated by technocrats who have relatively narrow power bases in the political system and thus are more susceptible to lobbies by bureaucratic interests. It is expected that as decisionmaking process becomes more institutionalized, the role of the bureaucracies in decisionmaking will increase in significance. The importance of their structures and processes should become more evident.

Notes

1. Most Western China watchers and some Chinese scholars who have never worked in a government bureaucracy at senior levels are often confused about lines of authorities in the Chinese political system, particularly in cases where a dual leadership is involved. Generally speaking there are three sets of relationships in the Chinese system: (1) *yewu guanxi*—professional relationship, (2)

xingzheng guanxi—administrative relationship, and (3) *zuzhi guanxi*—organizational relationship. The third refers to the relationship within the CPC hierarchy.

2. Guojia Jigou Bianzhi Weiyüanhui, (ed.), *Zhongguo Zhengfu Jigou* (China Government Organization) (Beijing: Zhongguo Renshi Chubanshe, 1991), p.#215. The staff sizes used here do not include some semi-autonomous operations run by these bureaucracies that are financially independent of government funding. Nor do they include certain logistical support staff. The Ministry of Machine Building and Electronics Industry was reorganized into two separate ministries in 1993—the Ministry of Machine Building Industry and the Ministry of Electronics Industry.

3. Ibid., pp.#221–222.

4. Both the Confidential Communications Bureau and the Office of Interpretation and Translation were originally subordinate organs of the General Office. In the mid-1980s, both became independent departmental ranking organs. The General Office though maintains professional oversight over the Confidential Communications Bureau.

5. Although nominally the Secretariat is under the administrative jurisdiction of the General Office, the secretaries to the Minister and Vice and Assistant Ministers operate independently by virtue of their function as personal assistants to the MFA chiefs.

6. For a more detailed description of the confidential document exchange system, see Yan Huai, "*Zhongguo Mimi Wenjian Gaiyao* (Notes on China's Confidential Documents)," *Papers of the Center for Modern China,* Vol. IV, No. 12, 1993, pp.#14–15.

7. Currently Foreign Minister Qian Qichen has three secretaries because of his Vice-Premiership. Personal Communications, October 4, 1994.

8. *China Government Organization.*

9. Ibid.

10. The Personnel Department handles only personnel matters concerning professionals up to the level of chiefs of departments. Ministerial-level personnel matters fall largely under the jurisdiction of the Organizational Department of the CPC. Non-professionals are managed through the personnel division of the Administration Department.

11. Journalists from Hong Kong, Macao, and Taiwan fall under the jurisdiction of the State Council's Hongkong Macao Affairs Office and Taiwan Affairs Office.

12. The department was since reorganized into six divisions with the First, Second and Third Divisions handling foreign journalists from North America and Oceania, Europe, and Asia and Africa respectively. The Fourth Division is now responsible for news analysis. The Fifth for news briefings—now twice a week and the Sixth for comprehensive affairs. Personal Communications, July 1995.

13. Other offices are manned by people from other bureaucracies. For instance, the Cultural Affairs Offices are manned by officials of the Ministry of Culture, the Commercial Offices and Economic Counsellor's Offices by the Ministry of Foreign Trade and Economic Cooperation, the Defense Attache's Offices by officers of the People's Liberation Army, the Offices of Education by the Ministry of Education.

For Chinese representations in international organizations, the UN headquarters in New York, Geneva and Vienna are largely staffed by the MFA. Specialized organizations are normally staffed by various bureaucracies designated as their respective *guikou danwen*—coordinating body within the Chinese system. For instance, the World Bank and the International Monetary Fund are represented by the Ministry of Finance, the United Nations Education, Science and Culture Organization (UNESCO) by the Ministry of Education, the World Health Organization by the Ministry of Health.

14. Personal communication, October 26, 1994.

15. In the mid-1980s, Ambassador Wang Bingnan, President of the Friendship Association, decided to promote its own cadres unilaterally in the course of revamping China's civil service, thus breaking ranks with the MFA. As a result, many cadres who had a similar rank with their counterparts in the MFA in the past are now one grade higher. This prompted the MFA to stop sharing human resource pool with the Association, thus terminating most chances for the Association's professionals to work in Chinese missions abroad. Although the Association managed to create a few positions in a few selected missions with their own budget, the mobility of most of its professionals to serve overseas is seriously handicapped.

16. The main reason for monitoring the VOA instead of the BBC is because the VOA is regarded as an operation of the US government. Despite of its denials, its views are often regarded as reflecting, at least partially, US government views, which are much more relevant to the MFA.

17. The CNN news watch started in 1985. Personal recollections.

18. *Cankao Ziliao* known as *Da Cankao* is "a daily comprehensive collection of information on international current events and politics through overseas public sources and chiefly caters for leading cadres above the county/regiment level." *Zuixin Zhongguo Qikan Quanlan* (A Complete Overview of the Latest Chinese Periodicals) (Beijing: Xiandai Chubanshe, 1989), p.#11. It is classified as a *"jimi* (strictly secret)" publication. Before the Cultural Revolution, its circulation was more tightly restricted among officials above provincial/army rank. Prior to 1984, it was published twice a day in morning and afternoon editions. Since then it becomes a daily with each issue averaging around 100 pages. Yan Huai, "Confidential Documents," p.#13.

19. Until recently every department had one person on night duty. This practice is now discontinued. Personal communications, August 1994.

20. Most come from American and British newspapers like *New York Times, The Washington Post, The Christian Science Monitor, Los Angeles Times, Times, The Guardian*, etc. They are sent in their original form every day by the overseas branch offices of Xinhua. For this service the MFA pays Xinhua a subscription fee. Personal recollections.

21. Personal recollections.

22. Personal communications with ID sources, August 1994. One of the reasons is that the current generation of ministerial leadership is fluent in foreign languages and has direct access to information of foreign sources.

23. According to the Chinese Secrecy Act, there are three levels of secrecy classification: *jüemi* (top secret), *jimi* (strictly secret), and *mimi* (secret). *Zhonghua Renmin Gongheguo Baoshou Mimi Fa* (Secrecy Act of the People's Republic of China) in *Zhongguo Falü Nianjian 1989* (China Yearbook of Law 1989) (Beijing: Falü Chubanshe, 1990), p.#130.

24. Personal recollections.

25. Its influence on the central leadership is thought to be greater than on ministerial leadership mainly because by the mid 1980s most of the MFA ministers were professionals who are fluent in at least one foreign language, thus having direct access to original material and less dependent on processed material.

26. The MFA generates a whole host of internal publications. However as far as those that have an impact on decisionmaking, only these three are really important.

27. There are generally three levels of urgency in cable communications: *ji* (urgent), *teji* (very urgent), *teteji* (extremely urgent). Ironically an incoming cable listed as urgent is often regarded as not urgent. As a result in order to attract attention, incoming cables are routinely listed by their authors as very urgent. Personal recollections.

28. Yan Huai, "Confidential Documents," p.#15.

29. For an analysis of this phenomenon, see Yan Huai.

30. Depending on the preferences of each individual minister, some secretaries are also asked to make comments or attach memos on the cables or documents clarifying the situation or making suggestions.

31. One of the experimental departments was the Protocol Department. By the late 1980s, much of the protocol work began to be processed on computers. The division of the Information Department which is in charge of the MFA official position press statements also began to store information in computers. However in general they were the exceptions rather than the rule. Personal recollections.

32. The system of secretarial support that is common in Western bureaucracies does not exist in China. Desk officers do all the secretarial work. There are normally only two or three secretaries at departmental level mainly for the circulation and safekeeping of documents and diplomatic cables, and to a less extent secretarial support for departmental leadership. Personal recollections.

33. Secured telephone communication among Chinese central bureaucracies in Beijing and between Beijing and the provinces is conducted through the 39th Exchange of Beijing which is located inside Zhongnanhai. Because of the color of the telephones used for such communications, it is often referred to as *hongji*—red telephones. Every MFA minister has one in his office, while there is only one in every MFA department. Li Zhisui, *Mao Zedong Siren Yisheng Huiyilu* (The Private Life of Chairman Mao) (Taipei: Shibao Wenhua, 1994), p.#200. Fan Shuo, *Ye Jianying zai 1976* (Ye Jianying in 1976) (Beijing: Zhonggong Dangxiao Chubanshe, 1990), pp.#230–231, 291, 303.

34. Personal communications with a senior MFA official, October 27, 1994, Washington, DC.

35. This situation is significantly changed with the introduction of the current Politburo Standing Committee. With the exception of Li Ruihuan, all its members speak one or more foreign languages and thus theoretically have access to unfiltered information from foreign sources.

36. Most younger leaders would read themselves, while older leaders prefer to listen to daily oral presentations. For a detail example of such practice, see Zhang Yünsheng, *Lin Biao Mishu Huiyilu: Maojiawan Jishi* (The Memoirs of Lin Biao's Sec-

retary: A Record of Events at Maojiawan) (Hong Kong: Cunzhen Chubanshe, 1988).

37. Provincial authorities prove particularly ingenious in lobbying foreign affairs bureaucracies in Beijing. In order to obtain MFA permission for a travel plan to the Middle Eastern Muslim countries, Hei Boli, Chairman of the Ningxia Hui (Muslim) Autonomous Region, once sent a full carriage load of water and other melons to the MFA in the middle of a very hot summer in the mid 1980s. Since 1990, lobbying the central bureaucracies by provincial authorities has apparently been elevated to an art known in the capital as *paobu qianjin*—"double time march." In mandarin Chinese, the phrase sounds the same as "walk the lobbies of ministries and in flows money."

3

The Case of the MFA—
Its History, Cadres' Corps, and Political Culture

Despite leadership changes and political turmoil, the MFA has remained one of the most important institutions of Beijing's foreign affairs establishment. Although as one of the largest central bureaucracies it has had its share of problems typical of such a bureaucracy, its political culture, formed through long years of management of the nation's diplomacy, continues to have a strong effect on other foreign affairs institutions as it provides a steady stream of senior foreign affairs managers to these institutions. An examination of its past history, the experiences of different generations of the cadres' corps and its political culture can help shed light on the relevance of some Western assumptions about the policy impact of its political culture and provide some clues to the outlook of the institution, its current leadership and cadres' corps, which will continue to play a significant role in the formulation and implementation of the country's foreign policy.

Its History and Cadres' Corps

The Pre-Revolution Years

The Foreign Affairs Commissariat The CPC started to conduct foreign affairs one year after its founding in 1921, when it joined the international communist movement—the Comintern in 1922. Since then the CPC maintained extensive contacts with the Comintern. When the Nationalists led by Jiang Jieshi (Chiang Kai-shek) began to slaughter the Communists in 1927, the Communists started a rebellion in Guangzhou in December 1927 and set up a short-lived "Soviet government" with its own "foreign ministry" and "Commissar of Foreign Affairs." The regime lasted only two days before it was crushed by the Nationalist forces.[1] This was followed by the official establishment of the "People's Commissariat for Foreign Affairs" in November 1931 under the Communist "Soviet

Republic" in the Communist-controlled enclave in Jiangxi Province. Wang Jiaxiang, who would later become PRC's first ambassador to the Soviet Union and Vice Minister of Foreign Affairs and Director of the CPC International Liaison Department, became the "People's Commissar for Foreign Affairs."[2] As the Communists were preoccupied with their survival, there was no indication that the existence of the "Commissariat" was anything more than a name. Wang, nevertheless, was the point man of the Communist leadership to maintain contacts with the Comintern through its representative Otto Braun who was sent to the Jiangxi "Soviet" by the Comintern in October 1933 as a military advisor.[3]

The CPC Southern Bureau in Chongqing   After the Long March, Wang Jiaxiang would become in November 1935 "Foreign Minister" of the northwest office of the central government of the "Soviet Republic," now in Shaanxi Province. He would later be succeeded by Bo Gu.[4] A "foreign office" was reportedly in existence by 1937 in the Yenan Communist base area with Bo Gu, the Communist leader replaced by Mao during the Long March, as "the Foreign Minister of the Chinese Soviet" and Wu Xiüqüan, who later became PRC ambassador to Yugoslavia, as its secretary-general.[5]

In mid 1937, as a result of the Xi'an Incident, the Communists set up offices in Wuhan, Xi'an, Lanzhou, Taiyüan, Chongqing, Changsha, Guilin, Guangzhou and Urumchi. Of these, the Lanzhou Office became an important Communist liaison station with the Soviet Union, which by then had also set up a diplomatic and a military representative office in the city.[6]

However the origin of the PRC's foreign affairs cadres' corps should be traced back to the period between 1938 and 1946 when the Chinese Communists established a representation in Nationalist-controlled Hankou and later Chongqing headed by Zhou Enlai.[7]

In 1938 the CPC Representation set up an international propaganda small group (*duiwai xüanchuan xiaozu*) targeted at Westerners particularly the Americans. Its main job was to translate Chinese Communist documents into English for dissemination in the foreign community in the war-time Nationalist capital. The group was headed by Wang Bingnan, who later as ambassador to Warsaw became chief PRC negotiator in the Sino-US Warsaw talks during the 1950s and 60s, and included as its members Wang's German wife Anna von Kleist, Bi Shuowang, Xü Mengxiong etc., all fluent in English.[8] Besides keeping in touch with a number of radical Western journalists like Edgar Snow, Rewi Alley, and Agnes Smedley, they also established a relationship with US diplomatic officials like General Stilwell, the then US Defense Attache in China.[9]

In October 1938, Hankou fell to the advancing Japanese army. The CPC Representation moved with the Nationalist government to Chongqing—its wartime capital. In 1939 Ye Jianying on behalf of the CPC Southern Bureau officially set up a foreign affairs group (*waishi zu*) under the leadership of Zhou Enlai, the CPC top representative. Wang Bingnan was appointed director and Chen Jiakang, who later became PRC ambassador to Egypt, deputy director. Its members over the years included Qiao Guanhua, Gong Peng (Qiao's wife who was serving as Zhou's English secretary/interpreter and spokeswoman), Li Shaoshi, Zhang Wenjin, Liü Guang, Chen Hao, Ma Lie and others.[10]

Other Communist representations under the jurisdiction of the CPC Southern Bureau in Guangzhou, Guilin and Hong Kong were headed by Lian Guan, Li Kenong and Liao Chengzhi.[11] All three would later become senior PRC diplomats. The three offices were subsequently closed as a result of Japanese occupation (Guangzhou in October 1938, and Hong Kong in 1941) and of Nationalist-Communist military conflict in January 1941 (Guilin). Some of their staff like Qiao Guanhua later joined Zhou Enlai's foreign affairs team in Chongqing.[12] The primary focus of Zhou's team was the American community in that city and the secondary focus was the British.[13]

One characteristic of this team is that unlike the CPC foreign affairs officers in the north (such as Russian-trained Wu Xiüqüan), most of the people at the Southern Bureau had received a Western-style education. Wang Bingnan was educated in Germany. Qiao Guanhua studied in Japan and did his doctoral dissertation in Germany.[14] His wife, Gong Peng, went to an American missionary middle school and to Yanjing (Yenching) University established by the Americans.[15] Zhang Hanfu was first educated in America and even joined the American Communist Party before going to study in Moscow.[16] Zhang Wenjin had studied in Germany.[17] Chen Hao and Ma Lie, who later became Zhou Enlai's foreign affairs secretaries and PRC ambassadors, were students recruited by Wang Bingnan for the foreign affairs team.[18]

Zhou's team in 1944 successfully made arrangements for American journalists to visit the communist controlled Yenan. In July that year the US Army set up an observers' mission there known as the Dixie mission. Huang Hua, a Yanjing University graduate who interpreted for Edgar Snow, served as an escort to the American team. Also involved in dealing with the Americans was Ke Bainian, who later became PRC ambassador to Rumania and Denmark.[19]

Throughout the War, the Communist representation under Zhou Enlai was run like a diplomatic mission in the Nationalist-controlled Chongqing. Most of his team had their first diplomatic training during this period. Some of the rules and regulations established during this period would later become official diplomatic disciplines of the PRC.

The Marshall Mission At the end of WWII, China was again on the brink of a civil war. General George Marshall was called up by President Truman from retirement to mediate between the Chinese Nationalists and Communists. The Marshall Mission as it was known set up a three-men team with George Marshall, Zhang Qün and Zhou Enlai representing the three parties of the U.S., the Nationalist Government and the Communists. Wang Bingnan and Zhang Wenjin remained Zhou's personal aides.[20] Under them, the Beiping (Beijing) Executive Headquarters was created to implement the truce agreement signed by the two sides in January 1946. The communists were represented by Ye Jianying. Ye was assisted by Li Kenong, who as secretary general headed the staff office, Huang Hua, who was in charge of the information section, and Ke Bainian, the publication and translation section.[21]

In addition, some 40 truce teams composed of representatives of the three parties were set up at various locations in northern China and Manchuria to monitor the local situation where the Nationalist and Communist forces confronted each other. Some two hundred communists participated in the work of these teams. Most of them senior military officers. These participants would constitute the largest source of men with "diplomatic" experience in the nascent PRC foreign affairs in the early 1950s. Most noted among them were Wu Xiüqüan, Geng Biao, who later became PRC ambassador to Sweden, Denmark, Finland, etc., Huang Zhen, who later became PRC ambassador to Hungary, France and the United States, Huang Hua, later ambassador to Canada, the UN, and Foreign Minister.[22] The characteristic of this group was that most of them were Long March veterans with only limited education and very brief foreign exposure.

The Central Foreign Affairs Group and Local Foreign Affairs Offices
The Marshall Mission collapsed in November 1946. Zhou Enlai and his team returned to Yenan on November 19, 1946.[23] The CPC Central Committee decided to officially establish a Foreign Affairs Group (*waishi zu*) headed by Ye Jianying and Wang Bingnan under the leadership of Zhou Enlai. The group collected most of the communists' foreign affairs and language expertise in preparation for the conduct of foreign affairs after their takeover.

Among the first acts that the group took was to set up the Foreign Language School by combining the then North China United University and the Foreign Language Institute. The Foreign Language School would later play a prominent role in the training of PRC's foreign service officers. Ye also successfully persuaded the British Communist David Crook and his Canadian wife Isabel to teach there.[24]

In March 1946 Zhou sent some members of his Nanjing Bureau team to Shanghai to set up an office. Among them were Qiao Guanhua and Gong

Peng. With the outbreak of the civil war, the Shanghai office was forced to be closed and the Qiaos moved to Hong Kong in September 1946, and together with Zhang Hanfu, they set up the Hong Kong branch office of Xinhua News Agency, which to this day has remained PRC's official representation in Hong Kong. The main task at the time, however, was to win British support and possible recognition of the future Chinese communist regime.[25] The CPC Northeastern Bureau also maintained a foreign affairs office headed by Zhou Qiüye,[26] who would later become PRC ambassador to Yugoslavia and Australia.

In the fall of 1948, the North China People's Government created the first Communist local foreign affairs office headed by Li Dihua.[27] In January 1949, Beiping (Beijing) foreign affairs office was established. It was headed by Ke Bainian and Li Dihua. In May 1949, Zhou Enlai convened an important foreign affairs conference making arrangements for the Communist takeover of other big cities. He made the first round of appointments: Zhang Hanfu would head the Shanghai foreign affairs office, Huang Hua Nanjing, Zhang Wenjin Tianjin, Li Dihua Wuhan, and Cao Ruoming Guangzhou.[28]

MFA: The Formative Years

On October 1, 1949, Mao officially declared the founding of the People's Republic of China. The MFA was officially established with Zhou Enlai as its first Foreign Minister.[29] The initial size of the bureaucracy was very small with a staff of around 170 people. Its cadres' corps consisted of (1) foreign affairs officers of the CPC Foreign Affairs Group and those who had been engaged in long term underground and United Front work in the Nationalist-held areas, (2) high ranking PLA officers and CPC officials, (3) selected liberal arts college graduates. A small number of ex-diplomats of the Nationalist Government were also retained as advisors.[30]

MFA Ministerial and Departmental Appointments On December 18, 1949, the first round of appointments of senior officials of the MFA was announced.[31] The three Vice Foreign Ministers were Wang Jiaxiang, Li Kenong and Zhang Hanfu. Wu Xiüqüan was appointed Director of the Department of USSR and East European Affairs, Ke Bainian American and Oceanian Affairs, Huan Xiang West European and African Affairs, Xia Yan Asian Affairs, Dong Yüeqian International Affairs, Gong Peng Department of Intelligence. Wang Bingnan became the Director of the General Office. Some adjustments were soon to be made. Wang Jiaxiang would become the first PRC ambassador to the Soviet Union. He was replaced as Vice Foreign Minister by Zhang Wentian, who had originally been designated as PRC representative to the United Nations. Xia Yan never assumed the post, and Chen Jiakang took the position instead.[32]

The appointments at the ministerial level were all veteran CPC leaders with considerable exposure in foreign affairs. Some like Zhou Enlai, Wang Jiaxiang and Zhang Wentian, once held leading positions above that of Mao within the party. With the exception of Zhou Enlai, all received extensive training in the Soviet Union and thus were fluent in Russian. Zhang Hanfu was also educated in the U.S. and fluent in English.

At the departmental level, it was apparent that Zhou had retained some of his closest aides of the Chongqing and Marshall Mission days. These included Wang Bingnan, Chen Jiakang, Dong Yüeqian and Gong Peng, who had a Western educational background, and only joined the Communist revolution during WWII.

General Ambassadors Within three months of the founding of the PRC, 10 countries recognized the new regime. All were communist countries of Eastern Europe and Asia.[33] To cope with the situation, Zhou Enlai quickly assembled a group of generals in Beijing and gave them a short training course before sending them off to missions abroad.

They included Yüan Zhongxian, Huang Zhen, Geng Biao, Ji Pengfei, Han Nianlong and Wang Youping. Yüan Zhongxian's "diplomatic" experience was his involvement as the communist army's chief negotiator in April–July 1949 with the British over the Amethyst Cruiser Incident.[34] Huang Zhen, Geng Biao, Han Nianlong were all participants in the failed Marshall Mission. Yüan became the first PRC ambassador to India, Geng to Sweden and other North European countries, Ji to East Germany, Huang to Hungary, Wang to Rumania and Han to Pakistan.

The selection of generals with very limited foreign exposure to head PRC missions abroad was part of Mao's deliberate policy known as "starting a new kitchen (*ling qi luzao*)."[35] To ensure absolute loyalty, the new regime with few exceptions would not use any diplomatic personnel of the Nationalist Government but build up its own cadres' corps from scratch. The policy also indicates a distrust of those who had a Western education, most of whom were retained in the home office instead of posted abroad. Mao told the generals, half jokingly, that one reason he sent them to do diplomatic work even though they did not know foreign languages was that he needed not to worry that they might defect.[36] Mao could count on their loyalty.

The Overseas Communists The new foreign affairs cadres' corps was soon reinforced by a small but important group of Communists who had operated overseas. Among them were Xiong Xianghui, who had served as Nationalist General Hu Zongnan's aide before going to study and got his master's degree in 1948 at Western Reserve in Cleveland; Tang Mingzhao, a University of California graduate who had worked as a Communist organizer and newspaper publisher in the U.S. until 1950 when he returned to work for the MFA; the Pu brothers—Pu Shouchang, who later became Zhou's English interpreter, Pu Shan and Pu Shouhai, all Harvard PhDs; Ji Chaozhu, who studied chemistry at Harvard before becoming Zhou's fifth English interpreter and now serving as UN Undersecretary-General; Bi Jilong, a George Washington University MBA who returned in 1950 and later served as UN Undersecretary-General; Gong Pusheng, Gong Peng's sister who had a master's degree from Columbia University and later became Director of the Department of International Organizations and ambassador to Ireland; Yan Baohang, who was educated in Britain and father of Yan Mingfu—former Director of the CPC United Front Work Department,[37] and Hu Jibang, a Communist undercover, served as a third secretary in the Nationalist Embassy in Moscow.[38] The last two helped train the first group of communist general ambassadors. Most of them though fluent in English and very knowledgeable of foreign affairs started out in lower level positions under supervision.

Training a New Generation of Diplomats Meanwhile Zhou Enlai set up schools to train a new generation of diplomats. Among the most important institutions that have provided over the years a steady flow of foreign affairs personnel to the MFA are the Peking Foreign Language Institute (formerly the Foreign Language School, now University of Foreign Studies), the Foreign Affairs College, Harbin Russian Language School.

In the early 1950s, the MFA designated the People's University, Peking Foreign Language School and the Department of Oriental Languages of Beijing University as its main training ground for its professionals. In 1955 the State Council approved the establishment of the Foreign Affairs College under the control of the MFA for the training of low and middle level officers. In 1959, the Peking Foreign Language School merged with the Peking Russian Language Institute and became the Peking Foreign Language Institute (PFLI) or *Beiwai* for short. Three years later, PFLI was officially designated as the human resource development base of the MFA.[39]

In addition the MFA began to send language students to study overseas, mostly in the Soviet Union and East European countries. One of them was Qi Huaiyüan who had been a student at the Harbin Russian Language School before being sent to East Germany to study German. He would later become Vice Foreign Minister, and Director of the State Council's Foreign Affairs Office and most recently Chairman of the Friendship Association. Most of the new recruits would start out doing interpretation and translation for their supervisors, who in most cases did not know foreign languages. Some through interpreting for their superiors formed bonds of what later became patron-client relationships.

Steady Expansion

The Second Wave The first wave of diplomatic recognition of the PRC lasted one year from October 1949 to October 1950. The 10 countries that recognized the PRC in 1949 were all Communist countries of Eastern Europe and Asia. In 1950 the PRC made more progress in the non-Communist world. Among the eight countries that granted official recognition were Nordic countries such as Sweden, Denmark, Finland, a neutral country—Switzerland—and such newly independent Asian neighbors as India, Indonesia and Burma. However when China entered the Korean War, the momentum came to a halt. With the exception of Pakistan which established diplomatic ties with Beijing in 1951, no other country exchanged diplomatic recognition with Beijing in the three years between 1951 and 1953.

When the process resumed in 1954 after the signing of the Korean armistice, it was at a far slower pace, averaging about three recognitions per year. By the end of the 1950s, a total of 33 countries had established diplomatic relations with China, including the U.K. and the Netherlands which maintained their diplomatic relations with Beijing at the charge d'affaires level.

The second wave came in the early 1960s when a large number of former European colonies in Africa gained their independence. It culminated in 1964 when within one year a total of six nations recognized Beijing. The most important breakthrough was France, the first major Western power to switch to full diplomatic recognition of Beijing. During this period between 1960 and 1965, Beijing's diplomatic success in bringing the total recognition to 50 came almost exclusively from Africa. Cuba (1960), Laos (1961) and France (1964) were the only exceptions.

The MFA's cadres' corps had also expanded greatly. By 1960 the MFA's staff size had grown by ten times to 1897. Although the majority of its senior officials above the departmental level were still veterans of the 1921–1949 revolutionary war period with limited professional knowledge and language expertise, more than half of its young professionals had had at least eight years of professional experience.[40]

With the rapid expansion of Beijing's diplomatic relations which led to a shortage of senior staff, the political leadership faced a choice in senior overseas post appointments. They could either fill those senior posts by promoting the young professionals from the ranks of its cadres' corps, who had since the early 1950s survived political movements and served mostly as interpreters and desk officers, or bring in from outside the MFA non-professional Communist cadres who had been working as high-ranking party, government and military functionaries.

Although rationality might point to the selection of foreign affairs professionals, Mao and Zhou chose the latter. As the country approached the middle of the decade, the political environment became increasingly radicalized. Mao in the midst of a polemic battle with the Soviet Union again started to stress "class struggle" and the importance of "red" over "expert." After the 1957 "Anti-rightist Campaign" in which Mao first mobilized the intellectuals in an attempt to destroy his political enemies in the party but had to crack down on them when it backfired, Mao found the intellectuals totally distrustful. Besides, most of the young professionals who joined the MFA after 1949 still held fairly junior positions and thus had no leadership experience.

As a result, between 1961 and 1965, particularly in 1964 and 1965, a large number of "amateur" diplomats of ambassadorial and counsellor ranks were selected from the ranks of senior officials of party apparatus, local governments and the military. Examples include Han Kehua, who had been a leader of the Hubei Province before appointed ambassador to Hungary and later France, Jiao Ruoyü, a former party and government official of Shenyang appointed ambassador to North Korea, Wang Ruojie, a former PLA general based in Zhejiang Province before being appointed ambassador to Yemen in 1964, Lu Guangxian, a former President of Hangzhou University before being appointed ambassador to Mauritania in 1965, Wang Rensa, who had been First Party Secretary of the Suzhou Prefecture before joining the MFA and became ambassador to the Central African Republic, Chad and Liberia, Liü Pu, formerly party secretary of the Anshan Iron and Steel Corporation, became ambassador to Malta, Mexico and Liberia, etc.[41] Most of them had no foreign language skills and no diplomatic experience except for a short training course provided by the MFA. As overseas posts were regarded as situated in a "hostile environment," like the general-turned predecessors, it was their party loyalty instead of professional skills that was valued.

Training and Recruitment   The Peking Foreign Language Institute and the Foreign Affairs College under the direct leadership of the MFA continued to be the main sources of recruitment for the MFA. A number of other specialized language institutes were set up in the 60s, including the Peking No. 2 Foreign Language Institute, the Shanghai Foreign Languages Institute, Guangzhou Foreign Language Institute, Xi'an Foreign Language Institute, etc.

Aware of the difficulties for a Chinese to learn a foreign language, Zhou Enlai, with an eye on a long term solution, in 1964 decided to start foreign language training at an earlier age by setting up foreign language schools in a number of major Chinese cities—Beijing which had two, Shanghai, Guangzhou, Hangzhou, Xi'an, Tianjin, and Dalian.

Characteristic of such schools, the Beijing Foreign Language School at Hepingmen was attached to the Peking Foreign Language Institute. It started at the third grade of primary school and finished at the tenth grade of senior high. Its recruitment was conducted through a highly competitive three-part (oral, written and physical) examination process which was open to all second graders city-wide. In conformity with the prevailing political environment of the mid 1960s, there was also a check of each candidate's family background to make sure he or she came from a politically correct family. Most came from party, government or military cadre families, few from city workers' families, almost none from farmers' families.[42]

These were boarding schools with nurses and caretakers at the primary level similar to those in the West. The pupils would have a chance to return home every Sunday. These schools later on became highly elitist with a very high percentage of children from diplomatic professionals' families.[43] The whole concept and system would come under heavy attack during the Cultural Revolution and most would be disbanded. However a high percentage of the students would end up in post-Cultural Revolution foreign affairs institutions. A few have since become prominent in these institutions. One of them is Yang Jieshi, who has recently been promoted to Assistant Foreign Minister from Minister of the Chinese mission in Washington. Widely considered a rising star, Yang had his first foreign language exposure while attending the Shanghai Foreign Language School.[44]

At the same time, Beijing continued to dispatch college or post-graduate students to study abroad. Because of the Sino-Soviet split, the focus gradually shifted away from the Soviet Union and Eastern Europe to Northern and Western Europe. Significantly a number of students began to study in universities in Britain and France.

The Third Wave In 1966 Mao launched the Cultural Revolution which also adversely affected China's foreign relations. As radicalism spread to its foreign missions, a number of countries suspended or broke off relations with Beijing. The total number of recognitions fell from its 1965 peak of 50 to 45 in 1967. The disruption in the MFA was relatively short-lived thanks to Zhou Enlai's personal intervention.[45]

Beijing's first diplomatic breakthrough came in 1970 when Canada, breaking ranks with the United States and other Western allies, recognized Beijing. This was followed by the Sino-US rapprochement and Beijing's return to the UN in 1971. Japan and nearly all Western countries one after another recognized Beijing in the early 1970s.

The demand for qualified personnel to fill overseas posts was enormous. For appointments to senior diplomatic posts, the MFA, in a major departure from past practice of recruiting amateurs from party, government and military apparatus, was able to promote experienced professionals from its own ranks and draw on the foreign service professionals of other foreign affairs institutions which had been dismantled during the Cultural Revolution. These institutions included the Commission for Foreign Cultural Relations, the Foreign Affairs Bureau of the Ministry of Education, the Commission for Overseas Chinese Affairs, etc. Most noticeable was Qian Qichen, current Vice Premier and Minister of Foreign Affairs, who had been a foreign affairs official of the Ministry of Education.

However the supply of qualified foreign service officers at the entry level was seriously disrupted by the Cultural Revolution. From 1966 to 1970, MFA's traditional recruitment channels—the Peking Foreign Language Institute and the Foreign Affairs College—had no enrollment. Those who had enrolled before 1966 spent most of their time in factional fighting and had little time to study. In 1969 they were sent to the countryside in Shayang, Hubei Province, to receive "reeducation" by doing farm work. Returning to Beijing in late 1971, they would enter a one-year crash course before some of them could enter the foreign service. With the radical elements purged, they represented MFA's first new recruits in eight years.

To meet the rapidly rising demand to fill its desk and overseas posts, the MFA under Zhou's direction resumed sending students to study overseas in 1973. In addition to the traditional training grounds in Eastern and Western Europe, some were also sent to African nations like Ethiopia and Tanzania. Most had to give up their previous language training in English, French, Spanish or Russian to concentrate on such obscure languages as Flemish, Icelandic, Rumanian, Maltese, Swahili, etc.

Unlike the past, this new group of students were mainly recruited from graduates or students of foreign language schools in Beijing, Shanghai, Shenyang, Changchun, Tianjin, Hangzhou and Guangzhou, most of them in their teens. Some of them have since risen to prominence, such as Yang Jieshi as mentioned earlier, and Wang Guangya, current Director of the International Affairs Department. There were a few college students too. One of them was Zhou Wenzhong, then a student of the Institute of Foreign Trade.[46]

For the first time, as an experiment, a group of primary school pupils were selected from the Beijing Foreign Language Schools to study in England, living with families friendly to China like British journalist Felix Green, and in New York as family members of Chinese diplomats to the United Nations. This experiment proved a failure as the kids forgot their Chinese as quickly as they picked up English, and thus discontinued.[47]

However, these were only drops in a bucket, the only real solution lay in restoring the traditional domestic training institutions. Thus in late 1971, the Peking Foreign Language Institute, still in the countryside in Shayang, Hubei Province, resumed its enrollment. The first class since the Cultural Revolution was more than 800 in size. Although they were known as "worker-peasant-soldier students (*gong nong bing daxüesheng*)," most of the students in *71 Jie*—Class '71—were in fact city middle school students who had been sent to the countryside, factories or who entered military services in the late 1960s.[48] A few were selected directly from Beijing middle schools including the Beijing Foreign Language School formerly at Hepingmen and by then at Weigongcun.[49]

There were among them also a substantial number of children of high-ranking, mostly military officials, including a daughter and a daughter-in-law of Marshal Ye Jianying, a daughter of the Communist Party boss of Xinjiang, Seypidin Ayze, a son of Commander Han Xianchu of the Fuzhou Military Region, a daughter of Xü Guangyou, Deputy Political Commissar of the Beijing Military Region, a son of Vice Foreign Minister Liü Xinquan, a daughter of Vice Foreign Minister Pu Shouchang, a daughter of Wu Ruilin, Deputy Commander of the PLAN South Sea Fleet. There were indeed a few country boys. Most of them did not fare too well. One exception was Zhang Yesui, who was born and grew up in the Hubei countryside and has since become Deputy Director of the International Affairs Department.[50]

This class would remain in the Hubei countryside for one academic year, with time divided between doing farm work and learning foreign languages, before returning to their Beijing campus in summer 1972. The enrollment was suspended in 1972 because of a political debate over the source of enrollment and whether an entrance exam should be required. It resumed in 1973.

The Class of 1973 saw an even higher percentage of high-ranking, not only military but also civilian cadres' children as the downfall of Lin Biao saw a growing number of high ranking party officials returning to power. Concentrated in the English Department, they included those of Ye Jianying, Li Xiannian, Chen Geng (deceased PLA Chief of General Staff), Sichuan Party boss Li Jingquan and Qiao Shi, current Chairman of the NPC Standing Committee. Also in Class '73, there was Zhang Yümei, sister of Zhang Yüfeng—Mao Zedong's nurse and private secretary.[51] After their graduation, most of the children of senior military officials would congregate in the PLA General Staff Department, particularly in the Bureau of Military Attaches. Some of them have been instrumental in shaping a more outward looking PLA. For instance one of the prime movers behind the setting up of the China Institute of International Strategic Studies (CIIS) was Chen Zhiya of Class '73, son of the deceased

PLA Chief of General Staff, General Chen Geng. Chen junior studied at Harvard Kennedy School of Government in 1986–1987.

Since Class '73, enrollment became regularized. Class '71 graduated in February 1975. A large number of the graduates went to the MFA and its affiliates which at the time also included the State Tourism Bureau. Although a few recent graduates from language departments of Beijing University and from foreign language institutes of Shanghai, Dalian had entered the MFA earlier, the graduates of PFLI Class '71 represented the second major infusion of new recruits since the Cultural Revolution. Unlike their predecessors of the Cultural Revolution generation, this group was deemed to have received a relatively comprehensive and complete training in school. A substantial number of them were immediately dispatched overseas to receive further training. This time all for major languages: English in Britain, Australia and New Zealand, French in France, German in West Germany, and Spanish in Spain. In 1980, the MFA began to send mid-career officers to study in the U.S., mainly at the Fletcher School of Law and Diplomacy, Tufts University and the School of Advanced International Studies, Johns Hopkins University. Except for a brief interruption after 1989, the program has continued to this day.[52]

The Slowdown Since 1980 Beginning in the early 80s, the Chinese political leadership began to place a lot of emphasis on professionalization and rejuvenization of its cadres' corps. By the mid 1980s, most of the senior diplomats were in their 60s. A mandatory retirement age of 60 was set for male officials below the vice ministerial rank and 55 for female officials.[53] With a few exceptions made in the case of some veterans of the general diplomat generation, most had retreated to more ceremonial positions like the Chairman of the Friendship Association (Wang Bingnan) and Director of Chinese People's Institute of Foreign Affairs (in the case of Han Nianlong). Ji Pengfei however would remain the Director of the Foreign Affairs Office of the State Council for some time. Exceptions were also made in regard to some critical diplomatic posts like ambassadors to the U.S., U.N., France etc. (most of them Zhou Enlai's aides of the 40s).

The result of this policy was the retirement of the generation of "amateurs," most of whom by then had already had several overseas tours of duty, and the coming of age of those intellectuals who entered the foreign service as professionals in the late 40s and early 50s. A few assumed leadership positions in the MFA and many became chiefs of overseas missions. This group included Qian Qichen, current Vice Premier and Foreign Minister, Zhu Qizhen, former ambassador to the U.S., Zhou Nan, current Director of HK Xinhua News Agency, Qi Huaiyüan, current Chairman of the Friendship Association.

By 1995, most officials of the 50s' generation have retired with some more prominent figures taking up positions like the Chairman of the Friendship Association (Qi Huaiyüan in 1994), the Director of the Chinese People's Institute of Foreign Affairs (Liü Shuqing 1993) and the Vice Chairman of the NPC Foreign Affairs Committee (Zhu Qizhen 1993). Those who entered the service in the 60s begin to assume ministerial and ambassadorial positions. Examples: Qin Huasun, Chinese Ambassador to the UN, Li Zhaoxin, Assistant Minister for American Affairs, Liü Huaqiü, Director of the State Council's FAO. Many of the 70s generation have assumed divisional responsibilities and a few departmental positions, mostly deputy positions, such as Wang Guangya, Director of the International Affairs Department, Zhang Yesui (PFLI Class '71), Deputy Director of the International Affairs Department, Shen Guofang (PFLI Class '74), Director of the Information Department. Yang Jieshi's appointment as Assistant FM heralds the coming of age of this generation.

After the fall of the Gang of Four, college enrollment through competitive entrance exam was reintroduced in 1978. By the time this new class graduated in the early 1980s, the PFLI had already won its long battle with the MFA to rid itself of the "step-son" status and gained official independence. This coupled with China's rapidly opening up to the outside world, the MFA, having lost its near monopoly over overseas assignment and travel, can no longer expect to attract the best and the brightest, who tend to seek opportunities in the business world, which often offers the same foreign travel opportunities but better financial rewards.

By the mid 1980s, the MFA began to have a serious problem in attracting well qualified new recruits. The situation however had not become unmanageable since the days of rapid expansion were largely over. The MFA relied instead on the Foreign Affairs College which has a very limited capacity to supply new graduates and for retraining those MFA officials with no language ability (mostly retired young confidential communications specialists) to staff some administrative and logistic support positions in overseas missions.

In order to make up the shortfall, the MFA also tried to recruit from some second or third rate colleges in places like Inner Mongolia and Fujian Province. The qualities tended to be poor.[54] In the mid 1980s, the MFA also began to recruit through examinations that are open to society, similar to the US foreign service exam. There have also been problems with this process.[55] To this day, this problem is still not adequately resolved.

The Political Culture

Factionalism in the MFA

Factionalism in the MFA did not exist before the Cultural Revolution. However as a major bureaucracy, tensions and personal conflicts were as routine as in any foreign affairs bureaucracy in the world. Political movements also exacted their tolls. Yet the MFA often fared much better than others as Zhou would carefully shield it from the extremes of these movements.[56]

Factionalism During the Cultural Revolution When the Cultural Revolution first started in spring 1966, the MFA under the direct supervision of Zhou Enlai was relatively calm. However following the instruction of Liü Shaoqi and Deng Xiaoping,[57] Foreign Minister Chen Yi organized and dispatched a number of work teams to the colleges under the jurisdiction of the foreign affairs sector such as the Peking Foreign Language Institute and Foreign Affairs College. Of them, seven were led and composed of cadres of the MFA.[58] For instance the work team sent to the PFLI was led by Vice Foreign Minister Liü Xinqüan, who would soon become the primary target of the radicals of the PFLI.[59]

When Mao returned to Beijing on July 18, 1966, he denounced the sending of work teams as a means by Liü and Deng to suppress the young radicals and ordered their immediate recall.[60] Mao's subsequent actions galvanized the radicals in the PFLI which split into two main factions—"the Red Flag Detachment" and "the Rebel Regiment." "The Rebel Regiment" faction was the more radical of the two in that it advocated the toppling of Foreign Minister Chen Yi and his two principal Vice Ministers, Ji Pengfei and Qiao Guanhua.[61]

Slowly the raging battles outside the MFA began to affect the MFA cadres' corps. On September 9, 1966, Mao commented on a report supposedly written by a friendly Austrian who criticized some PRC diplomats in Vienna for living in a "bourgeois" life style: "Get revolutionized, otherwise, it is very dangerous."[62] As a result of this so-called 9/9 Instruction, in December 1966, the MFA decided to recall ambassadors and other diplomatic officials home in two separate groups to "participate in the Cultural Revolution." By late 1967, all ambassadors except for Ambassador to Egypt, Huang Hua, were in Beijing. Most of the senior diplomats were subject to "struggle sessions" by their respective embassy staff.[63]

Some young MFA staff officers set up factional organizations to carry out "revolution" from within. On January 18, 1967, an "MFA Revolutionary Rebel Liaison Station" was launched.[64] As spring changed into summer, the rebels within the MFA and of the PFLI became increasingly radicalized. Following a speech by Wang Li on August 7, 1967 in which he extolled the radicals to seize power in the MFA,[65] the radicals headed by Yao Dengshan, the newly returned charge d'affaires to Indonesia, seized power in the MFA for 14 days, during which the British Embassy Chancery was sacked on August 22.[66]

On September 1, 1967, appalled by the radical actions, Zhou Enlai supported by Mao instructed that the radicals return their control of the MFA to the professionals and the MFA start repudiating the ultra-left. 26 ambassadors including Geng Biao and Huang Zhen wrote to Zhou who personally met them and gave them instructions.[67] So ended the brief reign of extreme radicalism in the MFA.

The anti-left trend initiated by Zhou encouraged some senior officials of the MFA to make a counter-attack. In early 1968, a group of ambassadors led by Geng Biao and Huang Zhen wrote posters criticizing some ministerial officials for supporting the ultra-left. On February 13, 1968, 91 departmental chiefs and senior diplomats wrote a wall poster that attacked the radicals and reaffirmed their loyalty to Mao and sought to protect Chen Yi. This "91 Persons' Big Character Poster Incident" however had an opposite effect in that it re-energized the left for a short period of time.

The overall situation changed when Mao began to send the PLA to take control of the country. The radical faction within the MFA and some of its ministerial supporters like Xü Yixin and Luo Guibo were discredited. In early 1969 most of the MFA people were sent to "May 7 Cadres' Schools" in Jiangxi, Hunan and Hubei. Those identified as ultra-leftists were purged during the process and would not return to the MFA. Those who survived would be blacklisted and kept in low desk positions.[68]

In the MFA leadership, veteran CPC leader-turned diplomats like Zhang Wentian, Wang Jiaxiang, and Zhang Hanfu, would not survive mainly due to their political problems with Mao in the past. Vice Foreign Minister Liü Xiao though survived the Cultural Revolution was in such bad health that he could no longer function in the MFA. Ji Pengfei and Qiao Guanhua became the real winners as Chen Yi became dysfunctional due to political trouble and physical illness.[69] Winners of this round also included most of the departmental ranking officials of the MFA. In 1969 ambassadors began streaming back to their overseas posts.

There were other winners who would become important figures in future new factional battles, namely Wang Hairong, Mao's niece who joined the foreign service in 1964 and was quickly promoted to Director of the Protocol Department,[70] and Tang Wensheng (Nancy Tang), the American-born daughter of Tang Mingzhao, who served as Zhou Enlai's sixth English interpreter and was promoted to Deputy Director of the Department of American and Oceanian Affairs.

"The Lord v. the Young Mistresses"[71]   The diplomatic breakthrough with the United States in 1971 was followed by the PRC's entry into the UN. Western countries one after another recognized Beijing, ending its long diplomatic isolation. These events greatly helped the MFA return to normalcy, even though it was still operating understaffed.[72]

Although there were very few new faces in the MFA, one was particularly important—Zhang Hanzhi, a former PFLI lecturer, who joined the MFA in March 1971.[73] Soon in early 1972, Zhang would bring two of her close female PFLI associates to the MFA—Zhao Jia, who is now a partner of the Chicago-based American law firm Baker & McKenzie, and Zhang Youyün, who later became a Counsellor in the Chinese mission in London.[74]

Following the Lin Biao Incident of 1971, Mao's health began to deteriorate. In 1972 Mao began to lose sight and speech. As he further retreated from the front line, even Zhou Enlai had few chances to talk to him directly. Instead his niece Wang Hairong and Tang Wensheng became his liaison with the Politburo.[75] Wang and Tang, by then known as the "two young mistresses (*liangwei xiaojie*)," began to see their personal power expand rapidly, as the two became Mao's ears and mouth. They also began to attract a following in the MFA. Most of their followers were relatively young—professionals working at low level positions. For a time Zhang Hanzhi remained one of their closest associates.[76]

In early 1972 when Mao's conditions suffered a serious downturn, Mao indicated he wanted Zhou to be his successor. However later Mao became suspicious that Zhou was too much on the right. On July 4, 1972, Mao criticized Zhou and the MFA. He did it again in December.[77] This attack on Zhou and the MFA would continue in 1973. In July, Mao made a harsh comment on an MFA analysis of the international situation as having "right tendency." Qiao Guanhua, the then Vice Minister in charge of American affairs, was a prime target.[78] After Kissinger's visit on November 10–14, 1973, Wang and Tang reported to Mao that Zhou had failed to ask for Mao's opinion and report to Mao. Mao asked to convene Politburo meetings to criticize the "right" mistakes of Zhou during his discussions with the top US diplomat.[79] In late 1973 and early 1974, Mao launched another political campaign to "criticize Lin Biao and Confucius" which was targeted at Zhou Enlai.

The rift between Qiao Guanhua, Lord Qiao as he was known in the MFA, and Wang Hairong and Tang Wensheng, the two Young Mistresses, began in late 1971 and early 1972, ostensibly over policy differences. The Young Mistresses under the instruction of Mao attacked the right tendencies of the MFA as represented by Qiao and implicitly by Zhou Enlai. Wang by virtue of her status as a liaison officer for Mao rose quickly in the MFA hierarchy. By May 1972 she was already Assistant Foreign Minister.[80]

In November 1974, Qiao Guanhua became the Foreign Minister replacing Ji Pengfei, who was transferred to the nominal National People's Congress. Qiao's power however was seriously compromised. Zhou Enlai was hospitalized since June 1, 1974 for cancer treatment.[81] As Mao retreated further into seclusion, only the Young Mistresses had access to him. Instructions concerning foreign policy came from the Young Mistresses.[82] Qiao became a puppet.

Meanwhile with Mao and Zhou too sick to be effective, a major battle was raging between Deng Xiaoping, who since December 1974 assumed Zhou's overall responsibility for the day-to-day work of the government, and the Gang of Four.[83] Mao who initially sided with the moderates in May 1975 would finally throw his weight behind the Gang of Four by late October, convinced that Deng intended to undo his accomplishments during the Cultural Revolution.[84] In mid October 1975, a new political campaign "to counter the rightists' attempt to reverse the verdicts" was unveiled to unseat Deng Xiaoping and aimed at the old cadres that had only recently been rehabilitated.

Wang Hairong on October 25, 1975 conveyed to the MFA party nuclear group Mao's criticism of Qiao's "rightist" stance in his talks with Kissinger and Japanese Foreign Minister early in the month at the UN in New York.[85] Starting from October 27, Qiao was forced to make self-criticism. By this time Qiao had already married Zhang Hanzhi, who had had personal connections with Mao. Zhang however refused to take things lying down. She would instead make her case with Mao through her personal connections.[86] Mao after meeting with US President Gerald Ford on December 12, 1975 admonished the Young Mistresses to go easy on "the old guys."[87] Thus the battle line was drawn. For the first time since the Cultural Revolution, the MFA staff was divided into two major factions: the Lord Faction represented by Qiao, and the Young Mistress Faction represented by Wang Hairong and Tang Wensheng.

The Lord Faction supporters tended to be MFA officials in senior and supervisory positions, like ambassadors and departmental chiefs, while the Young Mistress Faction was more characterized by younger and lower ranking professionals. However this distinction was not absolute.[88] In a way it represented a challenge by the young intellectuals to the amateur-turned-professional diplomats who had no language training but by then still occupied most of the senior positions. It probably also underlined some disgruntlement on the part of the young intellectual professionals for the slow pace of promotion. For instance, in the early 1970s, Zhou Nan, the current PRC chief representative in Hong Kong, who joined the MFA in early 1950, was a mere Second Secretary in the Chinese UN mission after more than 20 years of professional service.[89]

The factional fighting was largely confined to the MFA home office in Beijing. However a few missions abroad were also affected. For instance, in the Chinese mission in Washington, Counsellor for political affairs Qian Dayong was a supporter of the Young Mistress faction.[90] He reported directly to the Young Mistresses against Ambassador Huang Zhen for allegedly "prosecuting young cadres." The situation became so intolerable that in August 1975 Huang cabled Mao to offer his resignation. This was part of the reason for Mao to make the "go easy" remark and voice his support for Huang in December 1975.[91]

1976 proved to be a dramatic year in Chinese history. On January 8, Zhou Enlai, the most authoritative figure for the MFA officers died. The two factions were left to themselves to battle it out. Deng, already paralysed in late 1975, fell in April. Hua Guofeng, a humble provincial leader from Hunan, assumed overall leadership of the whole country. Qiao, having lost his ultimate patron Zhou Enlai who had protected him in successive past political movements, began to shift his loyalty behind the Gang of Four whose march to ultimate power in China in early 1975 seemed unstoppable.[92] This would prove a strategic and fatal mistake for Qiao.

Qiao made other tactical mistakes that would lead to his ultimate downfall. He failed to show proper respect for earthy Hua Guofeng and even joked about his briefing sessions with the Acting Premier as "coaching the crown prince."[93] On July 30—two days after the Tangshan earthquake, he ordered an evacuation of all foreign diplomatic missions in Beijing without obtaining prior approval of the top leadership. Finally Qiao allegedly failed to heed the instruction from Beijing at the time of the fall of the Gang of Four to delete a sentence from his UN speech delivered on October 5, 1976.[94]

The Gang of Four was arrested on October 6, 1976. When Qiao returned from the UN on October 17, wall posters were all over the MFA linking him with the Gang. He was soon removed from the seat of the Foreign Minister and replaced by Huang Hua.[95] Qiao's removal failed to resolve MFA's factional infighting. Despite open support for the Young Mistresses voiced by Li Xiannian, who took charge of foreign affairs after the fall of the Gang of Four, wall poster attacks on them continued. It was not until the removal of the Young Mistresses later in 1977 that a superficial normalcy gradually returned to the MFA.[96] Even then it was widely believed by the supporters of the Young Mistress Faction that Huang Hua was on the side of the Lord Faction and discriminated against them.[97] The problem persisted under the surface until 1982 when Hu Yaobang had to send Wu Xueqian, an outsider from the CPC International Liaison Department, to take over the ministerial leadership.

Summary. Compared with most other bureaucracies, factionalism in the MFA was mild during the Cultural Revolution. Radicalism was mostly spearheaded by the students of the PFLI. The reign of the left was relatively brief in the MFA due to the importance Mao and Zhou attached to foreign affairs. Most of the radical elements during the brief reign of radicalism were purged in the later stages of the Cultural Revolution leaving little traces of factionalism of the period.

The factional struggle of the 1975–1976 period proves more enduring and relevant today as no clear-cut result was produced from the fighting. Most of the participants in the factional infighting are now in their 50s and are holding senior positions. The legacy of this period of factionalism is mainly reflected in the appointments. For a period of time in the late 70s and early 80s, the Mistress Faction was believed to be at a disadvantage as most senior officials tended to sympathize with Qiao. The situation began to change with the coming of age of Qian Qichen, who is said to be more balanced toward supporters of the Young Mistress Faction. As senior officials began to reach their retirement age in the early 80s, senior appointments tilted toward a more balanced treatment of the supporters of the Young Mistress Faction.

However by 1995 most participants of the 1975–76 factional fighting are on the verge of retirement, if not having already done so. The traces of the Lord v. Young Mistress factionalism will soon disappear from the MFA. Already most of the departmental chiefs belong to the new generation that entered the foreign service after the Cultural Revolution. As fresh recruits, most of them remained neutral, and very few participated in the Lord v. Young Mistress factional fighting.

It is important to note that the impact of factionalism in the MFA on China's foreign policy formulation was minimal. It was mainly because decisions have been tightly controlled by the paramount leader and a few members of the leading nuclear circle. Although at times foreign policy issues have been exploited by factions for tactical advantages in the domestic political power struggle, there has been no evidence of major foreign policy differences among these factions. Factionalism does have an impact on personnel as it chiefly centered around power and influence. As factionalism is a sensitive issue, it is not openly talked about. Those in senior positions are very careful so as not to give the impression of playing the factional card, since, after all, factionalism officially is against party principles.

Patron-Client Relationship

Factionalism in the MFA was more characteristic of the special historical period during and immediately after the Cultural Revolution. There are sufficient reasons to believe that it is only a transient phenomenon. During the upheavals in May and early June 1989 that led to an unprecedented military crackdown, no faction emerged in the MFA from this period of great turmoil even though the MFA like many other bureaucracies had its share of participants in the demonstrations.[98]

The more enduring feature of the foreign service corps is perhaps what is known in Western literature as patron-client relationship. This kind of relationship is not unique to the MFA or for that matter to China. Although much of the Chinese political culture seems founded on this kind of relationship, an exploration of its historical root however is beyond the scope of this study. The following is only intended to highlight some such relationships that have existed in the MFA and its significance in the dynamics of MFA's political culture.

From 1949 to the Cultural Revolution When the MFA was established in 1949, three sets of patron-client relationships at the senior levels emerged from its formative years. For the simplicity of this study, they are categorized as the Russian Group represented by Vice Foreign Ministers Wang Jiaxiang and Zhang Wentian, the Chongqing Group under Zhou Enlai represented in the MFA hierarchy by Vice Foreign Minister Li Kenong and Director of General Affairs Wang Bingnan, and the Third Field Army Group which included newly recruited general-turned ambassadors like Yüan Zhongxian, Ji Pengfei, Han Nianlong.

What was common with most of the people in the Russian Group category was their extensive training in the Soviet Union in the 20s and 30s and they had since maintained contacts with the Soviet Union and Comintern. Wang Jiaxiang, Zhang Wentian and Wu Xiüqüan went to the Soviet Union in 1925 and received five years of extensive military and Marxist theoretical training in Moscow. After returning to China in 1931, they continued their interactions with the Soviet Union and Comintern. Wang Jiaxiang went to Moscow for medical treatment and would become one of the Chinese representatives to the Comintern. Wu Xiüqüan would serve as an interpreter to Otto Braun, the Comintern representative in China between 1932 and 1939. Later as the director of the CPC's representative office in Lanzhou from 1938 to 1941, Wu would continue to serve as a chief liaison officer with the Soviet military and diplomatic representatives in Lanzhou.[99]

Zhang Wentian and Wang Jiaxiang for a time in the CPC history served in the leadership positions and had conflicts with Mao. At the time of the Long March, Zhang was Chairman of the Soviet government, Wang Vice Chairman of the CPC Military Commission. Both belonged to the Moscow faction that was in command of the Red Army at the time and opposed to Mao who was left outside the decisionmaking circle. Although during the Long March, Wang and Zhang were instrumental in orchestrating the political comeback of Mao at the Zunyi Conference, Mao would never trust them, considering the two potential political rivals.[100] As a result both would be very cautious so as not to give any impression of cultivating personal loyalty within the MFA.[101] Toward the end of the 1950s with the fall of Zhang Wentian and the departure of Wang Jiaxiang and Wu Xiüqüan, the limited influence of this group in the MFA quickly dissipated.[102]

As examined earlier, the Chongqing Group's chief patron was Zhou Enlai. Under him, Wang Bingnan (General Office), Chen Jiakang (Asia), Ke Bainian (America), Dong Yüeqian (international organizations) and Gong Peng (information) would dominate senior positions at departmental level in the MFA. The commonality with this group was that in addition to their association with Zhou Enlai during the Chongqing years in the 1940s, most of them were either educated in the West or received a Western style education. Their diplomatic experience was also centered on interactions with the West. Unlike the Russian Group, this group in general was not politically involved in CPC's inner party struggles and thus avoided political prosecution during successive political movements. A few did get tangled up in political movements. Qiao Guanhua was almost branded a rightist during Mao's anti-rightist campaign in 1957 and was again accused of "right leaning" in 1959. A number of them were in trouble during the Cultural Revolution. However they could count on Zhou Enlai's intervention to save them.

Mention must be made of Zhang Hanfu, Vice Foreign Minister, who represented a special case. Although educated first in the US and joined the US Communist Party, Zhang would go to Moscow to study and became a researcher in Comintern's oriental department. During WWII he joined Zhou Enlai in Chongqing in running a communist newspaper. Zhang Hanfu like Wang Jiaxiang and Zhang Wentian was once a powerful figure in the CPC. His experience in the early years linked him to the Russian Group. However since WWII, he seemed to have come under the patronage of Zhou Enlai.

The Third Field Army (TFA) Group refers to those generals who were recruited in 1949 to serve overseas as MFA's first generation of ambassadors. A high proportion of them came from the Third Field Army under the command of Chen Yi who would in 1958 succeed Zhou Enlai to become Foreign Minister. In the Chinese military, the patron-client relationship follows the field army lines of the 1945–1949 civil war period.[103] The TFA generals included Yüan Zhongxian, former Political Commissar of the TFA 8th Army Group and the TFA Chief of Staff, Ji Pengfei, former Deputy Political Commissar of the TFA 7th Army Group, and Han Nianlong, former Political Commissar of the 33 Army of the TFA 9th Army Group. They were later joined by Li Yaowen and Zhong Qidong, both TFA divisional political commissars who later became Vice FMs, and Kang Maozhao, a former TFA regimental political commissar who later became Chinese ambassador to Cambodia.[104] This group was noted for their impeccable political background, having fought in WWII and the Chinese civil wars. They had the trust of Mao and most of them survived successive political movements under the patronage of Chen Yi.

After the Cultural Revolution The Russian Group did not survive the Cultural Revolution. As noted, even before the start of the Cultural Revolution, most of the people in this group had left the MFA for different reasons. Because of their political opposition to Mao in the past, Wang Jiaxiang and Zhang Wentian came under heavy attack during the Cultural Revolution. Wang died in January 1974 and Zhang would also die during the Cultural Revolution. Wu Xiüqüan after five years of imprisonment returned to the military. Thus at the end of the Cultural Revolution this group left no visible contacts in the MFA.

Zhang Hanfu's fate was similar to Wang Jiaxiang and Zhang Wentian. He died in prison in 1972. He was survived by his wife Gong Pusheng, Gong Peng's sister and former Director of the Department of International Affairs and Treaties, and Xie Qimei, his brother who later became Undersecretary-General of the UN.[105] Both have since retired.

By the end of the Cultural Revolution, most of the senior people of the Chongqing Group were no longer in active service in the MFA. Qiao Guanhua proved most successful and was promoted to the post of Foreign Minister by Zhou Enlai. Others included Zhang Wenjin and Han Xü who later became Vice Foreign Ministers and ambassadors to the US. Huang Hua should probably be included in this group even though he did not stay in Chongqing during WWII when he was personal secretary to Zhu De. He came under Zhou's patronage since 1949.

The survivors of this second generation have their own proteges. Under Huang Hua, who served as Foreign Minister from 1977 to 1982, there were Zhu Qizhen, former ambassador to the US and current Vice Chairman of the NPC Foreign Affairs Committee, Zhou Jüe, former ambassador to France and current Deputy Director of the Information Office of the State Council, Wen Yezhan, former Vice Foreign Minister and ambassador to Canada. Cha Peixin, current Deputy Director of the Foreign Affairs Office of the State Council and former Minister in the Chinese mission to Ottawa, was a rising star under Han Xü but lost favor since the departure of Han from the MFA. Yang Jieshi, current Minister in Washington, however, would come out of Han's patronage and maintain his upward mobility.[106] Liü Xiaoming, Deputy Director of the American Affairs Department, rose quickly under Zhu Qizhen.[107] With Zhu's departure, his promising career seems less assured now as it once was. Hua Jünduo, ambassador to Australia, first went to Australia as Ambassador Zhou Qiüye's interpreter and later came under the patronage of Zhu as an expert on Oceanian affairs. Zhu at the time was Counsellor for political affairs.

Qiao Guanhua's son Qiao Zonghuai was sent to Hong Kong in early 1983 first as an unofficial representative and later Deputy Director of the Chinese representation in Hong Kong.[108] He later joined the MFA as ambassador to Finland and to North Korea. The junior Qiao represents another special case, as he could not forgive his father's marriage to Zhang Hanzhi and cut his personal ties to his father.[109] He came to the MFA as an outsider with no previous experience in the MFA. Thus it would be inaccurate to say that he inherited senior Qiao's influence in the MFA.

The Third Field Army Group survived the Cultural Revolution almost unscathed thanks to their impeccable revolutionary credentials during the Chinese civil wars when they were senior enough to prove their loyalty to Mao and the party through military battles, yet junior enough not to get tangled in political struggles in the upper echelons of the CPC.

Among this group Ji Pengfei would exert a long lasting influence in the MFA. From 1969, when Foreign Minister Chen Yi was exiled to Shijiazhuang, to 1974, when Qiao Guanhua took over the MFA, Ji presided over the day-to-day operations of the MFA.[110] After a brief association with the NPC and the International Liaison Department, Ji would become Director of the Foreign Affairs Office of the State Council after the fall of the Gang of Four, thus assuming again a supervisory position over the MFA's work.[111] Ji Pengfei's reign in the MFA thus was the longest. He actively promoted a whole family of senior MFA officials. Most of these officials promoted in the 70s were the so-called *sanba shi* (Type 38) cadres.[112] They included He Ying, a former Director of African Department who was promoted to Vice Foreign Minister in 1972, Fu Hao, former Director of the General Office who was later made a Vice Foreign Minister, Gong Dafei who was also made a Vice Foreign Minister.

Ji has also spawned a younger generation of MFA officials. Notable among them are Qi Huaiyüan, former Vice Foreign Minister and Director of State Council's FAO, and Liü Huaqiü, former Vice FM and current Director of the State Council's FAO. Qi's association with Ji dated back to the early 1950 when he worked under Ji as a young interpreter in the Chinese mission in East Germany. Liü's relationship is much more recent. From the early to mid 1980s Liü worked as Ji's aide in the State Council's FAO.[113] When Ji was heading the State Council's FAO, both men rose quickly in the MFA hierarchy and for a time both were poised to take over the FM position. Since Ji's retirement, however, neither has fared too well. Both men have not been able to succeed Qian Qichen as FM and instead kicked upstairs in the difficult position of Director of the FAO.[114] Of lesser importance is Liü Hongxiao, current Director of the MFA General Office.

Liü originally joined the MFA as a confidential communications technician. He later became Ji Pengfei's secretary. During the Cultural Revolution when Ji was in political hot water, Liü stood by his boss by refusing to "expose Ji's crimes." For this Ji would not forget. Liü would remain Ji's personal assistant until the mid 1980s, when as a reward for his loyalty and long years of service, he was appointed Minister of the Chinese Embassy in France even though he speaks no foreign language and has little professional expertise. However with the retirement of Ji and in the current climate that stresses professionalism, Liü probably has reached the upper bound limit of his career in the MFA.

Finally, mention should be made of Cong Jün, the only sibling of Chen Yi who joined the MFA. Cong attended the elitist Peking Foreign Language School at Hepingmen and did her undergraduate studies in Britain and postgraduate studies at the Fletcher School. Although being the daughter of Chen Yi and a favorite of Deng Xiaoping, she has been treated respectfully, it is no guarantee for a successful career. After serving as deputy division chief of the American Division for some time, she is "borrowed" to work for Deng Xiaoping's youngest daughter—Deng Rong. Her husband, Wang Guangya, on the other hand, has fared far better, being one of the few of the 70s generation to become a Departmental Director in 1995. There is no evidence however to suggest that his success has anything to do with the Third Field Army Group.

The Information Department Group   In order to solve the problem of factionalism in the MFA, Wu Xüeqian was appointed FM in 1982. Wu belongs to Hu Yaobang's Communist Youth League group. Most of his career had been associated with external liaison work of the CPC. He was considered in the MFA an outsider. When Hu fell at the end of 1986, Wu's position within the CPC became precarious. It was further weakened after the Tiananmen crisis in June 1989. Besides bringing in a couple of officials from the International Liaison Department,[115] Wu during his 6 years in the MFA did not built up a base there.

It was the ascendancy of Qian Qichen in the MFA in 1982 that has given rise to a new set of patron-client relationships. In 1982 Qian surprised many in the ministerial party election of representatives to the 12th Party Congress by getting the highest vote. He was subsequently elected on the 12th Party Congress as a CPC Central Committee member, a seat that would guarantee him a ministerial position. He was promoted from Director of the Information Department to Vice FM. Qian would remain one of the three nuclear members of the MFA party group/committee.[116]

Even before he took over the responsibility of personnel from Yao Guang, Qian began to promote those who worked under him during his directorship in the Information Department (ID). Huang Guifang, a former deputy division chief of the ID and later ambassador to Malaysia, became Wu Xüeqian's personal aide. The pace accelerated after he took over personnel. Li Zhaoxing, former ID deputy division chief, rose quickly to become Assistant and Vice FM. Qin Huasun, also a former ID deputy division chief, became Assistant FM for international organizations before being appointed ambassador to the UN. Ma Yüzhen, ambassador to the UK and deputy director of State Council's Information Office, was ID First Division chief and later ID Director. Shen Guofang, current Director of Information, had served as Qian's aide for 10 years. He is also an ID veteran.[117]

However not everyone in the ID has benefited from Qian's rise. Yao Wei, a former official of the Ministry of Public Security, was chief of the ID First Division under Qian. However in the early 80s, Yao bypassed Qian—his immediate supervisor—and obtained permission directly from FM Huang Hua—his patron, to take up a fellowship in the U.S. By the time he returned from the U.S., Huang had long gone from the MFA. Yao was subsequently "exiled" to the Institute of International Studies.[118] Slowly but systematically Qian would ease most of Huang Hua's people out of important MFA posts.[119]

By 1995 close associates of Qian Qichen have dominated senior positions of the MFA. Qian's men represent a new generation of professional foreign service officers. Unlike some appointments under other patron-client relationships mentioned above, most of Qian's men are professionally competent, having received their education in Chinese colleges after 1949, fluent in foreign language(s), having extended foreign affairs experience both at home and in missions abroad. Although members of the CPC, they have relatively weak party loyalty and little baggage from experience in the Chinese civil war. They are the closest thing to civil servants that the MFA has ever produced. The only drawback for this generation is perhaps the narrowness of their diplomatic experience, most of which is confined to one or two geographical regions or functional areas.

The patron-client relationship is an enduring phenomenon of the Chinese bureaucratic system. Like factions, it mainly affects personnel selection and appointments rather than policy choice. For instance the Russian Group did not demonstrate any leaning to the Soviet Union during the Sino-Soviet split. Wang Bingnan and Qiao Guanhua would lead the diplomatic battles with the U.S. at the UN, in Panmunjom and Warsaw. In an era when foreign policy decisionmaking power was highly concentrated in the hands of a strongman, policy subversion carried a very high political cost and therefore was practically non-existent.

Today personal loyalty is likely to guarantee a better understanding of the chief patron's intent and nuances of certain policy and thus facilitate better policy implementation. However this kind of relationship occasionally may have a subtle impact on policy formulation when the chief patron's associates would provide data and information that support the patron's policy preference or undermine the position of other policy choices.

Notes

1. Donald W. Klein, "The Management of Foreign Affairs in Communist China," in John Lindbeck (ed.), *China: Management of a Revolutionary Society* (Seattle: University of Washington Press, 1971), p.#306.

2. The Chinese communists convened its first national congress of "The Soviet Republic of China" on November 7–23, 1931 in Ruijin, Jiangxi Province. A "Provisional Central Government of the Soviet Republic of China" was officially established. Mao was elected chairman of the "People's Commissariat of the Central Executive Committee." Wang Jiaxiang became the "People's Commissar for Foreign Affairs." After the second national congress of the "Soviet Republic" on January 24–February 1, 1934, Wang would become "Foreign Minister." He Hushen, Li Yaodong and Xiang Changfu (eds.), *Zhonghua Renmin Gongheguo Zhiguan Zhi* (A Record of the Official Posts and Appointments of the People's Republic of China) (Beijing: Zhongguo Shehui Chubanshe, 1991), pp.#137–138.

3. Wu Xiüqüan, *Huiyi yü Huainian* (Memoirs and Cherishment), (Beijing: Zhonggong Zhongyang Dangxiao Chubanshe, 1991), p.566.

4. He Hushen et al.

5. Klein, p.#145. Edgar Snow, *Red Star over China* (New York: 1938), p.#50.

6. The Lanzhou Office also received communists from other Asian countries who were apparently stopping over on their way from or to the Soviet Union, including Ho Chi Minh of Vietnam. Wu, pp.#167–171.

7. The CPC Politburo meeting held between December 9 and 14, 1937 made a decision to set up an official representation called CPC Central Committee Delegation in Wuhan—the then wartime capital of the Nationalist government. The delegation headed by Zhou Enlai, Wang Ming, Bo Gu, and Ye Jianying would take the main responsibility for CPC's *external affairs* such as negotiating and coordinating with the Nationalist government, and dealing with the foreign community. At the same meeting, a decision was made to set up the CPC Changjiang (Yangtze River) Bureau to direct CPC's activities in southern China. The Bureau would be headed by Xiang Ying, Zhou Enlai, Bo Gu, and Dong Biwu. At their first joint meeting in Wuhan, it was proposed to merge the two since their functions and personnel tended to overlap. The proposal was approved. Since then the new body was known as the CPC Delegation *externally*, but *internally* as the CPC Changjiang Bureau which later became the CPC Southern Bureau. Wang Ming was appointed its secretary and Zhou Enlai deputy secretary. Other members included Xiang Ying, Bo Gu, Ye Jianying, Dong Biwu and Lin Boqü. This practice of "one institution, one team of staffers but with two name plates" is still widely applied today. Liao Xinwen (Assistant Fellow, CPC Central Committee Office of Document Research), "*Kangzhan Chuqi Zhou Enlai zai Wuhan Huodong Ceji* (A Short Record of Zhou Enlai's Activities in Wuhan in the Early Days of the Anti-Japanese War)" in Li Haiwen, Run Yün and Li Jing (eds), *Zhou Enlai—Zhihui, Yongqi, Zhongcheng de Huashen* (Zhou Enlai—An Embodiment of Wisdom,

Courage and Loyalty) (Beijing: Zhonggong Zhongyang Dangxiao Chubanshe, 1992), p.#93.

8. Anna von Kleist was born in Germany in 1907 and received her PhD from Berlin University. She married Wang Bingnan in 1935 and went to China with Wang in 1936. During WWII, she worked for the CPC Southern Bureau until 1945 when she separated with Wang. She would stay in China until 1955 when she returned to East Germany. She moved to West Germany in 1961. For her experience during WWII, see Anna von Kleist, *Ich Kämpfte Für Mao* (Hamburg: Holsten Verlag, 1973).

9. Wang Bingnan, *Zhongmei Huitan Jiünian Huigu* (Nine Years of Sino-US Talks Remembered) (Beijing: Shijie Zhishi Chubanshe, 1985), p.#33.

10. The CPC Central Committee officially approved the establishment of the CPC Southern Bureau on January 13, 1939. Headquartered in Chongqing, the Southern Bureau was headed by Zhou Enlai as its Secretary, with Zhou, Qin Bangxian (Bo Gu), Kai Feng, Wu Kejiang, Ye Jianying and Dong Biwu as members of its Standing Committee. It had an International Research Office headed by Zhang Hanfu. Cao Runfang and Pan Xianying (eds.), *Zhongguo Gongchandang Jiguan Fazhan Shi* (A History of the Evolution of CPC Organs) (Beijing: Dangan Chubanshe, 1988), p.#199.

11. Klein, p.#308. Qiao Guanhua, "*Tongnian, Shaonian, Qingnian* (Childhood, Teenage, Youth)" in Zhang Hanzhi (ed.), *Wo yü Qiao Guanhua* (Qiao Guanhua and I) (Beijing: Zhongguo Qingnian Chubanshe, 1994), p.#319.

12. Qiao, p.#334.

13. Ibid., pp.#336–341.

14. Ibid.

15. Feng Yidai, "*Zhongguo Waijiaobu Cainü—Gong Peng* (A Female Talent of the Chinese Foreign Ministry—Gong Peng" in Han Zhang (ed.), *Waijiao Zhenwen Lu* (Anecdotes of Diplomacy) (Taiyüan: Shanxi Gaoxiao Lianhe Chubanshe, 1994), pp.#284–285.

16. Zong Daoyi, "*Lianheguo de Siwei Zhongguo Fumishuzhang* (The Four Chinese Undersecretary-Generals of the United Nations)" in Han Zhang (ed.), p.#273.

17. In the second half of 1944, the CPC Southern Bureau decided to send a group of secret CPC member students of the Southwest Union University to Yenan. When they passed through Chongqing, Zhang Wenjin was retained to become a member of the Foreign Affairs Group due to the need for foreign language expertise at the CPC delegation. Zhang Wenjin, "*Zhou Enlai he Wojia Sidai Ren* (Zhou Enlai and the Four Generations of My Family)" in Xiao Yü (ed.), *Zhou Enlai* (Chengdu: Sichuan Renmin Chubanshe, 1992), p.#321.

18. Chen Hao, "*Danxin Yi Pian, Hongtu Wan Jüan* (A Loyal Heart and Many Grand Plans)" in Cheng Hua (ed.), *Zhou Enlai he ta de Mishumen* (Zhou Enlai and his Secretaries) (Beijing: Zhongguo Guangbo Dianshi Chubanshe, 1992), pp.#176–177. Quan Yanchi, *Zouxia Shengtan de Zhou Enlai* (Zhou Enlai Desanctified) (Beijing: Zhonggong Zhongyang Dangxiao Chubanshe, 1993), p.#183.

19. Klein, p.#310.

20. On May 5, 1946, the Nationalist Government returned to its formal seat of government—Nanjing. Zhou Enlai and his team moved with the Nationalist Government and set up the official CPC representation there, known internally as

the CPC Nanjing Bureau. Its leading members included Zhou Enlai, Dong Biwu, Ye Jianying (resident in Beiping), Wu Yüzhang (resident in Sichuan), Lu Dingyi, Deng Yingchao and Li Weihan. Under its jurisdiction, a Foreign Affairs Committee was set up with Zhou Enlai as its Secretary, Liao Chengzhi and Wang Bingnan as Deputy Secretaries. It had a Secretariat headed by Zhang Wenjin, a Research Division headed by Qiao Guanhua, an Information Division headed by Gong Peng and a Liaison Division headed by Chen Jiakang. Cao Runfang et al, pp.#219–220. Wang Bingnan, p.#40. Quan, p.#26. Zhang Wenjin succeeded Gong Peng to become Zhou's personal secretary and interpreter. Zhang Wenjin, p.#321.

21. Wu Xiüqüan, p.#207. Klein, p.#310.

22. For a list of participants of the Marshall Mission who later became senior PRC diplomats, see Klein, Appendixes A–E.

23. Quan Yanchi, p.#30.

24. David Crook, originally from Hamptead in north London, was a veteran of the Spanish Civil War of 1936–1939 fighting on the side of the Spanish communists. He first went to China after the Spanish Civil War. Enlisted in Britain's Royal Air Force during WWII, he worked for the intelligence service in Sri Lanka and Burma before being demoted and sent back because of his links to the Communist world. Crook and his Canadian wife—the daughter of missionaries working in China—returned to China in 1947 and came to the Communist-controlled area in 1948 from Hong Kong through Zhang Hanfu's introduction. Originally to spend 18 months to investigate and complete three academic books on land reform, they instead end up spending the rest of their lives in China training foreign language personnel. Other foreigners teaching there included William Hinton, and George Hatem. Li Dihua, "*Jianguoqian Waishi Gongzuo de Pianduan Huiyi* (Reminiscence of Some Aspects of Foreign Affairs Work Before the Founding of the PRC)" in Pei Jianzhang et al (eds.), *Xinzhongguo Waijiao Fengyün II* (New China Diplomacy II) (Beijing: Shijie Zhishi Chubanshe, 1991), pp.#163–164. Lorien Holland, "Forty Years On, English Communist Keeps His Faith in Mao," *AFP,* May 14, 1996.

25. Qiao Guanhua, pp.#351–352.

26. Wu Xiüqüan, p.#213.

27. Li Dihua, p.#165.

28. Ibid., p.#170.

29. On the morning of September 30, 1949, Zhou told the Foreign Affairs Group that from then on the work of the Central Foreign Affairs Group was accomplished, and they could officially begin to conduct diplomacy. Zhang Rong and Kong Fanjing, "Zhou Enlai and Wang Bingnan" in Xiao Yü, p.#317.

30. Gan Bushi, "*Zhou Enlai yü Xin Zhongguo de Waijiao Duiwu Jianshe* (Zhou Enlai and the Development of New China's Diplomatic Contingent)" in Pei Jianzhang (ed.), *Yanjiü Zhou Enlai Waijiao Sixiang yü Shijian* (A Study of Zhou Enlai's Diplomatic Thought and Practice) (Beijing: Shijie Zhishi Chubanshe, 1989), p.#308, 314.

31. *Renmin Ribao* (People's Daily), December 18, 1949.

32. Wu Xiüquan, p.#231.

33. Countries officially recognized the PRC in 1949 are USSR, Bulgaria, Rumania, Hungary, North Korea, Czechoslovakia, Poland, Mongolia, East Germany and Albania.

34. The Royal Navy's cruiser Amethyst was caught in the artillery gun fire in the Yangtze River on April 20, 1949, when the communist troops stormed across the river. Yuan was the Political Commissar of the 7th Army Group of the Third Field Army. For details about the ensuing negotiations between the Chinese communists and the British, see Kang Maozhao, "*Yingjian Zishiying Hao Shijian* (The British Amethyst Incident)" in Pei Jianzhang, Vol. 1, pp.#33–47.

35. The other two components of Mao's foreign policy were "leaning to one side (*yi bian dao*)" and "cleaning up the house before inviting guests (*dasao ganjing wuzi zai qingke*)," which mean alliance with the Soviet Union and abolishment of all treaties and derecognition of all foreign missions before reestablishing new relations. See Chapter 4.

36. Zhu Lin, *Dashi Furen Huiyilu* (Memoirs of An Ambassador's Wife) (Beijing: Shijie Zhishi Chubanshe, 1991), p.#10.

37. Yan Baohang became a close confidant of the Young Marshal, Zhang Xüeliang and served as his chief diplomatic liaison with the British and the Americans. In September 1937 he secretly joined the CPC. In 1949, he was first appointed Deputy Director of the General Office. He died in prison in 1968 during the Cultural Revolution. *Zhonggong Nianbao 1988* (Taipei: Institute for the Study of Chinese Communist Problems).

38. Han Zhang.

39. Gan Bushi.

40. Gan Bushi.

41. George P. Jan, "The Ministry of Foreign Affairs in China Since the Cultural Revolution," *Asian Survey*, V. 17, June 1977, p.#524. Personal recollection.

42. Personal recollections.

43. Ibid.

44. Ibid.

45. The MFA during the Cultural Revolution is dealt with in more detail in the following section on factionalism within the MFA.

46. Zhou was moved from the post of Consul-General in Los Angeles to Washington to take charge of the Embassy after China recalled its ambassador to protest Taiwan President Lee Teng-hui's US trip in 1995. With the rank of Minister, he acted as Charge d'Affaires.

47. Personal recollection.

48. In the Chinese college system, dropouts are few. So are those unable to graduate on time. Thus class identification refers to the year of enrollment instead of graduation.

49. Personal recollection.

50. Ibid.

51. For more about Mao's relations with Zhang Yüfeng, see Li Zhisui, *Mao Zedong Siren Yisheng Huiyilu* (The Private Life of Chairman Mao) (Taipei: China Times Publishing Company, 1993). Li's claims are disputed by Zhang and others. Although Zhang became Mao's nurse during the Cultural Revolution, it was not

until early 1975 that she was officially appointed Mao's confidential secretary managing Mao's documents. The appointment was proposed by Mao and approved by the party center after Mao's long time confidential secretary Xü Yefu was hospitalized because of cancer. Ye Yonglie, *Jiang Qing Zhuan* (A Biography of Jiang Qing) (Beijing: Zuojia Chubanshe, 1993), p.#532.

52. Personal recollections.

53. A cabinet minister's official retirement age is 65. Personal recollection.

54. As one example, one young female officer started an affair with a married foreign representative in Beijing at her first diplomatic cocktail party—one month after she entered the MFA, in violation of the MFA regulations. Personal recollections.

55. One of the recruited was Bai Weiji, who actively took part in the demonstrations in May and early June 1989 and left the MFA after the military crackdown. Arrested on May 5, 1992, he was convicted one year later of "selling state secrets" to foreigners and sentenced to ten year imprisonment. His wife, Zhao Lei, a fresh recruit of the MFA, was also convicted (for translating) and sentenced to six years in jail. For more details, see Lena H. Sun, "Casualties of A Paper War in China: Every Day, Citizens are Arrested, This Time, They were My Friends," *The Washington Post,* July 25, 1993.

56. For instance, Qiao Guanhua barely escaped the fate of being branded a "rightist" during the 1957 Anti-Rightist Campaign thanks to the personal intervention of Zhou Enlai. Zhang Hanzhi, pp.#11–12.

57. Mao deliberately stayed away from Beijing according to Li Zhisui, p.#442.

58. Melvin Gurtov, "The Foreign Ministry and Foreign Affairs During the Cultural Revolution," *The China Quarterly,* Oct–Dec 1969, p.#67.

59. Personal recollection.

60. Li Zhisui, p.#454.

61. Zhang Hanzhi, p.#16.

62. Personal recollection.

63. Zhu Lin, p.#144. Gurtov, p.#72.

64. Gurtov, p.#73.

65. Until his downfall in summer 1968, Wang Li was a key member of the Central Cultural Revolution Small Group. Wang would claim that Mao had in fact read in advance his infamous speech on August 7. Patrick E. Tyler, "Old Leader from China's Cultural Revolution Still Seeks Rehabilitation," *The New York Times,* April 9, 1996. For his account of the Cultural Revolution, see Wang Li, *Xianchang Lishi: Wenhua Dageming Jishi* (Eyewitness to History: A Record of Events in the Great Cultural Revolution) (Oxford: Oxford University Press, 1993).

66. Ibid. Yao became a hero—"red diplomat" in "the struggle against imperialism, revisionism and reactionaries" after leading the fight in the besieged Chinese Embassy in Jakarta following the military coup in 1965.

67. Zhu Lin, p.#151.

68. Personal recollections.

69. Nominally Chen Yi would remain the Foreign Minister until his death on January 6, 1972. In fact Chen was exiled to Shijiazhuang from October 20, 1969 to October 21, 1970. He only returned to Beijing in 1970 for medical treatment after

it was discovered that he had cancer. Chen Xiaolu, *Jinian Chen Yi* (In Memory of Chen Yi) (Beijing: Wenwu Chubanshe, 1991). Since April 1970, Ji Pengfei had been Acting Foreign Minister and became Foreign Minister after Chen's death.

70. Wang first worked as an apprentice in a Beijing chemical plant before passing the college exam and entering the Russian Department of Beijing Normal College. Having completed her studies in four years, she was assigned to the MFA and was sent to the PFLI for further training. The training ended in November 1965. Zhou Enlai first put her in the Secretariat of the MFA General Office. Nominated by Zhou, she was later appointed Director of the Protocol Department. She became Assistant FM in spring 1972 and Vice FM in 1974. Ya Wen, "*Wang Hairong Jiashi* (Wang Hairong's Family History)," *Qiao Bao,* February 17, 1995, p.#33.

71. Qiao Guanhua was widely known in the political leadership and the bureaucratic circles as *Qiao laoye*—Lord/Master Qiao. The nickname is said to have come from Deng Xiaoping in the early 60s. It originated from a popular Chinese classical comedy movie *Qiao Laoye Shang Jiao* (Lord Qiao Mounting on a Sedan Chair) released in the late 1950s. Zhang Hanzhi, p.#74.

The Young Mistresses—*xiaojie*—refer to Wang Hairong, Mao's niece, and Tang Wensheng. The nickname the Young Mistresses originated from Mao, because both were unmarried. One of them—Wang Hairong would remained single to this day. Personal recollections.

72. At one time in the early 1970s the size of its staff was reduced to around 300. Personal recollections.

73. Zhang was born an illegitimate child adopted by Zhang Shizhao, a noted scholar and at one time Minister of Education in the Nationalist Government. Although never a Communist, Zhang Shizhao helped Mao Zedong when Mao was a revolutionary agitator in Beijing University in the early 1920s. He had since maintained a long standing friendship with Mao and Zhou. In December 1963, Zhang Shizhao took his daughter to see Mao on Mao's 70th anniversary. At Mao's request, the young Zhang began teaching Mao English as his personal English tutor for several months. During the Cultural Revolution, she joined the less radical PFLI "Red Flag Detachment" after being rejected by the more radical "Rebel Regiment" for her politically incorrect family background. In 1968 she was branded by the radicals as a "traitor" because of her connections with David Crook, who by then had been charged as a "British spy" because of his work with the British intelligence service during WWII and was subsequently imprisoned for five years and 100 days. Zhang wrote to Mao who in turn lent his support to Zhang. After giving her the mandate in 1970 to carry out "education reform" in the PFLI then relocated to Hubei, Mao in March 1971 personally sent her to the MFA "to become a female diplomat." Zhang Hanzhi, p.#18.

74. Personal recollections.

75. Wang and Tang's liaison role would end in late September 1975. Li Zhisui, pp.#551–554, 576.

76. Zhang had known Wang since 1964 when Wang was in training in the PFLI. Zhang personally coached her. Ya Wen.

77. Li Zhisui, pp.#550–551.

78. Zhang Hanzhi, pp.#51–52. For details, see Chapter 5.

79. Ye Yonglie, p.#497.

80. It was impossible to be certain whether the rift was really caused by policy differences or over political power. Qiao Guanhua, whose first wife Gong Peng died in 1970, became the most eligible bachelor in the MFA. His rift with the Young Mistresses, both single, coincided with his budding romance with the newly divorced Zhang Hanzhi, who, until then a good friend of the Mistresses, would receive repeated warnings from Wang about their relationship. Zhang Hanzhi, pp.#33–57.

81. Quan Yanchi, pp.#379–381.

82. Zhang Hanzhi, pp.#74–75.

83. Deng took charge of the day-to-day work of the State Council, while Wang Hongwen took charge of the work of the party Politburo and Ye Jianying of the CMC. Ye Yonglie, p.#514.

84. Since late September, Mao appointed Mao Yüanxin as his liaison officer replacing Wang Hairong and Tang Wensheng. Mao Yüanxin was said to be instrumental in bringing down Deng Xiaoping. Li Zhisui, p.#576.

85. Mao was said to be unhappy with Qiao because of his failure to point out to Kissinger that Washington and Moscow were pursuing a "new Munich conspiracy" and of Qiao's apparent eagerness to sign a peace treaty with Japan in his talks with the Japanese Foreign Minister. These were termed as mistakes of the right. Zhang Hanzhi, pp.#82–83.

86. By then Zhang Hanzhi no longer had personal access to Mao. She made Qiao's case indirectly through an old PFLI friend, who passed the message through Zhang Yümei, then a PFLI student, to her sister Zhang Yüfeng, Mao's private secretary. Personal recollections.

87. Zhang Hanzhi, pp.#83–84.

88. Some senior MFA officials of the general ambassador generation were jealous of Qiao's diplomatic talents and could not forgive Qiao for replacing Ji Pengfei as FM.

89. Personal recollections.

90. Qian fell out of favor after the exit of Wang Hairong and Tang Wensheng in 1977. He was "exiled" to the Institute of International Studies to become a leading American affairs scholar. Personal recollections.

91. Zhu Lin, pp.#239–241.

92. According to Qiao, his move in March and April 1976 was intended to save the MFA by "exploiting the internal contradictions within the Gang of Four." Zhang Hanzhi, p.#99. This claim however is questionable since Jiang Qing had promised Qiao a vice premiership as early as late 1994. See *Zhongguo Gongchandang Zhizheng Sishi Nian* (The CPC's Forty Years in Power) (Beijing: Zhonggong Dangshi Ziliao Chubanshe, 1989), pp.#526–527.

93. On January 21 and 28, Mao proposed Hua Guofeng to be Acting Premier in charge of country's day-to-day work. The appointment was officially ratified by the Politburo on February 3, 1975. Li Zhisui, p.#584.

94. The critical sentence was "acting according to the established guidelines" which was the slogan used by the Gang of Four to confirm their positions after the death of Mao in their struggle against Hua Guofeng. Hua, on the other hand, used Mao's words "with you in control, I am at ease" to establish his own legitimacy.

On October 4, a cable was sent to Qiao at the UN to delete the sentence. Qiao, unaware of the political struggle in Beijing, was puzzled at its significance but complied. However *Renmin Ribao* (People's Daily) published the undeleted version thus giving ammunition to Qiao's opponents and a chance to unseat him later. Zhang Hanzhi, pp.#101–103.

95. Qiao's official replacement was announced by Li Xiannian on December 12, 1976. Chen Youwei, "*Qiao Guanhua Gaiguan Shinian reng wei Lunding* (The Verdict is Still Out Ten Years After Qiao Guanhua's Death)," *Shijie Zhoukan* (World Journal Weekly), October 3, 1993, p.#S–3.

96. The two Young Mistresses were initially sidelined. It was not until the early 1980s that Wang was given the title of a counsellor in the State Council's Counsellor's Office. Tang became Director of the Bureau for International Cooperation of the Ministry of Railways. Personal recollection.

97. It was somewhat ironic that Qiao found little support in the ministerial leadership, most of its members were former general ambassadors who were envious of Qiao's talents which were highly appreciated by Mao and Zhou. Qiao's base of support came from departmental ranking officials, who had been promoted under Qiao.

98. Most participants tended to be young professionals who had joined the MFA not long ago and thus had a lot of sympathies with the students. The most senior person involved was Hu Hongfan, former PRC ambassador to Venezuela and then Vice Chairman of the Friendship Association. The only known fatality associated with the MFA was the son of Qian Yongnian, an MFA longtime African specialist who was once Minister in Chinese missions to the U.S. and U.N. and at the time deputy director of the Foreign Affairs Office of the State Council. Qian as a result left the FAO and later became ambassador to Indonesia. Personal communications.

99. Wu Xiüqüan.

100. The landmark Conference solidified Mao's position as the *de facto* paramount leader of the CPC in that the military command of the Red Army was transferred from Otto Braun to Mao. After the conference, Zhang Wentian became the General Secretary of the CPC. Wang together with Mao and Zhou Enlai formed the supreme military command. For details of the conference and the roles of Zhang and Wang, see Wu Xiüqüan, pp.#117–125.

101. Zhang would lose his post as Vice Foreign Minister after the Lushan Conference in 1957 when he spoke out against the excesses of Mao's Great Leap Forward and was branded a member of the "Peng (Dehuai)-Huang (Kecheng)-Zhang (Wentian)-Zhou (Xiaozhou) Anti-Party Clique." Wang served as the first PRC ambassador to Moscow. When he returned in 1952, he was appointed Director of the CPC International Liaison Department. Although still a Vice Foreign Minister, his chief responsibilities were no longer with the MFA.

102. Wu as ambassador to Yugoslavia was criticized in 1958 for his pro-Yugoslavian views and left the MFA to become Deputy Director of the International Liaison Department under Wang Jiaxiang. Wu Xiüqüan, pp.#316–321.

103. The First Field Army was commanded by Peng Dehuai and Xi Zhongxün with 350,000 troops in 1949. The Second Field Army commanded by Liü Bocheng and Deng Xiaoping had 300,000 troops. The Third Field Army commanded by

Chen Yi and Su Yü had 600,000 troops and the Fourth Field Army commanded by Lin Biao and Luo Ronghuan had 900,000 troops. Xü Yan, *Jinmen zhi Zhan* (The Battle of Quemoy) (Beijing: Zhongguo Guangbo Dianshi Chubanshe, 1992), p.#11.

104. Jünshi Kexüe Yüan Jünshi Tushuguan, *Zhongguo Renmin Jiefangjün Zhuzhi Yange he Geji Lingdao Chengyüan Minglu* (The Evolution of PLA Organizations and A List of its Leaders at Various Ranks) (Beijing: Jünshi Kexüe Chubanshe, 1990).

105. Xie first became Minister/Counsellor in the Chinese mission in Washington, later Director of the Department of International Affairs. Han Zhang, p.#273.

106. Qian Qichen is said to be impressed by Yang's performance. Personal communications with senior MFA sources. His appointment in 1995 to Assistant Minister of Foreign Affairs seems to have confirmed this.

107. Liü, a graduate of the Fletcher School of Law and Diplomacy, Tufts University, went to the Chinese mission in Washington with Zhu in 1989 and as Zhu's personal aide attended most of Zhu's important meetings. Chen Mingming, the former ambassador's aide who was the first PRC student to graduate from the Fletcher School, felt left out and soon returned to Beijing. Personal communications.

108. Xü Jiatun, *Xü Jiatun Xianggang Huiyilu (shang)* (Xü Jiatun's Hong Kong Memoirs I) (Hong Kong: H.K. Lianhebao Youxian Gongsi, 1993), p.#16, 226.

109. For Zhang Hanzhi side of the family feud story, see Zhang Hanzhi, p.50. For the other side, see Jing Xi, "*Buzhangjia 'Beidao', Xin Furen Yaoqiü Gongan Jübu Qiao Shaoye* (Minister's Home 'Burgled,' New Wife Demanded Police Detain Young Master Qiao," *Ming Pao*, August 10, 1995.

110. It is ironic that Ji regarded by many as mediocre in his performance as FM and replaced by Mao with Qiao Guanhua would survive to become the supervisor of foreign affairs establishment. He never forgave Qiao when the latter was in serious political trouble after the fall of the Gang of Four. Chen Youwei, "The Verdict," October 10, 1993, p.#S–3.

111. Ji Pengfei has his own patron in the Standing Committee of the Politburo. He was a longtime associate of Li Xiannian from WWII New Fourth Army days when Li was a division commander of the Army. Li after the fall of the Gang of Four assumed overall responsibility of foreign affairs as the Head of the CPC Central Foreign Affairs Leading Small Group. After the death of Liao Chengzhi, it was at Li's strong recommendation that Ji was appointed Director of State Council's Hong Kong and Macao Affairs Office in 1983. Xü Jiatun, pp.#16–18.

112. The name originates from a type of Japanese rifle widely used during WWII. It refers to the second generation of CPC cadres who joined the Communist revolution movement around the beginning of the Anti-Japanese War in 1938.

113. Personal recollections.

114. The Director of the State Council's FAO is of ministerial ranking. However as Qian is both Vice Premier in charge of foreign affairs and FM. The FAO Director is sandwiched between the two offices.

115. One of them was Yang Zenya, who became Director of the Asian Department and later ambassador to Japan. His performance in the MFA has been considered mediocre.

116. For much of the 80s, the other two were FM Wu Xüeqian, who was also Secretary of the MFA Party Committee, and Yao Guang, executive Vice FM. Personal recollections.

117. Personal recollections.
118. Yao was no researcher. He later left the MFA and joined CITIC. He finally left CITIC and is now in the U.S. Personal recollections.
119. Most of them would just be retired after their last assignment abroad, which was perfectly legitimate since they had passed the official retirement age. Examples of this include Zhu Qizhen, Zhou Jüe, Wen Yezhan. Zhu would serve in semi-retirement as Vice Chairman of the NPC Foreign Affairs Committee. Zhou Jüe left the foreign affairs sector and became Deputy Director of the State Council's Information Office.

4

Main Actors— The Central Leadership

In Chapter 1, we have examined the Chinese political system and the foreign affairs sector in their vertically structured organizations. In such a vertical view, there is a multitude of elements involved in foreign policy decisionmaking. Since the late 1970s when China began to open up to the outside world, the number of elements in the Chinese system involved in foreign affairs is on the increase. This can lead to some degree of confusion as to who are the main players and what are their roles in the foreign policy process.

A horizontal view of the overall foreign policy decisionmaking structure reveals three basic types of actors: (1) the central leadership,[1] (2) major foreign affairs bureaucracies and institutions,[2] and (3) working level officials in the foreign affairs establishment.[3] This and the following Chapter will examine through case studies the roles of the top leadership, foreign affairs establishment and working level officials in the formulation of China's foreign policies.

There are four components in the central leadership: (1) the paramount leader or leading nucleus, (2) the nuclear circle, (3) members of the Politburo Standing Committee and (4) the other members of the Politburo, particularly its Beijing residents and the Secretariat. The concepts of the leading nucleus and nuclear circle have already been examined in Chapter 1. Normally the leading nucleus and the members of the leading nuclear circle are all members of the Politburo Standing Committee. In this study they are collectively referred to as the top leadership.

The most important characteristics of China's foreign policy decisionmaking are that it is highly centralized and that in terms of key decisions it is very much personalized. This is not only true when compared with practices in the West but also with decisionmaking in other fields and over matters purely of domestic concern. These key decisions include decisions that determine the basic orientation of the Chinese foreign policy, decisions over military operations that involve actual or potential conflicts with foreign powers and decisions in the formulation of regional policy and country policies towards key world powers like the United States, Russia and Japan, and major decisions concerning the implementation of these country policies. Also included are decisions concerning "sensitive" regions or countries, and "sensitive" issues that can have a major impact on China's relations either with a whole category of countries or with key countries.

The following are a number of case studies that focus not only on the dynamics but also the environment surrounding some specific foreign policy decisions made during the eras of Mao and Deng.

In the Mao Era

From 1949 to 1976, Mao Zedong, as Chairman of the CPC, of the CMC and till 1958 State President, dominated China's foreign policy formulation and decisions. Mao's role in the key decisions that determined the fundamental orientations of China's foreign policy, that propelled China into wars or military confrontations with foreign powers, and in decisions concerning the implementation of key country policy is illustrative of the centralized and personalized nature of these decisions.

The Three Key Principles

From September 1948 to January 1949, the Chinese Communist forces won a series of decisive victories in the Chinese civil war. A Communist victory was irreversible and imminent. In planning the decisive military campaigns that sealed the fate of the Nationalists, Mao convened a crucial enlarged Politburo meeting between September 8 and 13, 1948. Although the focus of the meeting was on military matters, Mao also determined that the establishment of a new Communist regime should be put on the agenda.[4] At the meeting Mao set the tone for the basic foreign policy orientation of the new regime: "As for the preparation of transition from New Democracy to socialism, the Soviet Union will help us, first of all helping us develop the economy."[5] Immediately after the meeting, Mao cabled Stalin to brief him on the decisions made during the meeting and requested to travel to Moscow in November to discuss face to face with Stalin. High on Mao's agenda were the basic orientation of the new regime, Soviet recognition and Soviet economic aid.[6] Mao cabled Stalin again on October 16: "(With regard to) convening a political consultative conference and establishing a provisional central government, they should be decided when I am at your place in November."[7]

Stalin however believed that the Chinese civil war was at a critical juncture and Mao must remain in China to personally direct the military operations. He instead suggested to have his Politburo member, Anastas Mikoyan, go to the CPC headquarters in Xibaipo. Mikoyan made the secret trip between January 31 and February 7, 1949, during which he was given in-depth briefings on the current situation and CPC's plans for the future including the new regime's basic foreign policy orientations and tactics.[8] Mikoyan mostly listened to what his hosts had to say. However he did raise some serious questions reflecting the concern of Stalin over the nature of the Chinese communist revolution.[9] Having had a public split with Tito of Yugoslavia just six months ago, Stalin worried that Mao could well be just another Tito.[10]

While assuring Mikoyan that an American intervention was manageable,[11] the prospect of American intervention remained a primary concern of Mao in early 1949. On January 8, 1949, Mao convened a Politburo meeting making plans for 1949 including the scheduled 2nd Plenum of the 7th Party Congress. Mao asked his commanders to prepare for a possible US intervention in the form of either direct involvement in the fighting or occupation of some coastal cities.[12] During the Communist military campaign to cross the Yangtze, precautionary deployment of the Communist forces was effected in anticipation of a possible American or American-British intervention.[13]

To allay Stalin's fear and to forestall a possible American intervention,[14] Mao finalized the basic foreign policy orientation of the new regime which was made public in his famous speech on the 2nd Plenum of the 7th Party Congress on June 30, 1949, four days after his personal envoy Liü Shaoqi arrived in Moscow:

> Externally, unite in a common struggle with those nations of the world which treat us as an equal and unite with the peoples of all countries. That is, ally ourselves with the Soviet Union, with the people's democracies, and with the proletariat and the broad masses of the people in all other countries, and form an international united front . . . We must lean to one side.[15]

However "leaning to one side" is only one component of a three-pronged diplomatic strategy devised by Mao. The other two components—*ling qi luzao* (starting a new kitchen) and *dasao ganjing fangzi zai qingke* (cleaning up the house before inviting guests)—were not made public.[16] The foreign policy implications of these principles were: (1) the new Communist government would not recognize and inherit diplomatic relations established by the Nationalist government; diplomatic status of foreign diplomats previously accredited to the Nationalist government would not be recognized by the new government and they would be treated only as resident foreign nationals; (2) all international treaties and agreements entered into by the previous government would not be inherited automatically and would be re-examined, some abrogated; foreign imperialist influences and privileges were to be eradicated before new diplomatic relations could be re-established on the basis of mutual respect for sovereignty, territorial integrity and mutual benefit. The bottom line was that the new regime would not rush to establish diplomatic relations with "imperialist countries" before its power was well consolidated.[17]

These three key principles were proposed by Mao and discussed in the meeting of the CPC Secretariat which constituted the present-day Politburo Standing Committee,[18] before it was officially ratified at an enlarged Politburo meeting in January 1949 and finally announced on the CPC plenum in March 1949. The implementation of the policy was apparently left to Zhou Enlai. For instance after the Communist forces captured the Nationalist capital Nanjing, the American Ambassador John Stuart, who once served as President of Yenching University remained behind trying to establish some informal contacts with the new Communist authority. On June 8, 1949, Stuart proposed to Huang Hua, a Yenching graduate and then Director of the Nanjing Foreign Affairs Office, that he visit Beijing to meet with Zhou Enlai. Huang, based on his personal understanding of the three principles, first turned it down. Zhou reversed that decision and made arrangements for the President of Yenching University to extend on June 16 an invitation to Stuart to "visit the University," ostensibly for the school's anniversary celebration. Huang under Zhou's instruction would confirm that a meeting in Beijing with Zhou was "possible." The trip was ultimately vetoed by the State Department.[19] Mao's three key principles would determine China's basic foreign policy orientation and diplomatic posture through the 1950s and placed the new regime on a course that ultimately led to a direct military confrontation with the U.S. in Korea.

Chinese Intervention in Korea Korea had long been a Chinese protectorate before the Japanese occupation. The post-War division of the peninsula saw the emergence of two opposing regimes nurtured by the United States and the Soviet Union. The North Korean Communist regime had had a long history of interaction with the CPC with its leader Kim Il Sung having fought in the Chinese Communist forces in Manchuria during WWII. A large number of ethnic Koreans also fought in the Chinese Communist army during the Chinese civil war.

As the threat of American direct intervention in the Chinese civil war began to recede in the second half of 1949, an estimated 50–70,000 ethnic Korean PLA soldiers returned to North Korea in the fall of 1949 and spring of 1950 at the request of Kim Il Sung.[20] Although he was aware of Kim's intention to reunify Korea through military means, Mao did not know an invasion was soon to take place until he was informed of it on May 13, 1950.[21] A surprised Mao directed Zhou to seek urgent clarification from Stalin. Although in his reply, Stalin indicated that he conditioned his approval on Mao's signing on to the idea, Mao was clearly put on the spot and felt compelled to give his blessing.[22]

When the war broke out on June 25, 1950, Mao had just endorsed a massive demobilization of the PLA. Truman's declaration of American intervention in Korea and "neutralizing" the Taiwan Strait did not alter the PLA demobilization plan. The plan for an assault on Taiwan was postponed, but the preparations for attacking Jinmen (Quemoy) remained on schedule.[23] Publicly, on June 28, Mao and Zhou denounced American actions focusing chiefly on its intervention in Taiwan. Gao Gang, Chairman of the Northeast Administrative Council, assumed the chief responsibility for providing logistic support for the North Koreans. The task for military preparations fell on Zhou Enlai, who on July 7 and 13 convened a national defense conference at which it was decided that as a precaution a Northeast Frontier Defense Force with the 13th Army Group as its core was to be set up. The CMC issued an order on July 8 for the 13th Army Group, which was originally designated as the national strategic reserve of the CMC to counter a possible US intervention in the Chinese civil war, to move to the Sino-Korean border area.[24] At the same time, Zhou quickly assembled a small group of military officers and dispatched them to Korea as embassy military attaches to keep a close watch on the developments.[25]

Mao endorsed all the precautionary measures but did not get personally involved in those details. He had no reason to do so. The war went well for Kim: by the end of July his forces had captured 90% of the total territory. However in mid August Kim's military offensive halted in a stalemate.

As early as July 8, Zhou predicted that "protracted warfare" in Korea looked "unavoidable."[26] Watching the ominous massive buildup of American forces in the Far East, Mao on August 4 for the first time raised the prospect of possible Chinese intervention in the Korean War. He told his colleagues at a Politburo meeting that if the Americans won the war, it would be a menace to China. Therefore the Chinese must come to Kim's aid in the form of "volunteers," although the timing of the intervention must be carefully considered.[27] Since then Mao began to get more deeply involved in the preparations. On August 5, he ordered the 13th Army Group to complete war preparations by early September.[28]

On the same day Mao raised the prospect of Chinese intervention, Malik, Soviet chief representative to the UN, offered an olive branch by formally introducing a proposal for peace talks which was welcomed by China. Mao and his generals watched closely the US reaction as a clue to real American intention. The proposal was rejected on September 1: the Americans were planning a counter offensive.

The Chinese strategists focused their attention on America's next move. After analyzing the history of the US 8th Army Corps and General MacArthur, the topography of Korea and troop deployments, the Chinese military reached an almost unanimous conclusion: the Americans were planning an amphibious landing in the "waist" of the Korean peninsula.[29] The Chinese anticipated a dramatic worsening of the situation in Korea.[30]

Mao was convinced that a war with the United States had become unavoidable. On August 1, MacArthur reached an agreement with Chiang Kai-shek on the defense of Taiwan. This was followed by the introduction of the American air force onto the island on August 4.[31] The Americans also accelerated their support for the French forces in Vietnam in early 1950. After the outbreak of the Korean War, American military advisors began to arrive in Vietnam. Mao faced a strategic choice: if a military conflict with the US was inevitable, in which of the three possible theaters—Taiwan, Korea and Vietnam—had he the greatest advantage? The conclusion was Korea where the logistic support was easier for the Chinese than for the Americans and he could count on Moscow to lend its support.[32]

Thus Mao made a strategic decision: if he had to fight with the Americans, it had better be in Korea. On September 9—six days before Inchon, the CMC ordered the 9th Army Group, the main invasion force for the battle of Taiwan that had been stationed in southern Jiangsu, to move to the north to serve as a strategic reserve for the 13th Army Group, thus effectively abandoning the Taiwan campaign.[33]

The American successful landing in Inchon propelled Mao to move simultaneously along two tracks on the diplomatic front. Intense high level consultations were initiated between the Chinese and the Soviets on possible joint intervention. An understanding was reached that the Chinese were to provide ground troops while the Soviets the air cover.[34]

Although he was prepared for a fight, Mao had not abandoned all hopes for a peace settlement even after the Inchon landing on September 15. To the pleas Kim's special emissary, Mao remained uncommitted, pledging only "to be the strong rear area for the Korean people." At the same time Mao was sending additional military experts to lay the groundwork for a Chinese intervention which, Mao told his senior official in Manchuria, Gao Gang, seemed inevitable after Inchon, Zhou under Mao's blessing wrote to Kim in his own name on September 20 urging him to "follow the principles of self-reliance and waging protracted warfare."[35] In other words, Kim should not count on the Chinese to come to his rescue.

Mao was still hoping that the Americans would stop at the 38th parallel after recapturing Seoul on September 28.[36] To deter further American advances, Mao instructed Zhou to issue a series of warnings. On September 21, Zhou told the Indian and Burmese ambassadors that "if the U.S. is bent on expanding the war in Korea and Taiwan, we are sure to resist and liberate Taiwan (from the Americans)." On September 30, Zhou warned that China will not stand by when "imperialists are subjecting its neighbors to wanton aggression."[37]

MacArthur exuberant from his Inchon success dismissed the Chinese warnings as "diplomatic blackmail." A South Korean division first crossed the 38th parallel on September 30. October 1, MacArthur issued an ultimatum demanding unconditional surrender. Late that night Kim met with the Chinese ambassador with an urgent plea for Chinese intervention and a cable to the same effect was sent to Mao. An urgent meeting of the Politburo was convened late on October 1 and continued on October 2. After a long debate in which Lin Biao and Gao Gang led the opposition to intervene, Mao nevertheless made a preliminary decision on October 2 to commit Chinese troops, although the nature, size and timing of a Chinese involvement remained an open question. The decision thus was not final: although Mao issued an advance order to the 13th Army Group to be ready to move, the decision was not communicated to Kim.[38]

To dispel the doubts expressed by his comrades, Mao needed final assurances from both the Soviets and Americans. He cabled Stalin proposing to send Zhou Enlai and Lin Biao to consult the Soviet leader. On October 3, at 1:00 a.m., Zhou called in the Indian ambassador, K.M. Panikkar asking Indian Prime Minister Nehru to pass a message to the UN. In the message which was really intended for the U.S., Zhou gave the most explicit warning to date: China "will take the matter into our own hands" if the U.S. did not halt its advance.[39]

Enlarged Politburo meetings continued from October 3 to 8 to overcome internal opposition. Although only Lin Biao and Gao Gang were known opponents, and Peng Dehuai and Zhou Enlai supporters of Chinese intervention, the majority of the participants had reservations over the wisdom and necessity of such a move. Mao dominated these meetings and used his personal prestige in forcing a consensus.[40] On October 7, the UN passed a resolution that authorized the UN forces to occupy the whole Korean peninsula. The Chinese interpreted the move as finally closing the door on any possible negotiated settlement. Mao was compelled to act and a decision was made to intervene massively. And on October 8 Peng Dehuai was appointed commander of the CPV forces in Korea. On the same day, Mao dispatched Peng to the CPV headquarters in Shenyang and Zhou to Moscow to firm up the Soviet support. He also cabled Kim Il Sung about his decision.[41] The decision was again put on hold on October 13 as a result of Zhou's talks with Stalin before a final decision was adopted on October 14 to enter the war.[42]

Throughout the crisis, Mao had focused his personal attention on the crucial issue whether the Chinese should intervene and if yes, under what circumstances? He let his chief lieutenants Zhou Enlai and Gao Gang handle the tactical issues such as communicating with the Soviets, Americans and Koreans, and preparations, both military and logistic, for the intervention. For instance when Mao decided to intervene and Zhou was to give Americans a last warning through the Indian ambassador, Zhou personally saw to it that an appropriate translation of his message was effected to ensure that the seriousness of the message was conveyed while at the same time no definitive commitment was made. Similarly, Zhou was credited for the Chinese intervention in the name of "volunteers" in order to avoid openly declaring war with the US and possible widening of the conflict to China proper.[43] The ultimate decision was made by Mao in spite of majority reservation. Mao, with an impeccable record of military successes during the Chinese civil wars, commanded tremendous respect among his CPC colleagues and PLA commanders, who despite personal reservations, were willing to support him once he made up his mind.

Rapprochement with the United States In the late 1960s, there were two significant strategic developments that fundamentally altered Mao Zedong's perception of the world. On the one hand, his number one enemy the United States, after a decade of escalating intervention in Vietnam, was embroiled in serious internal turmoil. By 1969, the United States under the newly elected President, Richard Nixon, was seeking to disengage from Southeast Asia. On the other hand, the Soviet Union under Leonid Brezhnev had undergone a massive military buildup and by the early 1970s achieved military parity with the United States. The nature of the Sino-Soviet rivalry had also undergone a significant change from polemic debate over ideology to military confrontation. Stationed across the Sino-Soviet and Sino-Mongolian border were more than one million Soviet troops equipped with nuclear weapons.

The American retreat and the Soviet advance were symbolized by the two doctrines in the names of the leaders of the two superpowers: the Nixon Doctrine of 1969 and Brezhnev Doctrine of 1968. The former enunciated by Nixon in Guam started the process of Vietnamization of the conflict in Indochina. The latter which advocated "limited sovereignty" for the Socialist states was used in August 1968 to justify Soviet invasion of Czechoslovakia. From Mao's perspective, the Nixon Doctrine was defensive in nature indicating American disengagement from Vietnam thus removing a major military threat to the Chinese security while the Brezhnev Doctrine was inherently offensive to justify the Soviet right to military intervention.

A series of border conflicts between the Chinese and Soviet forces in early 1969 accelerated the process of re-orientation of the Chinese foreign policy. Before the CPC 9th Party Congress, Mao on February 19, 1969 commissioned a series of studies by a group of PLA marshals of the international situation. The group led by Ye Jianying presented three reports with a policy recommendation to seek a diplomatic breakthrough with a rapprochement with the U.S.[44]

By summer 1969, rumors about a possible Soviet surgical nuclear strike against Chinese targets surfaced in a number of Western capitals. Mao ordered a massive evacuation and large-scale construction of air raid shelters in major Chinese cities like Beijing. The situation was so tense that Lin Biao, with the Soviet commando surprise attack on the Czech airport as a prelude to its 1968 invasion fresh in mind, was convinced that on board the special Soviet plane supposedly carrying the official Soviet delegation to the border negotiations were in fact Soviet commandos or a nuclear bomb—a prelude to a surprise attack, and he ordered to have the plane tracked until it landed at Beijing airport on October 9.[45]

Mao pondered over the survival of his besieged nation and regime—in the east Japan, in the south the US, in the west India and in the north the Soviet Union. As the United States was the real power behind Japan and India after the 1962 border war did not pose a realistic threat, Mao knew that he faced a strategic choice between the United States and the Soviet Union. The former he decided was the lesser of the two evils, since the US had never occupied any Chinese territory and was geographically much more distant. The strategy he was to adopt was a classic one called *yüan-jiao jingong*—making peace with the distant adversary while tackling the enemy in proximity.[46]

Mao's desire to mend fences with the Americans was reciprocated by the newly elected US President, Nixon, who early in his presidency sent out a diplomatic signal by announcing in July 1969 a relaxation of US restrictions on travel and commerce with China. Privately Nixon told his Pakistani and Rumanian hosts during his overseas trip in summer that he wished to open up a dialogue with the Chinese leaders. Following the withdrawal from the Taiwan Strait of two American destroyers on routine patrol duties instituted during the Korean War, Zhou Enlai ordered the quiet release of two Americans captured on July 16 after their boat strayed into Chinese waters near Hong Kong.

In early December Nixon instructed the US ambassador to Poland to contact Chinese diplomats on the resumption of bilateral ambassadorial talks.[47] Mao, who did not hide his preference for conservative politicians in the West, was heartened by the report from Zhou Enlai and was ready to reopen the talks, which had been used by the two sides to exchange propaganda, for serious negotiations on improving bilateral relations.[48] The talks which soon resumed proved a false start. After only two rounds, it was suspended again on May 18 due to Chinese public posturing after American incursion into Cambodia in early 1970.[49]

In June 1970, Nixon pulled his forces out of Cambodia. Mao in August personally authorized the visit by Edgar Snow, an American journalist considered a longtime friend of the Chinese Communist leadership dating back to the late 1930s. On October 1, Zhou personally made unprecedented arrangements to have the Snows appear on the Tiananmen rostrum by Mao's side for the Chinese national day celebration. Zhou also saw to it that the picture that appeared in the next day's official newspaper *Remin Ribao* contained nobody else but Mao, the Snows and an interpreter.[50] Though Zhou's subtle signal was completely missed by the White House, Nixon would pass some important messages of his own. On October 25, he told the visiting Pakistani President, Yehya Kahn, that he wanted a rapprochement with China and would not collude with Moscow against China and was willing to send a secret envoy to Beijing to open up a dialogue. Next day, he told the visiting Rumanian President the same thing and in his toast at the White House banquet he for the first time used the People's Republic of China in reference to Beijing.[51]

Nixon's message was passed to Zhou Enlai in Kahn's private talks with Zhou on November 10 in Beijing. After receiving this message, Mao instructed that to solve the problems between China and the U.S., Beijing must deal with those sitting in the White House (*dangquan pai*), thus giving a green light to direct official dialogue.[52] Four days later Zhou with Mao's blessing gave his reply: Beijing would welcome a visit by a special envoy from the US and the timing should be decided upon through the Pakistanis. Soon came Kissinger's reply that the invitation had been accepted. When the Rumanians passed the message in late November, Zhou went a step further in his reply by extending an invitation to Nixon. The invitation became public on December 18 when Mao in his interview with Snow said that Nixon was welcome to China either as President or as a tourist.[53]

In spring 1971 the Pakistani channel fell silent as the war in Indochina escalated. On January 31, 1971, Beijing at Zhou's intervention signed an agreement with the Japanese Table Tennis Association to participate for the first time since the start of the Cultural Revolution in the World Table Tennis Tournament to be held in April in Japan. On March 14, Zhou personally authored a report suggesting Chinese participation in the tournament. The report was approved by Mao. Another MFA preparatory document established guidelines for the Chinese players' interaction with the Americans: the Chinese should not initiate conversations or greetings with the Americans, and in a matchup should not exchange team flags but could shake hands ... Mao read the document without indicating his opinion.[54]

The Chinese delegation arrived in Japan on March 21 and started daily reports by telephone on their activities which included their contacts with the Americans. These reports were sent directly to Mao and Zhou. The interactions with the Americans attracted particular attention of Mao and Zhou who were engineering a Sino-US rapprochement. On March 30, the head of the Chinese delegation met his American counterpart who expressed some interest in visiting China as the US State Department had just announced on March 15 the lifting of restrictions on travel to China. The Chinese delegation asked for instructions. After some deliberation, the MFA and the State Sports Commission on April 6 jointly wrote an RFI suggesting that the move was premature and they should decline the American request. Zhou signed on to the idea by instructing the Chinese delegation to tell the Americans politely that there would be chances in the future for them to visit China. Mao initially approved Zhou's recommendation when he circle-read the MFA's RFI on the afternoon of April 6. However at midnight, Mao changed his mind and had the MFA instruct the Chinese delegation to extend an invitation to the Americans.[55] Zhou Enlai immediately after receiving the telephone call from Mao's office summoned Huang Hua and Zhang Wenjin of the MFA to emphasize the political significance of the decision and put the two in full charge of the arrangements for the visit.[56]

On April 7, a formal invitation was extended to the American delegation to visit China. The delegation arrived in China via Hong Kong on April 10. Zhou Enlai met the members of the delegation on April 14 and declared that the "door is open." One week later on April 21, Zhou, seizing the momentum, took the initiative by officially extending through the Pakistani President an invitation to the White House for high level talks. The invitation was officially transmitted to the White House by the Pakistani ambassador on April 27. On May 17, Nixon through the Pakistanis officially accepted the invitation and suggested a round of secret preparatory talks between Kissinger and Zhou Enlai, thus opening the process of rapprochement between the two countries.[57]

Throughout the whole process Mao not only made all the major decisions but also decisions concerning the implementation of the policy change. If Mao still needed to consult members of the top leadership in making major foreign policy decisions in the early 1950s, by the middle of the 1960s, Mao at the pinnacle of political power would make all major decisions by himself. The Politburo Standing Committee was but a rubber stamp.

In the Deng Era

On January 18, 1972 just one week after Alexander Haig and his advance team visited China to lay the groundwork for Nixon's historic visit, Mao suffered his first major attack. On January 21, for the first time facing the prospect of death, Mao designated Zhou to take over after his death. However Mao never fully trusted Zhou.[58] On May 18, 1972, it was discovered that Zhou Enlai had cancer. Mao knew very well that the radicals led by his wife would not be able to manage the nation's affairs. He needed somebody else. As early as January 10, 1972 at the funeral of Chen Yi, he indicated that Deng Xiaoping who had been in exile since the beginning of the Cultural Revolution might be rehabilitated.[59]

In February 1973 Deng returned to Beijing and on March 10, the CPC Politburo at the suggestion of Mao appointed Deng Vice Premier of the State Council. Soon at the 10th Party Congress in August Deng was made a member of the Central Committee and in December a member of the CMC. Meanwhile Zhou's health deteriorated rapidly. On June 1, 1974, Zhou finally checked into the hospital for a cancer operation and Deng assumed the overall responsibility of day-to-day operations of the government. On October 20, Mao decided to nominate Deng as first Vice Premier, Vice Chairman of the CPCCC and of the CMC and PLA Chief of General Staff. Deng's position was ratified at the Party Central Committee plenum and the 4th NPC held in mid January 1975. He began to take charge of foreign affairs. In mid 1974 Deng led the Chinese delegation to the UN Special Conference in New York at which he enunciated Mao's theory of "the three worlds." In 1975 he revisited France.[60]

By the end of 1975, the radicals began to make a political comeback thanks to Mao's nephew Mao Yüanxin, who starting in late September, replaced Wang Hairong and Tang Wensheng as Mao's liaison with the Politburo. Mao started a new political campaign in October to criticize Deng for "reversing the verdict of the Cultural Revolution." Zhou Enlai passed away on January 8, 1976 and a power vacuum emerged. On January 21, Mao Yüanxin in his report to Mao said that Hua Guofeng and Ji Dengkui, who had remained neutral in the political struggle, requested Mao to designate a person to take overall charge of the work at the Center. Mao nominated Hua Guofeng to be Acting Premier and Deng Xiaoping to take charge of foreign affairs only.[61] This did not last long as Deng was soon to fall in April and Hua Guofeng would take over foreign affairs. As Mao was in his death bed and Hua was new to foreign affairs, China's diplomacy was on autopilot. No major initiative was undertaken during this period of uncertainty.

Mao died in September and it was almost a year before Deng made his final comeback as Vice Premier of the State Council in charge of foreign affairs.⁶² Initially Deng like Mao dominated the foreign policy decisionmaking even though he was not the Chairman of the CPC. Following the Soviet invasion of Afghanistan, Deng moved quickly to normalize diplomatic relations with the US in late 1978 and launched a border war with Vietnam in early 1979. In making both decisions which left unmistakable marks of Deng's personal style, Deng like in the early Mao era had to overcome much inner party doubts and bureaucratic inertia.

Soon the dynamics of foreign policy decisionmaking began to shift away from that of the paramount leader toward the leading nuclear circle which through much of the 1980s included Deng Xiaoping, Chen Yün, Hu Yaobang and Zhao Ziyang. In 1982 at the 12th Party Congress, Deng Xiaoping, Hu Yaobang, Zhao Ziyang, Ye Jianying and Li Xiannian were elected members of the Standing Committee of the CPC Politburo. By then Ye Jianying was suffering from poor health and Chen Yün, never considering himself a foreign affairs specialist, did not take much interest in foreign affairs. Li Xiannian, though officially in charge of foreign affairs, was in a very weakened position in the party following the economic readjustment in 1979.⁶³ The key foreign policy decisionmakers were Deng Xiaoping, Hu Yaobang and Zhao Ziyang.

Although Deng remained the ultimate decisionmaker, he retreated in 1982 and let Hu and Zhao make most of the decisions concerning the implementation of the foreign policy re-adjustment initiated and outlined on the 12th Party Congress. The foreign policy readjustment came as a result of the fundamental change in CPC's focus after Deng's emergence as the new leading nucleus on the 3rd Plenum of the 11th Party Congress in December 1978. Economic development had become the centerpiece of the CPC program. The political campaign of "emancipating the mind" had also helped the new leadership to take a new and hard look at the country's international posture. The new "independent foreign policy" was formally announced by Hu Yaobang at the 12th Party Congress held in September 1982.⁶⁴ The central theme of the new policy was to create a favorable international environment for China's economic development program by gradually improving relations with the Soviet Union but not at the cost of relations with the West. The policy also envisaged a process of incremental change in China's relations with South Korea, Israel and South Africa—countries that had been on China's public black list—to serve the domestic economic needs.

Once the broad outlines and the guidelines were approved by Deng and ratified by the Politburo. Most of the important decisions that fell within the established guidelines were left to Zhao Ziyang and Hu Yaobang. Zhao came to Beijing as an outsider. For some time he did not take much interest in foreign policy issues. The initial phase of the foreign policy readjustment was presided over by Deng Xiaoping and Hu

Yaobang who managed to replace Foreign Minister Huang Hua with his protege Wu Xüeqian in 1982. Zhao's initiation came through his position as the top manager of the Chinese economy. Later Zhao developed a personal interest in relations with the U.S. and Hu an interest in relations with Japan. The following are three case studies of the role of members of the leading nuclear circle in making some of the foreign policy decisions in the 1980s.

Zhao Ziyang's Visit to the United States in 1984

During the American presidential election campaign in 1980, Ronald Reagan, the Republican candidate, repeatedly pledged that if elected he would move to restore "official relations" with Taiwan. The Chinese reacted strongly to Reagan's statement. In August Deng Xiaoping told George Bush, Reagan's running mate sent to Beijing to allay Chinese fears, that the Sino-US relations would stall if Reagan was to live up to his campaign rhetoric. Deng's warning, however, did not deter the Republican candidate from making new statements.

When Reagan entered the White House in 1981, bilateral relations were in a big chill mainly over the issue of US arms sales to Taiwan. As early as 1980, the Carter administration had decided internally to sell FX fighters to Taiwan. Reagan planned to announce the decision in late 1981. The Chinese indicated that they would react strongly and warned of a possible downgrading of the relations. In late 1981 bilateral negotiations were initiated to settle the issue of arms sales which resulted in a communique on August 17, 1982 placing limits on such sales.

However relations between Beijing and Washington did not stabilize. The two sides clashed repeatedly over such issues as the defection of a Chinese tennis player, old railway bonds, Taiwan's status in the Asian Development Bank, Chinese textile exports to the United States. Beginning in spring 1983, Washington introduced a new China policy. Relations improved after a relaxation of US export control over high technology items to China and an agreement reached over Chinese textile exports. In order to create further momentum in the relationship, it was agreed during US Defense Secretary Caspar Weinberger's visit to China in September 1983 that Chinese Premier Zhao Ziyang and US President Ronald Reagan would visit each other's country in 1984.

However Reagan for a period of time continued his occasional outbursts of pro-Taiwan rhetoric right up to the eve of Zhao's scheduled visit in January 1984.[65] The Chinese faced a dilemma. If Zhao went ahead with his planned visit, it could be interpreted as Chinese indifference to "American interference" in Chinese domestic affairs which could lead to bolder US actions. On the other hand cancelling the visit would deal a major blow to the relationship that had just started to show signs of improvement after a stormy period.

Zhao called an enlarged Politburo Standing Committee meeting after Reagan's statement on December 2, 1983, with the participation of the members of the Foreign Affairs LSG to discuss whether he should proceed with the planned trip. Deng Xiaoping, Ye Jianying and Chen Yün did not attend the meeting.[66] Hu Yaobang was known to be cool to the idea of business as usual in light of Reagan's strong pro-Taiwan stance.[67] The head of the Foreign Affairs LSG, Li Xiannian expressed his reservations about the trip under the circumstances. This was shared by others who suggested postponing the trip. Zhao however believed that the trip should go ahead. Instead of stressing the importance of making the trip, he asked the participants to think about the consequences of not going at this late moment. He argued that cancelling the visit would have such an adverse effect on the bilateral relationship, which had barely recovered from earlier conflicts, that it could substantially alter China's position in the global strategic triangular relationship to the detriment of China's fundamental national interest.

By then the established guidelines for the "independent foreign policy" were to improve relations with the Soviet Union at a slow but steady pace and in a deliberate manner so that it would not come at the expense of China's overall relations with the West, particularly the U.S., on which China depended for much of its capital and technological needs. Since the issue was not a clear cut one and there was no real opposition (rhetoric on Taiwan was after all more of an emotional issue), the Politburo agreed that the visit should go ahead. The decision later won the endorsement of Deng Xiaoping, and the MFA announced on December 6, 1983, that the visit was to proceed and preparations for the trip accelerated.[68] Zhao was proven correct in that after the exchange of visits in early 1984, bilateral relations stabilized and gained new momentum.

Policy Regarding Foreign Navy Ship Visit In early 1985 a bitter dispute broke out between the U.S. and New Zealand over the issue of visits by nuclear-armed vessels to New Zealand ports. The US and New Zealand are members of a 1951 mutual defense treaty known as ANZUS that also includes Australia. The dispute came at a time when the U.S. and the Soviet Union were locked in a rivalry over the deployment of medium range missiles in Europe. A grassroots antinuclear peace movement was sweeping through Western Europe. The Green Party of West Germany, which opposed the deployment of American Pershing II missiles in Germany, was gaining in popularity.

In 1984, David Lange, head of New Zealand's Labour Party, campaigned on an antinuclear platform and won the general election in July.

Prime Minister Lange's antinuclear stance was soon put to the test when in December 1984 the Pentagon formally requested permission to make a port call as part of ANZUS exercises in the South Pacific, known as Sea Eagle, scheduled for March. In the request, the U.S. maintained its policy of "neither confirming nor denying" the presence of nuclear weapons on its ships.

On February 4, 1985, Lange officially announced its government's rejection of the request based on the US refusal to provide assurances that there were no nuclear weapons on board the ships. The U.S. reacted angrily by cancelling the scheduled manoeuvers and threatened a broad range of further actions, including some that were not strictly military. The strong U.S. response was viewed as aimed at West European nations with strong domestic antinuclear peace movements. There was a concern in Washington that those nations might be emboldened to take similar actions concerning U.S. nuclear arms stationed on their territories.

In the face of the American threats, Lange stood firm and accused the U.S. of using "bullying tactics" in an attempt to "change a policy which has been embraced by the New Zealand people." At the same time he reaffirmed his country's desire to remain in ANZUS. The dispute reached an impasse with a virtual suspension of military ties between the two countries.[69]

The US-New Zealand dispute came at a time when three US Navy destroyers were scheduled to visit Shanghai in May 1985 based on an agreement reached during US Secretary of the Navy John F. Lehman Jr.'s visit to Beijing in August 1984. The port call would have been historic as it would be the first of this kind since US naval ships left China in 1949—36 years ago.

Coincidentally on April 13 that year, Hu Yaobang, General Secretary of the CPC, was scheduled to start an official visit to Australia and New Zealand. In a customary practice of the MFA Information Department, arrangements were made for Hu to meet Australian and New Zealand journalists prior to his departure. As the US-New Zealand dispute was the hottest topic in the South Pacific at the time, Hu was asked by a New Zealand journalist during the interview on April 10 whether Beijing would allow US nuclear-armed ships to visit its ports. Hu replied that the US Navy's port call would be "an informal visit" by "conventional warships." Asked further if this meant that Washington had assured Beijing that the visiting ships would not carry nuclear weapons, Hu said offhandedly, "That is already understood between China and the U.S. There is agreement. As they will enter Chinese territorial waters, that is our sovereignty, so they have to give their consent."[70]

While his statement on an informal visit by a conventional ship came from prepared cards of official positions,[71] the rest represented his own understanding of the situation which the MFA would have been happy had he kept it private.

China, since the explosion of its first atomic bomb in 1964, had adhered to a policy of no-first-use regarding nuclear weapons. Chinese Premier Zhou Enlai declared after the test that at no time and under no circumstance should China be the first to use nuclear weapons against any other country. In the 70s China undertook obligations in respect of declared nuclear-free zones. However Beijing had never formulated any policy regarding nuclear ships visiting Chinese ports. The question did not arise because China itself is a declared nuclear power. Prohibiting ships with nuclear weapons to make port calls did not make much sense. In fact since the early 1980s Beijing had already received naval ship visits from many countries including ships from known nuclear powers like France and Britain. Beijing on those occasions had not sought assurances that they carry no nuclear weapons.

Hu's (mis)statement came at a sensitive time and triggered an almost immediate uproar. Officials on both sides scrambled to respond. Diplomats of the US Embassy in Beijing called for clarification. Upon returning to his office from the interview, Zhu Qizhen, the Vice Foreign Minister for American and Oceanian Affairs who was present at the interview, asked for transcripts on the diplomatic exchanges concerning US ships' visits. Although US Embassy defense attaches had indicated *privately* that US Navy ships would not carry nuclear weapons, the same officials, now apparently under great pressure from Washington, insisted on the record that US policy was as it had always been to neither confirm or deny the presence of nuclear weapons.

Once the issue became publicized, both sides sought political cover by hardening their positions. A US State Department spokesman flatly rejected Hu's assertion by insisting that Washington had "given no assurances to the Chinese . . . that the visit would be by nonnuclear-armed vessels." He added pointedly, "No U.S. ship visits can take place anywhere in the world except under this policy."[72] Under the Chinese political culture, the MFA could not come out to repudiate its top political leader in the face of an open challenge from a foreign government and on an issue that China had no formal policy.

The PLA which had made all the preparations grumbled about Hu's mishap. The MFA in an effort to salvage the deal issued a statement on April 15 saying "US conventionally-powered naval vessels may call at a Chinese port on an informal, ceremonial visit." The statement deliberately skirted the question of nuclear arms. However during the heat of the moment, the two sides were unable to reach a compromise and the visit was postponed.[73]

Negotiations were restarted after a cooling period and the two sides finally reached a compromise. China would state its policy of allowing non nuclear-armed ships to visit its ports and expect other countries to respect this policy. The U.S. on the other hand would reaffirm its no confirmation no denial policy. Under this formula, US Navy ships visited Chinese port of Qingdao in 1986 and Shanghai in 1989. This formula thus became official Chinese policy regarding foreign naval ships' visits to Chinese ports.

The Case of a Russian Hijacker Although Politburo and Secretariat meetings are officially important venues for making important decisions. Most of the decisions of secondary importance are made on paper through endorsing/rejecting RFI documents of foreign affairs bureaucracies by members of the Standing Committee of the Politburo and other relevant members of the central leadership.[74] In such instances only when there is a significant divergence of opinion is a Politburo meeting warranted to resolve the differences.

On December 19, 1985, a Soviet civilian airliner on a domestic flight from Nerchinski Zavod, near the Sino-Soviet border of Siberia, to Irkutsk, about 700 miles to the west, was hijacked by its co-pilot named Shamil Alimuradov. After crossing the border near Manzhouli, the Antonov 24 carrying 50 crew and passengers was forced to land on frozen fields in the Ganan District of China's northeastern Heilongjiang Province, about 50 miles northwest of Qiqihar. The Foreign Affairs Office of Heilongjiang Province immediately notified the MFA and asked for instructions.

The hijacking came at a time when Mikhail Gorbachev was newly elected General Secretary of the Soviet Communist Party and the central leadership of the CPC had determined soon after his election that he represented a fundamental change in Soviet foreign and domestic policy orientation. Although Beijing would continue to insist on the Soviet removal of the three big obstacles as a precondition for improving the political relationship between the two countries, a process of rapprochement in other fields was already under way.[75]

The hijacking of a civilian aircraft with China as its destination was the first of this kind that Beijing had encountered. Previously in May 1983, a Chinese domestic flight was hijacked to South Korea. In the ensuing direct negotiations, Beijing insisted that the hijackers be extradited to stand trial in China, a request that Seoul refused.

Under these circumstances, the MFA almost felt embarrassed to have such a hot potato in its hand. It moved swiftly to first detain the hijacker and to transfer the rest of the crew and passengers including two naval officers of the Soviet Pacific fleet to Qiqihar. It initially proposed handling the hijacker and the rest separately by first repatriating the rest of the Russians promptly. This was quickly approved by the top leadership. On December 21, the rest of the crew and passengers returned to the Soviet Union each with a big gift bag of Chinese consumer items and liquor. It was not until December 25 that the MFA confirmed the story following an Associated Press report.

The Soviet Embassy in Beijing officially requested to have Alimuradov extradited to the Soviet Union. Over this thorny issue, the Department of Soviet and East European Affairs drafted an RFI that favored turning the hijacker over to the Russians. The MFA leadership signed on to the idea and submitted it to the central leadership for endorsement. The problem did not concern China's fundamental interest nor did it affect the basic orientation of China's foreign policies. It was strictly speaking a tactical issue which under normal circumstances would have been handled by the MFA. It was however submitted for approval by the top leadership because of its uniqueness as it could set a precedent for future cases and also because it concerned relations with a major power at a sensitive time.

As it was not a clearcut issue: while extraditing the hijacker might add a little goodwill, not to do so would not jeopardize the relationship either, Hu Yaobang and Zhao Ziyang circle-read the RFI with no comment. However when it reached Chen Yün's office, the veteran, who ironically was known in the West for favoring Soviet-style economics and who, in less than a month, was to give an emotional greeting to Ivan Arkhipov, the chief of Soviet economic advisors in the 1950s,[76] wrote two words, "*bu song* (not to return)," on the RFI with no further elaboration. Deng Xiaoping finally circle-read the RFI with no comment. The decision was thus made and a life spared from almost certain death if extradited. The Chinese authorities announced on February 21, 1986 that "after a judiciary investigation," Mr. Shamil Alimuradov would stand trial in a Chinese court for "unlawful seizure of a civilian aircraft." He was sentenced on March 4, 1987, to 8 years' imprisonment in China.[77]

This is a special case in that Chen Yün seldom expressed his opinion over foreign affairs issues. However it shows that when one key member of the leading nuclear circle like Chen, who once ranked above Deng Xiaoping, has a strong opinion over an issue that others do not care much about one way or the other, his view often prevails.[78]

Conclusion Almost all important foreign policy decisions since the founding of the PRC have been made by the leading nucleus, the leading nuclear circle and/or the Politburo Standing Committee. During the Mao era, it was Mao assisted by Zhou Enlai who made all important decisions. In the Deng era, the locus has shifted to members of the leading nuclear circle. As for the central leadership which hereby refers to the Politburo and the Secretariat, although the relative weight of the two organs changes from time to time in relation to each other due to political shifts within the CPC leadership, they generally serve the purpose of (1) a rubber stamp to lend legitimacy to decisions made by the paramount leader, the leading nuclear circle or the Politburo Standing Committee, (2) a consultancy for the paramount leader in some key decisions, (3) a forum for building inner-elite consensus or coalition, (4) an architect that provides the blueprint for a new foreign policy orientation often as pointed out by the paramount leader, and (5) a command center for the direction for achieving major foreign policy goals.

Notes

1. In the Chinese political system, there is a very strict definition of the term *zhongyang lingdao*—the central leaders, more often known in the Chinese media as *dang he guojia lingdaoren*—the party and state leaders. Officially the term refers to members of the CPC Politburo and Secretariat, Standing Committee members of the CPC Central Committee (CPCCC) Advisory Committee, Secretary of the CPCC Discipline Inspection Committee, President and Vice President of the State, Premier and Vice Premiers of the State Council, State Councilors, Chairman and Vice Chairmen of the National People's Congress (NPC) Standing Committee, Chairman and Vice Chairmen of the National People's Political Consultative Conference, President of the Supreme People's Court, Procurator-General of the Supreme People's Procurate, and Chairman and Vice Chairmen of the CPCCC Military Commission. Yan Huai, "*Zhongguo Dalu Zhengzhi Tizhi Qianlun* (Understanding the Political System of Contemporary China)," *Papers of the Center for Modern China*, No. 10, August 1991, pp.#15–16.

2. Main foreign affairs bureaucracies include the MFA, MOFTEC, International Liaison Department, Second Directorate of the PLA General Staff Department, and Xinhua News Agency.

3. Individuals here refer to the professionals below the ministerial rank.

4. Maomao, *Wo de Fuqin Deng Xiaoping* (My Father Deng Xiaoping) (Beijing: Zhongyang Wenxian Chubanshe, 1993), Shangjüan (Vol. 1), pp.#593–594.

5. Bo Yibo, *Ruogan Zhongda Jüece yü Shijian de Huigu* (A Reminiscence on Some Major Decisions and Events) (Beijing: Zhongyang Dangxiao Chubanshe, 1991), p.#36.

6. Yü Zhan and Zhang Guangyou, "*Stalin 'Kouxin' zhi Mi* (The Mystery of Stalin's 'Oral Message')" in Han Zhang (ed.), *Zhongnanhai Waijiao Zhenwenlu* (Diplomatic Anecdotes of Zhongnanhai) (Taiyüan: Shanxi Gaoxiao Lianhe Chubanshe, 1994), p.#2. Pei Jianzhang et al, (eds.), *Xin Zhongguo Wanjiao Fengyün I* (New China Diplomacy I) (Beijing: Shijie Zhishi Chubanshe, 1990), p.#16.

7. Bo, p.#36.

8. Ibid., p.#37.

9. One of the most contentious issues among Chinese scholars and ex-officials was whether Stalin asked Mao not to cross the Yangtze River. It is perhaps true that Stalin did not make that request explicitly as there is no archival evidence to prove that. However before Mikoyan's arrival, Stalin cabled Mao on January 10, 1949 about a request he had received from the Nationalists to mediate between the two sides. Although Stalin said he would respect Mao's opinion, he nevertheless indicated his interest in playing the role of a mediator for fear of a possi-

ble US intervention in the Chinese civil war should Mao seek a total victory. For an exchange of cables between Mao and Stalin over the issue of possible Soviet mediation, see *CWIHP Bulletin,* Issue 5, winter 1995/1996, pp.#27–29.

The fear of US intervention apparently was not Stalin's sole interest in seeing a less than total communist victory. Mikoyan also raised questions about the nature of the Chinese revolution: why do the Chinese distribute confiscated land to the peasants instead of going for collectivization? Why does Mao plan to have the participation of non-Communists and national bourgeoisie in the new regime? Why do the Chinese have so many non-Communist youth organizations? Bo, pp.#29–30. Yü & Zhang, pp.#4–5. Li Yinqiao, *Zai Mao Zedong Shenbian Shiwu Nian* (15 Years By the Side of Mao Zedong) (Shijiazhuang: Hebei Renmin Chubanshe, 1991), pp.#96–97.

10. Wu Xiüqüan, *Huiyi yü Huainian* (Memoirs and Cherishment) (Beijing: Zhongyang Dangxiao Chubanshe, 1991), p.#235, 244. Another indication of Stalin's worry about Mao being more nationalist than communist was Mikoyan's expressed concern over Mao's attitude toward Mongolia which under the Soviet control had declared independence from China. Yü & Zhang, p.#2.

11. Li Yinqiao, p.#97.

12. Mao Zedong, "The Present Situation and the Party's Tasks in 1949," *Mao Zedong Jünshi Wenxuan* (Selected Military Works of Mao Zedong) (Beijing: Zhanshi Chubanshe, 1981), pp.#328–329.

13. Ye Fei, *Ye Fei Huiyilu* (The Memoirs of Ye Fei) (Beijing: Jiefangjün Chubanshe, 1988), pp.#539–540.

14. The policy was also intended for a domestic audience, as some non-Communist independents wanted Mao to seek an accommodation with the United States and the West. In making the announcement, Mao intended to force them to make a choice and a clean break with the Nationalists and "imperialist forces." Bo, p.#38.

15. Mao Zedong, "*Lun Renmin Minzhu Zhuanzheng* (On the People's Democratic Dictatorship)," *Mao Zedong Xüanji IV* (Selected Works of Mao Zedong IV) (Beijing: Renmin Chubanshe, 1965), p.#1477.

16. Huang Hua, "*Nanjing Jiefang Chuqi Wo tong Stuart de Jici Jiechu* (Several Contacts I made with Stuart in the Early Days After Nanjing's Liberation)," *New China Diplomacy I,* p.#25.

17. Ibid. The reason behind the decision to make these two components of the policy "internal" was not revealed. Judging by the fact that Zhou Enlai made arrangements for US Ambassador John Leighton Stuart to visit Beijing in June 1949 (the trip was never made on orders of the US State Department), one can only assume that Mao would like to keep the option of establishing diplomatic relations with the West open.

18. The Secretariat, functioning as the Standing Committee of the Politburo, consisted of Mao, Liü Shaoqi, Zhu De, Zhou Enlai and Ren Bishi. Li Yinqiao, pp.#113–115. Huang Hua, p.#25.

19. Huang Hua, pp.#29–31.

20. Nie Rongzhen, *Nie Rongzhen Huiyilu III,* (Nie Rongzhen's Memoirs III) (Beijing: Jiefangjün Chubanshe, 1984), p.#744. Chen Jian, "The Sino-Soviet Alliance and China's Entry into the Korean War," *Cold War International History Project,*

Working Paper No. 1, Washington: Woodrow Wilson International Center for Scholars, June 1992, p.#11, 20.

21. There has been considerable disagreement among ex-officials and scholars as to the role of Mao played in the origination of the Korean conflict. N. Khrushchev claimed that Stalin, unsure of a possible American reaction, solicited Mao's opinion during Mao's visit to Moscow between December 1949 and January-February 1950. Mao dismissed the prospect as unlikely. As a result Stalin gave the go-ahead. N. S. Khrushchev, *Khrushchev Remembers* (Boston: Little, Brown, and Co., 1970), pp.#367–368. Shi Zhe, who accompanied Mao to Moscow and later served as Zhou Enlai's interpreter in early October 1950 during Zhou's trip to firm up Soviet support for the imminent Chinese intervention, dismissed Khrushchev's account. He claimed that Zhou demanded a Soviet explanation as to why the Chinese had not been informed of the invasion. Chen Jian, p.#21. Wang Li, who was a member of Mao's writing team during the Sino-Soviet split and later a member of the Central Cultural Revolution Small Group, claimed that Mao told him in person that a discussion of the Korean problem indeed took place among Stalin, Kim and Mao. However Mao was the only person who was opposed to an invasion because he believed that it would trigger an American intervention which would lead to a subsequent defeat for Kim. Sandwiched between Stalin and Kim, Mao signed on to the idea only reluctantly. Wang Li, *Xianchang Lishi: Wenhua Dageming Jishi* (Eyewitness to History: A Record of Events in the Great Cultural Revolution) (Oxford: Oxford University Press, 1993), p.#113. New revelations from Soviet archives lend credence to the view that (1) Mao on several occasions in 1949 and early 1950 expressed general support for Kim's plan to reunify the country by military means; (2) Mao was kept in the dark about North Korea's war preparations by both Stalin and Kim. (When Mao inquired in late March 1950 whether the Koreans had formulated concrete plans for reunification, Kim's ambassador in Beijing said that Kim was "undergoing medical treatment" even though Kim was in Moscow at the time when he solicited and finally obtained Stalin's official green light for his invasion plan.) Mao apparently was not informed of the war plan until he was told, much to his surprise, of Stalin's approval by Kim on May 13, 1950; (3) although Mao mentioned several times the possibility of "throwing in Chinese soldiers," Mao was clearly not serious about intervention even after being notified of Kim's plan as he soon approved a large scale demobilization of the PLA and continued plans for the Taiwan campaign. For the exchange of cables between Stalin and the Soviet ambassador to Beijing, see "More Documents from the Russian Archives," *Cold War International History Project Bulletin*, Washington: Woodrow Wilson International Center for Scholars, Issue 4, Fall 1994, pp.#60–61. For Mao's talk with the Korean ambassador, see Ignatiev's cable to Vyshinsky, April 10, 1950, *CWIHP Bulletin*, Issue 5, Winter 1995/1996, p.#38.

22. Wang Li. Mao who had just returned from his first trip to Moscow and signed a mutual defense treaty was under pressure to show his solidarity with the Kremlin. With Stalin's advice against his attempt to unify China fresh in his mind, Mao might feel that he could not let Kim down as Stalin had done to him.

23. Zhou Enlai in his capacity as Vice Chairman of the CMC told General Xiao Jingguang, PLA Naval Commander, on June 30, 1950 that the demobilization of

the ground forces was to continue while the building up of the air force and navy was to accelerate. The planned Taiwan campaign was to be postponed. Xiao Jingguang, *Xiao Jingguang Huiyilu II* (Xiao Jingguang's Memoirs II) (Beijing: Jiefangjün Chubanshe, 1988), p.#26. The preparation for attacking Jinmen went ahead. It was not until after September 15, 1950, when Americans landed in Inchon, that the planned attack on Jinmen was officially postponed. Xü Yan, *Jinmen zhi Zhan* (The Battle of Quemoy) (Beijing: Zhongguo Guangbo Dianshi Chubanshe, 1992), pp.#143–145.

24. Chai Chenwen and Zhao Yongtian, *Banmendian Tanpan* (The Panmunjom Negotiations) (Beijing: Jiefangjün Chubanshe, 1992), p.#28.

25. At the outbreak of the war, China had only a commercial office of the Northeast Administrative Council in the North Korean capital. Even though it had exchanged diplomatic recognition seven months earlier on October 6, 1949, its ambassador was recovering from an illness in China. The first group of officers left Beijing on July 8 and arrived in Pyongyang on July 10. Chai & Zhao, pp. #22, 29–34.

26. Ibid.

27. Bo, p.43.

28. "Mao Zedong and the CPC Central Committee to Gao Gang, August 5, 1950," *Jianguo yilai Mao Zedong Wengao I* (Mao Zedong's Manuscripts Since the Founding of the PRC) vol. 1, (Beijing: Zhongyang Wenxian Chubanshe, 1987), p.#454.

29. On August 23, the Office of Operations of the PLA General Staff Department held a meeting in the Jüren Hall of Zhongnanhai to study the military situation in Korea. The meeting concluded that as the next step the American forces would launch an amphibious landing operation. The most probable and threatening site for such an operation would be Inchon. See Lei Yingfu, "*Yin Rong Wan Zai, En Hui You Meng*" in Cheng Hua (ed.), *Zhou Enlai he ta de Mishumen* (Zhou Enlai and his Secretaries) (Beijing: Zhongguo Guangbo Dianshi Chubanshe, 1992), p.#114. It was immediately reported to Zhou, who sensing the significance of the conclusion, notified Mao right away. Mao believed it was highly probable and asked Zhou to transmit the danger immediately to Kim Il Sung and Stalin. On August 31, Deng Hua, Hong Xüezhi and Xie Fang, commanders of the 13th Army Group, reported jointly to Beijing that they believed that the American forces would attempt to land in the rear of Kim's forces—the Seoul or Pyongyang region. On September 7, Chai Chenwen on recall back to Beijing presented an official assessment from the Chinese Embassy to Nie Rongzhen, PLA Acting Chief of Staff, with an estimate that the American forces would attempt to land in Inchon or other areas. It was immediately transmitted to Mao. Wang Bo, *Peng Dehuai Ru Chao Zuozhan Jishi* (A Record of Peng Dehuai in Battle in Korea) (Shijiazhuang: Huashan Wenyi Chubanshi, 1992), p.#49. Chai & Zhao, pp.#58–59.

30. This is also reflected in the pessimistic attitude of Lin Biao, who was Mao's first choice to lead the Chinese intervention forces. Around September 8, after listening to Chai Chengwen's report on the situation, Lin asked Chai whether Kim, who at the time still controlled 90% of the territory, was prepared to retreat into the mountains to wage a guerilla warfare if necessary. Chai and Zhao, p.#59.

31. Most Chinese books claim, without citing sources, that MacArthur and Jiang Jeshi (Chiang Kai-shek) reached an "agreement" to set up a US "military

liaison group in Taiwan" and the Taiwanese naval and air force were placed under the command of the American general to "jointly defend" the island. And on August 4, an American team arrived in Taiwan to set up "a forward command" for the 13th Aviation Wing of the US Air Force. See Xü Yan, p.#145, Li Changjiu and Shi Lujia, *Zhong Mei Guanxi Erbai Nian* (Two hundred Years of Sino-US Relations) (Beijing: Xinhua Chubanshe, 1984), p.#170. The available official US records seem to contradict the claim as no "official" agreement was recorded. And it was seven days after MacArthur's visit that a Survey Group led by the general's Deputy Chief of Staff, Major General Alonzo Fox arrived in the island to assess Chiang's military needs. But exactly what was discussed one-on-one between MacArthur and Chiang remains a mystery. MacArthur made a statement after arriving back in Tokyo: "Arrangements were completed for effective coordination between the American forces under my command and those of the Chinese Nationalists, the better to meet any attack which a hostile force might be foolish enough to attempt." See George H. Kerr, *Formosa Betrayed* (Boston: the Riverside Press Cambridge, 1965), p.#406, Joseph C. Goulden, *Korea: the Untold Stories of the War* (New York: Times Books, 1982), p.#153, and William Sebald, *With MacArthur in Tokyo* (New York: W.W. Norton, 1965), p.#154.

32. Xü Yan, p.#145.

33. Ibid.

34. There is no archival evidence available yet to confirm the exact timing when these consultations started. Some scholars believe that the consultations started before the Inchon landing. Huang Chenxia and Jurgen Domes, *P'eng Te-huai* (Stanford: Stanford University Press, 1985), p.#60. Chen Jian, p.#24. Others say they happened after Inchon. Chai & Zhao, *Kangmei Yüanchao Jishi* (A Record of Events in the War of Resistance Against US Aggression and Aiding Korea), p.#55. Zhang Xi, "Peng Dehuai Shouming Shuaibing Kangmei Yüanchao de Qianqian Houhou," *Zhonggong Dangshi Ziliao*, No. 31, 1989, p.#123. Xü Yan, *Diyici Jiaoliang: Kangmei Yüanchao Zhanzheng de Lishi Huigu he Fansi* (The First Trial: A Historical Review of and Reflections over the War Against US Aggression and Aiding Korea) (Beijing: Zhongyang Guangbo Dianshi Chubanshe, 1990), p.#22. Recently declassified Soviet cables suggest that consultations started as early as July. Stalin in a cable to Zhou Enlai on July 5, 1950, gave his endorsement to a Chinese plan to concentrate nine divisions on the Chinese-Korean border for intervention "in case the enemy crosses the 38th parallel." And he promised "We will try to provide air cover for these units." *CWIHP Bulletin*, Issue 5, p.#43.

35. The Northeast Frontier Force had long requested to send a 4-men advance team to Korea. It was only approved after Inchon. To keep the options open, they had diplomatic status of military attaches of the Chinese Embassy. When they were in Shenyang after September 17, Gao Gang showed to Chai Chengwen a letter from Mao indicating a Chinese intervention looked inevitable. Chai and Zhao, *Banmendian*, pp.#69–70.

36. Zhou Enlai was told by Indian Prime Minister Nehru after the recapturing of Seoul on September 28 that the Foreign Ministers' meeting of the US, Britain and France held between September 12 and 18 decided that the UN forces would not cross the 38th parallel and whether to cross the line was to be decided by the UN. Chai & Zhao, *Banmendian*, pp.#64–65.

37. Ji Ming & Liü Qiang, p.#4.

38. Chai & Zhao, *Banmendian*, p.#72. There is considerable confusion over what transpired in the Politburo meeting on October 2. The Chinese have declassified a cable by Mao to Stalin on that day informing him of a decision to send Chinese troops to Korea. However a recently declassified Soviet version of Mao's cable that day, in response to one by Stalin to Mao one day earlier urging Chinese intervention, called the Chinese version into question. It showed a "preliminary" decision by the Chinese leader NOT to advance "a few" divisions to Korea as urged by Stalin. The Chinese version could have been misdated as the Chinese firmed up a decision in the following days. But Chinese sources also reveal that on October 2, the CMC issued an order to the 13th Army Group to be ready to move which was received at 2:00 a.m. on September 2. At 11:00 the 13th Army Group replied that all would be ready by the 15th and its commander communicated to his armies that they should be ready to move by October 10 (Wang Bo, pp.#49–50). Mao's cable, the Soviet version, could be a ploy to bargain with the Soviet leader.

39. Chai & Zhao, *Banmendian*, pp.70–71. One version of the event alleges that Zhou told the Indian ambassador that Beijing "has to be concerned." The warning was thus weaker than his previous address on September 30. Micheal H. Hunt, "Beijing and the Korean Crisis, June 1950–June 1951," *Political Science Quarterly*, V. 17, fall 1992, p.#462. This is apparently inaccurate. According to Pu Shouchang who translated for Zhou, Zhou urgently called him to his office late that night and gave him 30 minutes to come up with an accurate translation of the Chinese expression *women yao guan.* The key word was *guan* which in Chinese conveys implicitly intervention. Zhou wanted the other side to understand the seriousness of the Chinese warning but at the same time remained ambiguous about the nature of the commitment. Harvard-educated Pu remembered that he had read in US newspapers about how crimes in New York had driven some citizens to "take the law into their own hands" and decided with the approval of Zhou to use the expression. The message got across clearly since Panikkar asked for no further clarification and immediately cabled the Indian Prime Minister. Personal communications, March 8, 1995.

40. Wang Bo, pp.#10–14, 20–21. Although Peng's attitude has been well known, Zhou's support for the intervention was only recently revealed by his secretary for military affairs, Lei Yingfu, p.#116.

41. Chai & Zhao, *Banmendian*, pp.#72–75.

42. Available primary and secondary source materials offer little to clarify what transpired during Zhou Enlai's October 9–16 visit to the Soviet Union. According to a Chinese source, when Zhou met Stalin late on October 9, Stalin promised to supply the Chinese forces with Soviet military equipment. But on the crucial question of air cover, he said that in order to avoid having its planes shot down and its pilot captured, the Soviet air force could only operate in the rear and it would be ready only after two months. Zhou could not persuade him to change his mind and had to cable Mao on October 10 about the result of the meeting and asked Mao to reconsider his decision. Faced with this new prospect, Mao quickly put the CPV on hold and called Peng Dehuai back to Beijing for another round of Politburo meetings on October 13 to reconsider the soundness of the previous

decision to intervene. After a brainstorming session, Mao decided to enter the war even temporarily without a Soviet air cover. He cabled the decision to Zhou Enlai and asked Zhou to stay a few more days in Moscow to seek further assurance from Stalin on two issues. First, instead of cash purchase, the Soviet military equipment would be provided on credit, so that the Chinese could retain US$2 billion for domestic economic development, thus making the war effort more sustainable. Second, the Soviets were to provide air cover in two to two and a half months' time not only for the Chinese forces in Korea but also for major Chinese cities. The requests were quickly approved by Stalin who promised Soviet credit and 16 fighter wings for air cover. After receiving Stalin's cable, Zhou on October 14 again cabled him to request additional bombers for the Chinese forces in Korea and for major Chinese coastal cities. But then Stalin changed his mind. He told Zhou that even after two months, the Soviet air force would only be stationed in China and would not venture into Korea to provide air cover for the Chinese ground forces. Zhou left Moscow on October 16. Mao would reconvene a politburo meeting on October 18 to discuss the situation. It was decided that the Chinese forces would enter Korea on October 19 without Soviet air cover. Nan Shan, "*Zhou Enlai san fang Stalin* (Zhou Enlai's Three Visits to Stalin)," *Wen Wei Po*, September 13–15, 1995. Another Chinese source claims that when Zhou communicated the Chinese decision to intervene, Stalin had second thoughts, fearing a world war and favoring Kim setting up a government in exile in China. Chai and Zhao, p.#75. This version is supported by Stalin's October 8 cable to Kim Il Sung confirming a cable from Mao on October 7 informing Stalin of Mao's decision to intervene, and also by the fact that subsequent Soviet air cover was limited to the Chinese-Korean border areas and Stalin's rejection to provide frontline air support to Chinese-Korean ground forces. It is also confirmed by the Soviet ambassador's cable to Stalin on October 14 reporting his meeting with Mao, who told him of a final decision to intervene since problems such as air cover were clarified and requested a credit for weaponry. *CWIHP Bulletin*, Issue 5, pp.#116–118.

Shi Zhe, Zhou's interpreter, however insisted that Zhou told Stalin of the Chinese decision not to intervene. Shi Zhe, *Zai Lishi Jüren Shenbian: Shi Zhe Huiyi Lu* (By the Side of Historical Colossi: Shi Zhe's Memoirs) (Beijing: Zhongyang Wenxian Chubanshe, 1991). This view is supported by a research paper by Alexandre Y. Mansourov who suggests that Stalin's "about-face" on the question of air cover is a myth since the Soviet leader had been consistent in willing to provide it. *CWIHP Bulletin*, Issue 5, pp.#94–107. This seems partially borne out by the fact that Soviet fighters started engaging American aircraft as early as November 1, 1950, over the Yalu River.

43. Another consideration was to assuage Stalin's fear that the Soviet Union would be dragged into a direct conflict with the U.S. due to its obligations to defend Chinese territory under the Sino-Soviet mutual defense treaty. Ji Ming & Liü Qiang, p.#8. You Ping, *Da Mu Qianhou de Jiaoliang* (The Trials Before and Behind the Big Scene) (Chengdu: Xinan Jiaotong Daxüe Chubanshe, 1993), p.#212.

44. The four PLA marshals taking part in the studies were Chen Yi, Ye Jianying, Nie Rongzhen and Xü Xiangqian. From March 1 to October 8, a total of 24 weekly sessions were held. Three reports were officially presented to Mao, with one

entitled *Dui Zhanzheng Xingshi de Chubu Guji* (A Preliminary Estimate on the Situation of War), July 11, 1969, and another *Dui Muqian Xingshi de Kanfa* (A View on the Current Situation) of September 17, 1969. It was Chen Yi, who was officially still the FM, who first suggested a resumption of Sino-US ambassadorial level talks to break the ice in Sino-US relations. However it was not clear who presided over the studies. According to Chen's son, Chen at Zhou Enlai's request presided over the study meetings. See Chen Xiaolu, *Jinian Chen Yi* (In Memory of Chen Yi) (Beijing: Wenwu Chubanshe, 1991), #497. Another source puts Ye Jianying as head of the group. See Fan Shuo, *Ye Jianying zai 1976* (Ye Jianying in 1976) (Beijing: Zhongyang Dangxiao Chubanshe, 1990), p.#71. Ye is favored here for the following two reasons: (1) Chen at the time was in deeper political trouble than the relatively trouble-free Ye; (2) staff support for the studies was provided by the Second Directorate of PLA's General Staff Department. Ye at the time was heavily involved in the day-to-day work of the PLA.

45. Based on the Soviet strategic deployment and intelligence information, Mao and Lin suspected that the Soviets were using the reopening of border negotiation as a smoke screen for a surprise attack on China. In mid October, a Politburo meeting decided to accelerated war preparations and Lin once ordered the Chinese strategic missile force to be on standby to fire. The Russian plane that carried the Soviet delegation was to arrive during noon time on October 9. That day Lin gave up his customary nap to keep track of the flight. Zhang Yünsheng, *Lin Biao Mishu Huiyilu: Maojiawan Jishi* (The Memoirs of Lin Biao's Secretary: A Record of Events at Maojiawan) (Hong Kong: Cunzhen Chubanshe, 1988), pp.#250–254.

46. Li Zhisui, pp.#494–495.

47. On December 3, 1969, the US ambassador to Poland tried to contact Chinese chargé d'affaires Lei Yang while both were attending a fashion show. It was not until it was over that the American got hold of Lei's interpreter and told him that he had received instructions from Washington to establish contact with the Chinese mission. By then Lei was already in his car. The interpreter promised to transmit the message.

Zhou who had been looking for an opening was excited upon receipt of the cable from Poland. He rushed to see Mao, saying: "(We) have found the way. Now (we) can knock on the door. (We) have got the door knocker." Mao quickly approved the reopening of talks with the U.S. Zhou cabled the Embassy next morning. Two days after the initial contact, an official invitation was extended to the US ambassador to visit the Chinese embassy which took place on December 11. The Sino-US Ambassadorial Talks subsequently resumed. Geng Biao, "*Zhou Enlai shi Xin Zhongguo Waijiao de Chuangshiren he Dianjiren* (Zhou Enlai is the Founder and Originator of the New China's Diplomacy)" in Pei Jianzhang (ed.), *Yanjiü Zhou Enlai Waijiao Sixian yü Shijian* (A Study of Zhou Enlai's Diplomatic Thought and Practice) (Beijing: Shijie Zhishi Chubanshe, 1989).

48. In giving his personal approval to the resumptions of the talks, Mao said: "It has been 11 years since the suspension of Sino-US Warsaw talks in 1958. It is time to start the talks anew for some earnest discussions. It appears that Nixon is sincere having transmitted messages several times indicating his willingness to have a dialogue with China." Li Zhisui, pp.#495–496, 542.

49. Wei Shiyan, "*Kissinger Mimi Fanghua Neimu* (The Inside Story of Kissinger's Secret Visit to China)," *New China Diplomacy II*, pp.#33–34.
50. Ji Ming & Liü Qiang, pp.#111–114.
51. Wei Shiyan, pp.#34–35.
52. Ibid., p.#36.
53. Ibid. Mao was said to suspect that Snow was a CIA agent. His interview with the American was intended to pass his messages directly to the US government. Li Zhisui, p.#510.
54. Mao only circled his name on the report with no comments. Qian Jiang, "'*Pingpong Waijiao' Shimo* (The Story of the "Ping Pong Diplomacy")," Han Zhang, p.#156.
55. Wu Xüjün, Mao's personal chief nurse, recalls that after the RFI was returned to the MFA, Mao was visibly uncomfortable with the decision. He took his usual dose of sleeping pills around 11 p.m. and was only semi-conscious when he mumbled to Wu to call the MFA to reverse the decision. Since Mao had established rules that what he said after taking sleeping pills would not count, Wu took considerable risks in deciding to inform the MFA about the reversal under an extraordinary set of circumstances. For more details, see Lin Ke, Xü Tao and Wu Xüjün, "*Lishi de Zhenshi* (The True Life of Mao Zedong)," (Hongkong: Liwen Chubanshe, 1995), pp.#305–311.
56. Han Zhang, pp.#165–168. Li Zhisui, p.#535.
57. Wei Shiyan, p.#37.
58. Li Zhisui, pp.524–529, 550–551.
59. Mao told Chen's widow Zhang Qian that Deng was different from Liü Shaoqi in that Deng's problem was that of a "contradiction among people" in nature. Li Zhisui, p.#550.
60. Ibid. Quan Yanchi. Zhang Hanzhi, p.#73.
61. Li Zhisui, p.#584. Fan Shuo, p.#65.
62. Deng was officially rehabilitated on the Party plenum in August 1978. The final consolidation of his power came in December 1978 at the 3rd Plenum of the 11th Party Congress.
63. In 1978 Hua Guofeng announced an ambitious modernization program characterized by large-scale import of Western industrial plants and technologies. The program caused considerable balance of payment difficulties. In spring 1979 the program known to its critics as *yangmaojin*—"rash foreign advance"—was scrapped. Li Xiannian, who was the Vice Premier in charge of the economy, was subject to criticism and later relieved of his economic responsibilities.
64. "The independent foreign policy" requires that China "must not be dependent on or attached to any big power or power bloc," that it "will not ally or establish strategic relations with any superpower and will not support one against the other," and that over major international issues, it will adopt positions and make decisions based on their own merits.
65. Ronald Reagan for instance told a group of high school students on December 2, 1983: "We have made it plain that in continuing and trying to build this relationship with the People's Republic of China on the mainland, we, in no way, retreat from our alliance and our friendship with the Chinese on Taiwan. We are not going to throw aside one friend in order to make another." *The New York Times*, December 3, 1983, p.#6.

66. It has become a practice for the veterans not to participate in some Politburo meetings due to old age and poor health. It is customary for their secretaries to sit in Politburo Standing Committee and Secretariat meetings and later report to them. The secretaries sometimes would present their boss's opinions and report back to their bosses on the meetings but have no right to participate in the discussion. Xü Jiatun, II, pp.#438—439.

67. It is somewhat ironic that at the time of his dismissal in late 1986, Hu was hailed in the West as a pro-democracy liberal. Yet Hu was never known to harbor many warm sentiments for the U.S. Hu was in fact a driving force behind Sino-Soviet rapprochement in the mid 1980s. On November 26, 1983 during his trip to Japan, Hu caused a diplomatic stir when he warned at a press conference that if the US administration's response to the Congressional bills regarding Taiwan was not satisfactory, Beijing would have to reconsider the planned exchange of visits by Zhao and Reagan. Earlier the US Senate Foreign Relations Committee passed a resolution on November 15 affirming Taiwan's right to determine its own future free from Beijing's coercion. Three days later an attachment of the Congressional appropriation bill supported Taiwan's continued membership in the Asian Development Bank. On November 30, 1983, Reagan in signing the appropriation bill stated that the attached resolution did not reflect the position of his administration which recognized Beijing as the sole legal government of China. *The New York Times,* November 27, December 7, 1983.

68. In making the announcement, the MFA made it clear that Beijing was still not satisfied with the US response but was willing to make the trip in spite of it. On the same day an article in *Renmin Ribao* called Reagan's remarks on December 2 "very puzzling." *Facts on File 1983,* p.#933.

69. *Facts on File 1985,* pp.#88–89.

70. *The Washington Post,* April 11, 1985.

71. It is the MFA practice to have its official positions on a variety of issues printed on a set of cards before Chinese leaders meet the foreign press. This is the job of the Fifth Division of the Information Department although the most official positions on regional issues are drafted by regional departments. Hu was known to have a habit of ignoring the official lines from time to time.

72. *Facts on File 1985,* p.#287.

73. To break the impasse, the MFA first suggested that the two sides adopt a formula under which the Chinese would state its policy of accepting nonnuclear-armed ships without commenting on if they had received assurances, and the Americans would confirm no change in their policy without restating it. It was hoped that in this way the two sides could avoid having to react to each other's statement. However this was not acceptable to the Americans. A US State Department official confirmed on May 6 that the three US Navy ships scheduled to visit Shanghai were conventionally powered but he repeated that the no confirmation, no denial policy would not be relaxed. *Keesing's Contemporary Archive 1985,* Vol. XXXI, p.#33923.

Britain, which has a similar no confirmation no denial policy, however, accepted the Chinese formula. On July 11–15, 1986, two British navy ships, the destroyer HMS *Manchester* and the frigate HMS *Amazon,* visited Shanghai, the first port call by foreign nuclear-capable ships since the dispute with the U.S. broke out. *Facts on File 1986,* p.#796.

74. An RFI document that needs approval of the central leadership is first submitted to the Foreign Affairs Office of the State Council which serves as the staff office of the Central Foreign Affairs LSG. The director of the Office, who represents the most senior bureaucrat, would in turn submit it to the Head of the Foreign Affairs LSG, who represents the central political leadership. If the Head of the LSG determines that the matter is within his competence, he may endorse/reject/revise the RFI. If on the other hand he believes otherwise, most often he will submit the RFI to the members of the Standing Committee of the Politburo and relevant members of the central leadership for endorsement by writing on its cover his comment or suggestion or simply the names of the leaders in their proper political order, from the paramount to the most junior leader. The document though will travel in reverse order, first going to the office of the most junior leader. The leader has a choice of either giving explicit endorsement or rejection, or writing his own opinion, or simply circling his name. The last choice known as *quanyüe*—"circle read"—proves tricky, as during the Cultural Revolution, Mao would claim that some of the decisions "circle-read" by him had in fact been made without his consent—for by circling his name he only indicated having read the document and it did not represent his approval. Lin Biao would routinely have his secretaries circle for him on most RFIs. Mao during his last years would also have Zhang Yüfeng circle for him. For a photo of an authentic document, see Chen Xiaolu, #474.

75. The three obstacles were the Soviet occupation of Afghanistan, the mass of Soviet military forces along the Sino-Soviet border and in Mongolia and the Soviet support for the Vietnamese military occupation of Cambodia.

76. Arkhipov visited China in March as Soviet First Deputy Premier and signed a protocol covering the exchange of engineers and technicians. During his visit, he had emotional meetings with Chen Yün, Bo Yibo and other CPC veterans with whom he had worked in the 1950s.

77. *Keesing's 1987,* p.#35065.

78. On the 8th CPC Party Congress in 1956, both Chen and Deng were elected members of the Standing Committee of the CPC Politburo. Of the 7 Standing Committee members, Chen ranked 5th and Deng ranked 7th.

5

Main Actors—
Institutions and Individuals

Foreign Affairs Institutions

Under the top leadership lie the foreign affairs bureaucracies of ministerial ranking. As they have been examined in Chapter 1, these bureaucratic institutions represent the foreign policy elements of the three major systems of Chinese political power: the party, the government and the military. Officially these institutions make decisions over the details in their implementation of foreign policy decisions made by the central leadership. According to their respective functions, they can be roughly placed into three main categories: (1) policy consultation, coordination and supervision—the Central Foreign Affairs LSG and the Foreign Affairs Office of the State Council, (2) policy recommendation and implementation—the Ministry of Foreign Affairs (MFA), the Ministry Of Foreign Trade and Economic Cooperation (MOFTEC), the CPC Central (Committee) International Liaison Department (ILD), the Second Directorate of the PLA General Staff Department (GSD), (3) information and research—Xinhua News Agency, the Third Directorate of the PLA GSD, academic foreign affairs research institutes. Of the bureaucracies and institutions, only the MFA, MOFTEC and ILD play official policy roles. Others only represent bureaucratic interests in foreign policies, with the PLA one of the newest.

A disproportionate length is devoted to the PLA and the defense industries in this Chapter not because of the important and independent policy roles they play, but to clarify some of the issues related to them that have received much international publicity. On the other hand the brief treatment of such important bureaucracies as MOFTEC and ILD should not be viewed as an indication of their insignificance. Rather it is because China's foreign economic policy and interaction with foreign parties are not the focus of this study.

The Central Foreign Affairs LSG and the Foreign Affairs Office of the State Council

The Central Foreign Affairs LSG is a non-standing body consisting of a Head and one or two Deputy Head(s) and ministerial officials from various foreign affairs bureaucracies. It was first established in 1958 with Vice Premier and Foreign Minister Chen Yi as its Head. Its members consisted of Vice FM Zhang Wentian, Director of the International Liaison Department Wang Jiaxiang, Director of the Overseas Chinese Affairs Committee Liao Chengzhi, Minister of Foreign Trade Ye Jizhuang and Liü Ningyi of the Trade Union.[1] During the Cultural Revolution, this body like many others disappeared with most of its members in political hot water. When it was re-established after the fall of the Gang of Four, Li Xiannian was appointed Head and Zhao Ziyang Deputy Head of the LSG. Its members consisted of Wan Li, Chen Muhua, Ji Pengfei and Foreign Minister Wu Xüeqian, Minister of Foreign Trade, Director of Economic Relations with Foreign Countries and Director of the CPC International Liaison Department.[2]

Following the 13th Party Congress, Li Peng took over the premiership from Zhao Ziyang who became the General Secretary of the CPC. Li Xiannian was replaced by Yang Shangkun as State President. The Central Foreign Affairs LSG was subsequently reorganized after the reshuffle. Li Peng became the Head of the LSG, and State Councillor and Foreign Minister (FM) Wu Xüeqian his deputy. Former Director of the State Council Foreign Affairs Office Ji Pengfei became LSG advisor. Its members included Vice FM Qian Qichen who would soon replace Wu as FM, MOFTEC Minister Zheng Tuobin, Director of the ILD Zhu Liang, President of the *People's Daily* Qian Liren, and Defence Minister Qin Jiwei.[3] Qin's membership was significant since it was the first time that the LSG was represented by a professional soldier of the PLA. In the past, Chen Yi was officially a PLA marshal and member of the CMC, thus theoretically representing the PLA interest. Through much of the 80s the military had no official representation at this level. Qin's membership thus was an acknowledgement of the PLA's interest in foreign affairs and the need to bring it on board for better policy coordination and implementation.

The Central Foreign Affairs LSG provides a forum for the members of the central leadership in charge of foreign affairs—politicians—to meet face to face with the leading officials of various party, government and military foreign affairs institutions—top bureaucrats—to discuss important issues, exchange views and come up with policy recommendations to be submitted to the top leadership for final decisions. When necessary, departmental level officials from relevant bureaucracies and academic specialists and influential journalists are also invited to sit in on some of the LSG meetings. Although the LSG is not a decisionmaking body, some decisions are in fact made in the LSG meetings. The ratification of these decisions by the central leadership is but a matter of formality. Other times decisions are made by the central leadership based on the recommendation of the LSG with minor modifications.[4] Decisions at this level often involve cross ministerial jurisdiction or interest.

The Foreign Affairs Office of the State Council, otherwise also known as the Central Foreign Affairs Office of the CPC, provides the staff work for the Central Foreign Affairs LSG. The Office represents the highest ranking foreign affairs bureaucratic institution. Its Director often plays the role of the highest ranking foreign affairs consultant in the bureaucratic systems to the central leadership. Manned mostly by ex-officials of the MFA, the Office has always been headed by a ministerial ranking ex-official of the MFA. With a staff size of only 20, it largely plays the role of an overall foreign affairs sectoral coordinator. It also supervises the implementation of decisions made by the central leadership.[5] Because it is mostly staffed by MFA officials who would return to the MFA after a period of time, the Office is often regarded as a bastion of MFA influence.

The Ministry of Foreign Affairs

The MFA plays a pivotal role in China's foreign policy decisionmaking. It is indisputably the most important foreign affairs institution in the formulation and implementation of China's foreign policy. There are two important roles played by the MFA in the foreign policy formulation and decisionmaking process. First, it plays a decisive role in the "tactical" aspects of foreign policy decisionmaking. Second, it plays the role of a reliable provider of "processed" information for the central decisionmakers.

Policy Interpretation When some key "strategic" foreign policy decisions are made by the central leadership, they are often no more than some vague concepts, basic policy orientations, broad policy guidelines and long-term policy goals, in a word—only the "bones." It is often up to the MFA to make "tactical" policy choices and work out detail plans for the realization of the policy goals—adding the "flesh and blood" to China's foreign policy.

In September 1982, Hu Yaobang proclaimed in the 12th Party Congress that China was to pursue an "independent foreign policy" under which it would make decisions on international issues based on an independent judgement on their own merits. The interpretation and implementation of such policy fell on the MFA. The main problem at the time was how to change the practice of basing the judgement of an issue or a country on the Soviet policy over the issue or toward that country—*yi sü hua xian*. Namely if a country was judged to be pro-Soviet, it must be an enemy, otherwise a friend. If the Soviet supports an issue China must oppose it.

The Korean Airliner Incident of 1983. In September 1983, a South Korean airline Boeing 747 with 269 people on board strayed into the airspace of the Soviet Far East. It was shot down by Soviet air force fighters over the Sakhalin Islands. None of the passengers or crew on board survived. The incident touched off a world-wide condemnation of the Soviet action. The initial Chinese reaction was to "deplore" such an action on the part of the Soviet Union.

The Reagan Administration took the lead in waging a massive worldwide propaganda campaign. An emergency meeting of the UN Security Council was convened on which a tape recording of Soviet ground-air communications supplied by the Japanese Self-Defense Agency was played. The US delegation to the UN pushed for a resolution condemning the Soviet action.

The Chinese delegation cabled the MFA for instruction over the UN Security Council vote on the resolution. A high level meeting was held after the morning ID4D news briefing, with the participation of all vice FMs and assistant FMs and the chiefs of relevant departments. There was a considerable divergence of opinion among the participants, with those handling US relations favoring a vote for the US-sponsored resolution, while those associated with Soviet affairs expressed serious reservations, pointing among others to new revelations that a US military RC–135 reconnaissance plane was flying in the vicinity, "tickling" the Soviet air defense system.

The majority came to be persuaded that it was a case of innocent people falling victim to the Soviet-US superpower rivalry. As a concrete manifestation of its independent foreign policy, China should side with neither superpower. Until new conclusive evidence came to light, it was decided that the Chinese Permanent Representative to the UN, Ambassador Ling Qing, was to express "shock" over and "deplore" the Soviet action in the debate but to abstain over the US resolution that "condemns" the Soviet action.[6] The Department of International Organizations was to draft an RFI in accordance with the decision and submit it to the central leadership for approval. The RFI was quickly approved and the vote instruction was cabled to the Chinese delegation in New York. The decision was taken in spite of strong American pressures and intense Soviet lobbying.

U.S. Invasion of Grenada in 1983. On October 16, 1983 a military coup took place in Grenada—a tiny Caribbean island republic that had been under the rule of a Marxist regime led by Mr. Bishop. On the order of General Austin, Mr. Bishop, Prime Minister of Grenada, was arrested together with a number of his ministers. The general claimed that Mr. Bishop had been ousted from the party's central committee for having "disgraced the party and revolution." On October 19, the situation turned violent when some 3,000 people marching on the barracks where Mr. Bishop was believed to be held were driven back by the military who opened fire on the crowd. There was considerable chaos following the shooting. As a result, the military authorities declared a 96-hour curfew and gave orders to shoot on sight. A Revolutionary Military Council was created on October 20 under the military leadership.

In the early morning of October 25, the U.S. launched a full-scale invasion of the island. The initial invasion force consisted of some 1,500 members of the 82nd Airborne Division and 400 Marines. The purpose of the invasion, according to the US administration, was to save the lives of several hundred American medical students trapped on the island.

It was evening Beijing time around 7:00 or 8:00 pm. The ID4D night duty officers had just started when they received flashes from wire services that Grenada radio reported a foreign invasion of the island was taking place amid heavy fighting. One officer immediately reached the Situation Room of the Secretariat by phone to report to the officers on duty about this latest development. He also tried to reach the officer on duty in the Department of American Affairs but the phone was busy. When he finally succeeded, it was Zhang Wenpu, Director of the Department, who happened to be on duty that night. Zhang explained that an official of the US Embassy was on the phone just then notifying him of the invasion. In the meantime officers of the Situation Room notified the FM and relevant vice FMs and the central leadership. As the event took place in a part of the world that Beijing had very little practical interest, no immediate further action was warranted besides notifying the various officials in charge.

The morning news briefing on October 26 was dominated by the invasion. The ID4D briefing team concentrated on the details of the situation in Grenada which was still developing. In concluding the presentation, it provided a very brief analysis by citing foreign sources that the invasion was an attempt by the U.S. to get rid of a Marxist regime in its backyard under the pretext of protecting American lives, and that to prevent the emergence of another Cuba had been a long-term foreign policy goal of the U.S., and the internal strife of Grenada only made it possible for the U.S. to achieve its objective.

When the briefing was over, the meeting turned to the question of how should China respond. Zhang Zai, chief of the U.S. Division, came to the meeting with a prepared text which "deplored" the US action. The wording had had the apparent endorsement of Zhu Qizhen, Vice Minister for American Affairs. Zhou Nan, then Vice Minister for West European Affairs, thought it was too weak. The majority agreed that this was a "naked aggression" by a superpower against a tiny country and therefore must be *condemned* irrespective of that country's ideological affiliation. Thus a decision was made that China would "condemn" the invasion and the Department of the American Affairs was to draft an RFI to be submitted to the central leadership for approval. As the issue was largely a matter of diplomatic posturing, the central leadership signed on to the decision without any reservations.[7]

Policy Control The decisionmaking power in regard to the implementation details of China's policies toward key countries has always been a prerogative of the central leadership. This is particularly true during a period of policy adjustment and change and when the implementation details could affect the posture of China's overall relationship with the major powers. These key countries fall into two categories: one because of their strategic importance in world affairs, second because of their geographical importance to China—*zhoubian guojia*—the periphery states. Countries in the first category would include the U.S., Russia, and Japan. Countries of the second category: Korea, the Indochinese states of Vietnam, Laos and Cambodia, India, Pakistan, and more recently Kazakstan and Mongolia. Of course countries like Russia and Japan straddle the two categories.

Once regional policies are worked out under the guidelines provided by the central leadership, country policies for non-key states are decided by the MFA, which makes sure that the policies for specific countries conform to China's overall strategy and its regional policy. Most of the decisions in this regard are made by the MFA.

Exceptions to this general rule are policies toward a few non key countries that if changed might affect the carefully constructed balance of China's regional policies. In the 1980s these "sensitive" countries included Israel, South Korea and South Africa, for shifts in China's policy toward Israel would affect its overall relations with the Arab world, and changes in Chinese policy toward South Africa might alienate most of its friends in Black Africa, and adjustment in China's policy toward South Korea would offend North Korea—a key ally.

Similar to policies toward "sensitive" countries, certain policies are also considered "sensitive" because of their wider implications. For instance when China began to export arms abroad on a commercial basis in the early 1980s, it was regarded as a normal trade issue with little oversight. However when exports of certain products and exports to certain regions of the world began to attract international reaction. Such exports became a "sensitive" issue.

Such policies toward "sensitive" countries and over "sensitive" issues are the prerogative of the central leadership. However it is almost impossible for the central leadership to micro-manage their intricate details and make decisions accordingly. For such "sensitive" policy decisions, a system has been put in place to manage and control them.

For policies toward "sensitive" countries, a strategic decision was made when China declared an independent foreign policy in 1982 and began to make foreign policy readjustments. The main focus of the foreign policy readjustment was over relations with the two superpowers. However, a decision was also made to adjust its relations with Israel, South Korea, South Africa and the Vatican. Since the main motivation behind these adjustments was largely economic, relations with the Vatican have not been seriously pursued.[8] The initiative for these policy readjustments came from the MFA and other bureaucracies. For instance the Department of West Asian and North African Affairs felt strongly that China should not be "more Arabic than the Arabs" in its relations with Israel. In light of the normalization of relations between Egypt, the most important Arab country in the Middle East, and Israel following Egyptian President Sadat's visit to Israel in 1978, China should not maintain its hardline stance toward the Jewish state but should recognize the reality of its existence and pursue a mutually beneficial relationship.

The central leadership approved the readjustment of policies toward these "sensitive" countries. It envisaged a long process of gradual and incremental changes that would lead to eventual normalization of relations, rather than a sudden shift which could cause major upheaval in China's traditional relations with its long-term allies in the Arab world, Black Africa and on the Korean Peninsula. It set no timetable but entrusted the MFA to control the overall processes and determine the pace and the timing of each subtle policy shift.

The method of ensuring compliance by ministerial ranking bureaucracies to MFA policy oversight is through issuing a central joint document mandating that all matters concerning the designated "sensitive" countries must have policy clearance from the MFA.[9] Similarly during the Iran-Iraq War, the two countries were designated as "sensitive" areas for Chinese arms exports. All direct arms exports were generally forbidden. Special cases must have special clearance from the MFA and be approved by the central leadership. Indirect exports must also have the clearance of the MFA.[10]

Beginning in the mid 1980s, exports of Chinese missiles were added to the "sensitive" items list. First it was the export of Chinese tactical anti-ship and anti-aircraft missiles. Chinese Silkworm missiles became the focus of Western attention as Washington claimed that the Iranians intended to close the Strait of Hormuz to oil shipping with the Silkworms it had acquired from China.[11] In the second half of the 1980s Chinese companies began to market ballistic missiles and related technologies abroad. This caused another uproar in the West. The informal arrangement was no longer adequate to coordinate Chinese policies in this regard. A coordinating body was thus created in September 1989 to oversee China's arms exports—the Military Product Export Leading Small Group.[12]

The Sale of DF–3 IRBMs to Saudi Arabia.[13] By the mid 1980s, Beijing had managed to establish diplomatic relations with most of the Arab countries. Of the three countries that had no diplomatic ties with Beijing—Bahrain, Qatar and Saudi Arabia, only Saudi Arabia was of any political significance. For some time Beijing had been wooing Riyadh, and officials of the two countries had met on international occasions or in third countries. For instance on November 19, 1985, Chinese Vice Premier Yao Yilin during his visit to Oman met with Saudi crown prince Abdallah bin Abd al-Aziz al-Saud, First Deputy Prime Minister of Saudi Arabia. The Chinese press hailed the meeting "marked a new page in the annals of relationship between China and Saudi Arabia."[14] In early December, Ismail Amat, Chairman of the Xinjiang Uyghur Autonomous Region, while leading a Chinese hajj mission to Mecca, met with Prince Abd al-Rahman bin Abd al-Aziz, Saudi Vice Minister of Defense and Aviation.[15] During his visit to the Middle East and the Gulf, Chinese Foreign Minister Wu Xüeqian underlined the commonalities of the two countries' policies on such issues as the Middle East, the Iran-Iraq War and Afghanistan and indicated that although it was ready, Beijing was willing to wait for the eventual normalization of relations between the two countries.[16]

The Saudis seemed to be in no hurry to switch diplomatic recognition from Taibei (Taipei) to Beijing. However in 1985, Riyadh became increasingly concerned about the direction of the Iran-Iraq War in which the Saudis sided with Iraq. By then the Iraqis became exhausted by the war and lost much of the initiative. The problem was further compounded by the introduction of surface-to-surface missiles into the war and the desperate warring parties began to target their missiles on each other's cities in order to terrorize the urban population—a tactic known as the "city war."

The Saudis had been actively supporting the Iraqis and were horrified by the prospects of missile strikes by the Iranians against key Saudi oil installations and cities which became highly vulnerable.[17] Riyadh first approached its traditional arms supplier—the U.S.—for the purchase of F–15E fighters and Lance surface-to-surface missiles which had a range of only about 70 miles. The Saudi request was repeatedly rebuffed by the US Congress where the Jewish lobby had been strong.[18]

In early 1986, Chinese Ambassador to the U.S. Han Xü was approached by Prince Bandar bin Sultan, his Saudi counterpart and son of the Saudi Defense Minister. Prince Bandar indicated that the Saudis were interested in purchasing Chinese missiles and for that purpose would like to visit Beijing.[19] The MFA, which had long been seeking a diplomatic breakthrough with the oil rich Middle East kingdom, quickly approved the visit.

In the second half of March 1986, Prince Bandar arrived in Beijing via Hong Kong on a private Royal Saudi jet operated by a British crew. The small Saudi delegation consisted of another Saudi prince, an official of the Saudi oil industries and a number of their personal staff.

Qi Huaiyüan, Chinese Vice Foreign Minister for the Middle East and Public Affairs, played the host. A small Chinese delegation was quickly assembled, consisting of officials of the MFA Department of West Asian and North African Affairs and the Foreign Affairs Bureau of the PLA General Staff Department. As the visit was hastily arranged, the MFA had difficulties to go through the normal bureaucratic process to have a Chinese civilian aircraft ready for the visit. The GSD was eager to help.

While the PLA General Staff Department ordered the PLA air force to provide a plane for the visit, the Chinese flew first to Shanghai with the Saudis in the Royal Saudi jet. Talks took place on the plane. While the Saudis indicated that they would continue to improve relations and expand bilateral exchanges with Beijing, they were not yet ready to sever ties with Taiwan. Apparently they were mainly interested in purchasing Chinese surface-to-surface missiles as a deterrent to possible Iranian or Israeli missile attacks and to use it as a leverage in dealing with the Americans. The Chinese did not press them for diplomatic recognition but were willing to improve exchanges in other fields first in order to build up the relationship. In a show of goodwill to their Chinese hosts, the two princes spent lavishly in a Shanghai shopping mall which was kept open specially for them that night. The Saudis were also taken to a major oil refinery near Shanghai next morning and two sides discussed in general terms possible cooperation in the oil sector.

In the afternoon a PLA Trident jet which had flown in from Beijing overnight took the parties to a Yantai PLA Navy aviation station. A Deputy Commander of the PLA strategic missile force—the Second Artillery—joined the parties in Shanghai. A Deputy Commander of the PLA Navy North Sea Fleet also flew in to show the Saudis some anti-ship missile batteries, known as the Silkworms, in Yantai. The Saudis did not show much interest in the largely obsolete weapon systems and the parties flew to Xi'an late that afternoon.

In Xi'an, the Saudis were taken to the Guided Missile Institute of the Second Artillery and were given an indoor demonstration of the preparations and mock firing of a DF–3 IRBM. Known in the West as CSS–2, the missile uses liquid propellant and has a range of approximately 2700 km.[20] To impress the Saudis, the PLA hosts emphasized that it was the first time that the missile and its launch procedures were shown to foreigners.[21]

Prince Bandar immediately expressed his interest in purchasing an unspecified number of DF–3s. Discussions continued on the way to and in Guangzhou about the possible implications of such a sale. The MFA was chiefly concerned about the possible U.S. and Israeli reactions. Since the Royal Saudi jet had a British crew, the MFA, apparently having more confidence in the CIA, assumed that Washington would soon be able to learn of the discussions.[22]

Prince Bandar was confident that he could manage the relationship with Washington. As for the Israelis who had launched air strikes against suspected Iraqi Osirak nuclear facilities in 1981, he believed that Tel Aviv would not be able to repeat the attacks successfully on Saudi Arabia, since the Saudis by then had AWACS planes manned by joint Saudi-American crews. After touring the Special Economic Zones in Shenzhen and Zhuhai, the Saudis left China for Hong Kong where the Royal Saudi jet had flown in from Shanghai earlier and was waiting for them.

An inter-ministerial discussion was initiated after the departure of the Saudis. Both the MFA and the Equipment Directorate of the PLA General Staff supported the sale although the two bureaucracies differed in their primary motives.[23] For the MFA, the sale would open up an opportunity to engage the Saudis in further bilateral relations that hopefully would lead to eventual diplomatic recognition as promised by Prince Bandar. For the PLA, the motive was purely commercial. The weapon system was obsolete and would have to be replaced in the not too distant future.[24] The Saudi purchase therefore would represent a windfall for the cash-starved PLA.[25] It was decided that the GSD was to initiate the RFI for central approval.

The MFA while supporting the sale also pointed out possible wider implications of the sale. As Moscow and Washington for many years had been engaged in intense negotiations over the deployment of medium-range missiles in Europe and Asia, the sales of the missiles to Saudi Arabia would not only put almost the whole Middle East but also southern parts of the Soviet Union under their targets. This could complicate superpower negotiations and drag Beijing into the talks as the Soviets had once suggested and Beijing vehemently rejected. To address these concerns, Zhao Ziyang, in approving the sale in principle, requested to have the missiles modified so that they would have a shorter range. The General Staff Department agreed. At the same time, it must solve the technical problem of fitting the missiles with a conventional warhead. As all DF–3s carry only nuclear warheads, the General Staff requested COSTIND to help design a conventional high explosive warhead. COSTIND was so confident that it promised to have it ready in ten months.

When the decision was communicated to the Saudis, Prince Bandar was not happy about the modified range and emphasized that the Saudis only intended to use them as a deterrence and would not strike out unprovoked against any target. Since range modification envisaged by COSTIND would only involve programming and not the hardware as the latter would be impractically costly and complex, it was in fact a myth. The GSD lobbied Zhao again. As the general manager of China's economy, Zhao apparently found the deal too lucrative to resist and finally signed on to the sale of unmodified DF–3s.

The CMC, whose day-to-day operations were conducted under its Executive Vice-Chairman and Secretary General, Yang Shangkun, was to provide overall leadership for the venture. Prince Bandar would make another secret trip to China to reach an agreement in principle for China to supply Riyadh DF–3 missiles with conventional warheads. Lieutenant General Cao Gangchuan, PLA Deputy Chief of the General Staff, and General Khaled Bin Sultan, Commander of the Saudi Airforce, would take over and chair a joint negotiating committee to draft an outline of the project codenamed by the Saudis as "*al-Saqr*" or "falcon" on December 16–23, 1986.[26]

It would take more intense negotiations before a final deal was clinched in the first half of 1987. The two sides signed an agreement for what was essentially a turn-key project in which the Chinese were also to construct the launch sites and related facilities, and provide training to Saudi personnel. To facilitate communications between the two sides, Beijing and Riyadh would set up liaison offices in Pakistan. A deputy division chief, who was one of the MFA's best Arabic interpreters, was "lent" to the GSD mission to monitor the project and provide liaison.[27] To ensure the success of the project, the CMC ordered a mini mobilization of the institutions involved, including COSTIND, the GSD and units of the PLA engineering corps.

Ironically at the height of preparations, a second ranking official of the US Embassy in Beijing called on an MFA official of the Department of American Affairs and casually gave the latter a draft text of what was later known as Missile Technology Control Regime (MTCR). He indicated that the provision of the text of the agreement by the exclusive club of six Western nations was but a matter of courtesy. He made no request for either Chinese participation or compliance. Because of the highly compartmentalized nature of the Chinese bureaucracy, the MFA official was unaware of the ongoing preparations for the missile sales handled by another MFA department—Department of West Asian and North African Affairs. The text was sent to print in another routine issue of *Waijiao Jianbao*.

When it came out the next morning, Vice Minister Qi Huaiyüan was quickly alerted. It was suspected that the Americans, as long anticipated, had detected the unusual developments as hundreds of Chinese engineers and technicians were ready to depart for the Saudi deserts. Qi quickly called a meeting of senior officials of the Department of West Asian and North African Affairs and an official statement was prepared in the event of an official American representation or media report. It turned out to be a false alarm. It was not until fall 1987, when the Chinese began delivering the missiles, that the American intelligence became alerted and not until January 1988, almost two years after the initial discussions, that U.S. intelligence was able to confirm the sale.[28]

The sale of the DF–3s not only proved economically profitable but also helped establish personal relations between leaders and foster goodwill among people of the two countries. It provided the basis for the eventual establishment of diplomatic relations between the two countries on July 21, 1990.[29]

Information Provider In addition to the role of policy interpretation and policy control in the implementation of foreign policy decisions, the MFA also plays an important role as an information provider for the central leadership. Among the Chinese bureaucracies, the MFA has been regarded as a more reliable provider of information by the central leadership. Its cadre's corps for a long time had been under the direct personal supervision of late Premier Zhou Enlai, and had been able to recruit the best and the brightest of Chinese college graduates and had enjoyed greater exposure to the outside world. It therefore has been considered to be of higher quality in terms of professionalism by the central leadership. Important diplomatic cables and *Waijiaobu Jianbao* are a must read for members of the leading nuclear circle in charge of day-to-day operations.

Much of the information provided by the MFA is *processed*, as opposed to the *raw* material generated by Xinhua News Agency. The MFA maintains some 140 diplomatic missions abroad. Diplomatic cables reach directly the desks of the central leadership. The MFA's internal publications also provide a constant flow of up-to-date, concise information about world developments and developments in China's relations with other countries. As the MFA sources are considered more reliable and its publications more readable, its input plays a much more significant role in shaping central leaders' *perception* of these developments. As a result, the MFA's policy recommendations and opinions in a majority of cases prevail over those of other bureaucratic institutions in the battles for the hearts and minds of the central leadership.

The Ministry of Foreign Trade and Economic Cooperation

The Ministry of Foreign Trade and Economic Cooperation (MOFTEC) is the primary bureaucratic institution responsible for the devise of China's foreign trade and economic aid strategies and planning, and for studying and implementing foreign trade and economic aid policies under the guidelines established by the central leadership[30] (see Appendix III). As decisions regarding China's foreign trade and economic relations with foreign countries are often considered politically less sensitive, the MOFTEC often has a higher degree of control over these decisions which often have a strong domestic linkage. The decisionmaking process is similar to that in the MFA, though many issues are handled by the powerful Central Finance and Economic LSG. Foreign economic policy has become one of the most important issues that affect China's relations with the rest of the world. As noted in the Introduction, this important and complex issue however is beyond the scope of this study.

The CPC International Liaison Department

The International Liaison Department (ILD) was officially set up to manage Chinese Communist Party's relations with other communist parties, modelled after the Soviet system. As the communist parties were ruling parties in the former Soviet Union and East European countries and still are in a number of Asian countries, the ILD has played an important role in the foreign policy decisions regarding those countries. As a legacy of the past, its research and study of Russian and other East European countries are considered of high quality. It is also instrumental in maintaining high level contacts with the leadership of Asian communist countries like North Korea and Vietnam. In the 1980s its information on the Khmer Rouge leadership was of vital importance to China's policy toward the conflict in Indochina. Since the late 1970s, it began to broaden its contacts to include non-communist political parties in foreign countries. However its impact on foreign policies in the non-communist world is weak. Overall its influence on foreign policy decisions has been on the decline.

Xinhua News Agency

With its widespread network abroad, Xinhua is the most important provider of unfiltered information for the central leadership and the whole foreign affairs establishment (see Appendix VII). Its daily publication, *Cankao Ziliao* (Reference Material), each averaging more than 50 pages, represents the most comprehensive world information coverage in China.[31] Its sources have been very diverse, including not only wire services reports, but also articles and commentaries of major international and national newspapers, magazines and other publications of most of the countries of the world. They are sent daily in their original language by Xinhua's local offices and translated and compiled by the *cankao xin-*

wen bianji bu (Reference News Compilation Department) at its headquarters in Beijing. This publication is intended for the central leadership and the foreign affairs professionals as well as for senior officials at provincial/army level.

There are occasions that certain information is considered so sensitive that it cannot even appear in *Cankao Ziliao*. It is then printed in a special edition called *Cankao Ziliao (Qingyang)* (Reference Material [Proof]). Almost always classified as top secret and highly restricted in its circulation, it deals with such sensitive or embarrassing issues as Chinese arms sales, defections, and alleged Chinese espionage activities.

The same department also publishes an internally circulated newspaper for mass consumption called *Cankao Xiaoxi* (Reference News). The restriction placed on its circulation has been progressively relaxed over the decades. In the 50s its circulation was restricted to high ranking officials. In the 60s it was extended to all officials including university students. In the 70s Mao further relaxed its readership to include ordinary workers and in the 80s it has become available to all Chinese citizens. Its contents are more strictly edited. Although some criticism of non-sensitive aspects of the Chinese society do appear in the newspaper, sharp criticism is often edited out.

Xinhua however is not limited to the role of a provider of *raw* information. It has its own research units, and its correspondents based in foreign countries also write indepth analyses on important international developments and the domestic situations of the resident country, as well as the country's attitudes toward international, regional issues and to China. The internally circulated biweekly *Guoji Neican* (International Affairs for Internal Reference) provides a forum for these internal analyses by its overseas correspondents.[32]

In places where China does not have diplomatic representation, reports and analyses by the resident Xinhua correspondent play a very important role in shaping the perception of the central leadership and Beijing's diplomatic establishment. Occasionally he is also mandated to carry out semi-official functions in setting up contacts with important local officials on behalf of Beijing and lobbying for the interest of China. The role of a Xinhua correspondent in the establishment of diplomatic relations with Mali is a good example.

Establishing Diplomatic Relations with Mali. On June 20, 1960, the French colonies of Senegal and Mali declared independence and established the Mali Federation. Two months later, however, the relations between the two former French colonies deteriorated. Senegal first announced its withdrawal from the Federation. Subsequently Mali on September 22 declared the establishment of the Mali Republic and announced its withdrawal from the French West African Community and its entry into an alliance with Ghana and Guinea. Senegal blocked all railroad transports with Mali, which caused great economic difficulties in that land-locked country.

Beijing, trying to break through its diplomatic isolation imposed by the West, saw opportunities in the newly independent African nations. It ordered its Xinhua correspondent accredited to Guinea, Wang Shu, to visit Mali. As soon as Wang arrived in Mali, he requested an interview with the Mali President. During the interview, Wang inquired about the possibility of Mali establishing diplomatic relations with Beijing. The president faced with great economic difficulties was positive about the idea and asked Beijing to send a delegation to negotiate the terms of diplomatic recognition and economic cooperation between the two countries. Wang explained the terms under which Beijing would exchange diplomatic recognition, particularly in regard to the question of Taiwan. The Mali president accepted the terms with no objection. Thus Wang's report went directly to Mao Zedong and Zhou Enlai, who immediately dispatched to Mali the Chinese Ambassador to neighboring Guinea. The deal was quickly sealed and on October 27, 1960, the two countries announced the establishment of diplomatic relations.[33]

However the most important function of Xinhua in foreign policy decision making is to serve as the "ears and eyes" of the central leadership by "providing in a timely, comprehensive and accurate manner a variety of reference information to the Center for its decisionmaking."[34]

The General Staff Department of the PLA (GSD)

The role of the PLA GSD in China's foreign policy decisionmaking is confined to the activities of its three Directorates: *zongcan san bu* (the Third Directorate) for signal and imagery intelligence gathering, known in the West as SIGINT and IMINT, *zongcan er bu* (the Second Directorate) for human-source intelligence—HUMINT and intelligence analysis, and *zongcan zhuangbei bu* (the Directorate of Equipment) for arms purchases and sales abroad. While the Second Directorate is an oldtimer, the Directorate of Equipment is a newcomer.

The Third Directorate With its headquarters located in Beijing the GSD Third Directorate is organized into eight regional bureaux, three stations and two schools. The regional bureaux are chiefly responsible for China's SIGINT operations targeted mostly at areas in China's periphery. The three stations located in Beijing, Shanghai and Xinjiang respectively are PLA's IMINT and SIGINT operators.

One of them, in the Xinjiang Autonomous Region, was a joint venture with the CIA set up to intercept telemetry from missile tests and space launches in the former Soviet central Asia. The station was set up under an agreement between Beijing and Washington in January 1980 with its equipment supplied by the Office of SIGINT of the CIA Directorate of Science and Technology. At Deng Xiaoping's insistence, the station with two posts was manned by the PLA Third Directorate. The CIA provided training for the Chinese technicians, and its experts visited the station periodically to give advice and service the equipment. The main targets of the operation were the two major former Soviet test sites at Tyuratam near the Aral Sea and at Sary Shagan near Lake Balkash.[35] The joint venture survived the upheavals in bilateral relations and dramatic changes in the former Soviet Union and Eastern Europe.

The Third Directorate runs two educational and training facilities located respectively in Luoyang and Zhengzhou, Henan Province. The PLA Foreign Language School located in Luoyang provides both foreign language and computer science training. The PLA Information Engineering Institute in Zhengzhou was established more recently focusing on computer science. When the MFA was preparing for the gradual opening up of relations with Israel in the mid 1980s, it scouted through party and government bureaucracies and could not find a single competent Hebrew speaker as no Chinese college had had Hebrew language instruction. It eventually succeeded in securing one young Hebrew speaker—from the GSD Third Directorate.

The Third Directorate therefore also serves as the "ears and eyes" for the central leadership in the foreign policy decisionmaking process, similar to that of Xinhua News Agency. The difference is that while Xinhua gathers information mostly from public sources, the Third Directorate eavesdrops on both public and secret communications of foreign countries and forces.

The Second Directorate Similar to the US Defense Department's Defense Intelligence Agency, the GSD Second Directorate manages the intelligence analysis and the HUMINT operations of the PLA. It has a Bureau of Military Attaches that selects and rotates Chinese military attaches abroad and provides direct guidance and supervision of their work.

The Second Directorate, like the MFA, also plays the role of a supplier of "processed" information with an emphasis on the strategic and military aspects of international issues for the central leadership through the two publications it generates—*Jünqing* and *Jünqing (Jianbao)*. For this purpose it maintains a large research staff. However the impact of its research products on the central decisionmakers is not obvious, since most of its works though of good quality are repetitive of some of the MFA researches.

One exception was research and staff support provided by the Directorate for a series of studies on international situations, commissioned by

Mao in 1969 and conducted by four PLA marshals. The studies resulted in a major policy recommendation for seeking rapprochement with the US. The chief of the Directorate, Xiong Xianghui, participated in the top level sessions.[36] The prominent role of the Directorate however needs to be viewed within the context of the chaos in the civilian sector which created a vacuum. The MFA was torn apart in factional fighting (See Chapter 3). And the CPC Central Investigation Department had merged with PLA's Second Directorate.[37]

The Second Directorate also maintains a language school for training staff officers for missions abroad. The school located in Nanjing, known in the past as the Second PLA Foreign Language School, is now called the PLA Institute for International Relations.

In opening to the outside world and in coping with the problem of mandatory retirement of a large number of military officers in the early 1980s, the Second Directorate in 1979 established the Beijing Institute of International and Strategic Studies (BIISS), which was later renamed the China Institute of International and Strategic Studies or CIISS. Largely staffed by retired or active military officers of the Second Directorate, CIIS provides a venue for academic exchanges and contacts with foreign researchers on strategic and national security issues—a window on the world.[38] It also helps make public some of the research works of the Second Directorate in its periodical *Guoji Zhanlue* (International Strategy).

The Directorate of Equipment   Finally since the early 1980s when the PLA obtained official authorization to market its surplus military equipment and weapon systems abroad, the military attaches abroad also serve as a liaison for the GSD Directorate of Equipment to promote military sales overseas.

The GSD Directorate of Equipment began to play the role of an arms merchant in 1983 with the incorporation of *baoli gongsi*—Poly Technologies Co. Ostensibly a subsidiary of the China International Trust and Investment Corporation (CITIC), Poly Technologies is in fact under the direct control of the GSD Directorate of Equipment.[39]

The entry of the PLA into the international arms market came as a direct result of the drastic downsizing and reorganization of the PLA. As early as in March 1980 when Deng consolidated his power after resuming responsibility of the military affairs, Deng told an enlarged meeting of the Standing Committee of the CMC that the PLA must cut down its size for the purposes of supporting the civilian construction and military modernization programs. In his first move, the CMC on September 15, 1982, issued an order for the reorganization and downsizing of the PLA. The previously independent PLA Artillery Corps, Armored Corps, Signal

Corps and Engineer Corps became directorates of the GSD. The Railway Corps was incorporated into the Ministry of Railway.

Deng was not satisfied and directed Yang Shangkun, then Executive Vice Chairman and Secretary General of the CMC, to push for more cuts. From 1983 on, Yang, who was in charge of the day-to-day operations of the PLA, devoted much time and energy toward this goal. The size of the PLA was drastically reduced from an estimated 4.2 million in 1982 to 3.4 million in 1984. This was coupled with a substantial reduction of military spending.[40]

To alleviate the pains of these cuts and to find new, extra budgetary sources of revenue, Zhao Ziyang under a strong PLA lobby opened the door for the PLA to market its surplus arms and military products on the international market following an earlier permission granted to the defense industry in 1980.

When the PLA entered the international arms market in 1983, it became an instant competitor with the Chinese defense industry under the umbrella organization COSTIND set up in 1982. Through much of the 1980s, both targeted the Iran-Iraq War as their prime market for what is essentially the same line of products. From time to time, their battle over market shares would spill over to the MFA whose endorsement, unless overruled by the central leadership, was necessary for sales in "sensitive" regions.[41]

The decision to allow the PLA to enter the international arms market came as a result of domestic considerations. It however would soon develop into a foreign affairs issue. Today it is one of the key issues in the bilateral relations between Beijing and Washington. The PLA through its arms sales has thus become unwillingly and accidentally entangled in Chinese foreign policy decisionmaking. As a result, now it has a seat in the Central Foreign Affairs LSG.

The General Political Department (GPD)

The GPD's main function is to carry out political work under the CMC within the PLA. However, one directorate of the GPD has become increasingly involved in overseas activities. The Directorate, known as *zongzheng lianluo bu* (the GPD Liaison Directorate), has its origin in WWII and the Chinese civil wars. Sometimes called the Enemy Affairs Department, it was set up in various PLA units during the war years to carry out what was known to the Chinese civilian systems as "united front work" in the ranks of the enemy forces. The main purpose during the war years was to instigate large-scale defections of the enemy forces.

This tradition continued after the founding of the PRC. The focus of its work has been on areas and countries in China's periphery, particularly those with forces that the PLA had combat experiences in the past—Taiwan, Korea, Japan. The main target of its research and operations has been Taiwan. This is illustrated by the appointment of Yang Side, former Director of the GPD Liaison Directorate, as Director of the Taiwanese Affairs Office of the State Council when it was established in the 1980s.[42]

Since the early 1980s with the opening of China to the outside world, the GPD Liaison Directorate also began to broaden its research and operations beyond the regions on China's periphery, even though Taiwan remains its main focus. Like the GSD, it has also set up an organization with a staff of around 300 as its own window on the world to expand its exchanges and contacts with foreign academic and research institutions.[43]

Its impact on China's foreign policy decisionmaking is minimal however. The exception is of course the issue of Taiwan, where its views were channeled directly to the central leadership through Yang Side, who as Deputy Head of the CPC Taiwanese Affairs LSG, presided over the day-to-day operations of China's Taiwanese affairs, and thus have a significant influence over decisions concerning Taiwan.

The PLA Navy

Like the GSD Directorate of Equipment, the involvement of the PLA Navy (PLAN) in foreign affairs has been recent and accidental. It has come as a logical result of its steady modernization program which has seen its operations gradually extended from shallow coastal waters to more distant maritime areas.

Although its first combat experience against a hostile foreign naval force took place in 1974 in the Paracel Islands in the South China Sea where it was caught totally unprepared, the PLAN's foray into foreign affairs came in the 1980s.[44] In 1980 a PLAN task force of 18 ships sailed to the South Pacific for the first test firing of Chinese ICBMs. In late 1985 and early 1986, Chinese naval vessels for the first time visited South Asia and participated in the establishment of a science station in the Antarctic.

As the Navy extends its range of operations, its ships sometimes have to operate independently in international waters. Occasionally, it got caught inadequately prepared in events that would provoke international reaction and serve as a catalyst for change in China's relations with foreign countries, particularly those on its periphery.

The 3213 Torpedo Boat Incident of 1985. On the night of March 21, a mutiny occurred on torpedo boat 3213 of the PLAN North Sea Fleet which had been on manoeuvers in the Yellow Sea. Having apparently been subjected to verbal abuses by senior officers, two sailors shot and killed six and wounded two senior officers and crew out of a total crew of 19. The two mutineers afterwards commandeered the boat and sailed in different directions until it ran out of fuel and started to drift in the sea.

Early in the morning of March 22, its distress signal was picked up by a nearby South Korean fishing boat which responded and towed the boat, located at the time near Sohuksan Island, to South Korea's Hawangdung Island, about 120 miles southwest of Seoul. From there South Korean naval vessels towed the disabled boat to Kunsan.

Meanwhile three vessels of the PLAN North Sea Fleet searching for the missing boat inadvertently entered South Korean waters. One of the Chinese ships was a destroyer, the largest surface combatant in the Chinese navy. South Korean jets and ships scrambled to respond to the intrusion. The Chinese and South Korean forces faced each other in a tense standoff.

As China and South Korea had no diplomatic relations and there were no direct communications with each other, the South Korean government urgently requested the US Embassy in Seoul to convey a message to Beijing. The US Embassy in Beijing called the MFA and passed the South Korean message that urgently requested an immediate withdrawal of the three Chinese vessels from the South Korean waters.

The MFA contacted by telephone the PLA GSD situation room which confirmed the presence of the Chinese vessels in South Korean waters. The commander of the Chinese destroyer reportedly told the GSD that he was not aware when they entered the South Korean waters. "Now we are already in, what can be done?" he asked.

The South Koreans, extremely nervous about the standoff, promised the Chinese through the South Korean Consul General in Hong Kong that the boat and all members of the crew including the mutineers would be returned to the Chinese. The MFA suggested the immediate withdrawal of the Chinese ships and obtained the approval of Hu Qili and Zhao Ziyang.[45] The message was conveyed to the South Korean government that (1) the Chinese ships would be withdrawn, (2) the Chinese asked for the return of the boat and all members of the crew, and (3) the Chinese would like to deal directly with the South Korean Government. Meanwhile an order was issued through the GSD for the Chinese ships to pull out of the South Korean waters.[46]

Previously in 1982 and 1983, when two Chinese pilots defected respectively to South Korea with their Mig fighters, Seoul rejected Beijing's request and sent the defectors to Taiwan. In May 1983, six Chinese nationals hijacked a Chinese domestic flight to South Korea. Seoul, insisting on having jurisdiction over the hijacking, refused to extradite the hijackers to China for trial. The hijackers eventually went to Taiwan after serving a brief sentence in a South Korean jail.

This time however a request by the Taiwanese Embassy on March 24 for an interview with the surviving crew was refused. On March 25, South Korea issued a statement denying any political motivation involved in the mutiny and claimed that all 13 survivors had expressed a wish to return to China. On March 28, the boat and all its surviving crew were returned directly to the Chinese in a ceremony held in the Yellow Sea.[47]

The PLAN in this case not only inadvertently affected the outcome of an event that involved China's relations with its neighbor but also demonstrated some of the problems it may create in China's relations with other countries as it extends the range of its operations. This is just one of the events that served to open the door of direct contacts between the two countries and ultimately led to diplomatic recognition in 1992.

The Sino-Vietnamese Naval Skirmish at Johnson Reef in 1988. The growing role of the PLAN in China's relations with its neighbors is better illustrated by its activities in the South China Sea which triggered concerns and responses from littoral states thus affecting the overall relationship with those nations.

In November 1987 the State Council and the CMC formally approved a plan submitted by the PLAN and State Oceanographic Bureau to establish a permanent presence in the Spratly Islands in the South China Sea, a group of islands that are contested by China, Taiwan, Vietnam, the Philippines, Malaysia and Brunei.[48]

For this purpose a naval task force was organized with some 20 ships that included guided missile destroyers and escorts from the South and East Sea Fleets. Codenamed No. 502 Formation, the operation was launched in January 1988. The Chinese forces were instructed to play a strictly defensive role. All the PLAN missile ships were under order not to carry any anti-ship missiles and to show it by having their empty launchers open to the views of Vietnamese and other unidentified aircraft. The mission was also apparently instructed not to contest the features already occupied by other contestants.[49]

By early August, China successfully set up permanent posts on a total of six reefs in the Spratlys. The Chinese action set off a round of island-hopping races between China and Vietnam. On several occasions, the two forces confronted each other in tense standoffs. A skirmish finally broke out over the control of Johnson Reef. The conflict which started as a fist fight soon degenerated into a naval fire fight that lasted 28 minutes with three Vietnamese ships sunk and some 80 Vietnamese soldiers dead or missing.[50]

It was later revealed that the naval commander gave the order to sink the Vietnamese vessels after the shootout broke out on the reef. He was said to have no time to obtain the authorization from the GSD, given the situation.[51] After the skirmish, the PLAN task force cabled the CMC for permission to launch an assault and take over the 20 or so islands and reefs occupied by Vietnam. The CMC, while congratulating the PLAN unit for its victory, rejected its request.[52]

Since then a bureaucratic battle followed with the MFA opposing more assertive Chinese actions in enforcing its claim over the Spratlys while the PLAN leads the bureaucratic interest group in arguing for the safeguard of the nation's maritime interest against foreign encroachments. With the central leadership groping for a right balance between the nation's economic interests and the need for a peaceful international environment, the bureaucratic battle is likely to continue in the near future. Indirectly, the PLAN has thus become an important player in China's relations with some of its Southeast Asian neighbors.

The Commission of Science, Technology, and Industry for National Defense (COSTIND)

Before 1982 China's defense industries were organized into six industrial ministries of the State Council which at the time had a total of eight industrial ministries.[53] Their research and development (R&D) came under the direct supervision of the Commission of Science and Technology for National Defense while the Office of National Defense Industry supervised defense industrial production.

In 1979, having consolidated his political power within the CPC, Deng Xiaoping set out to reduce the size of the Chinese military and streamline the defense industries. He established a new 16-character guideline for the defense industries as *jünmin jiehe, pingzhan jiehe, jünpin youxian, yimin yangjün*—to combine military with civilian production, to integrate peacetime with wartime production, to give priority to the production of military products, to use civilian products to maintain military production capabilities.

However defense industrial managers would soon discover that defense conversion under the so-called 16-character guideline was easier said than done. Defense conversion is a long term process that requires substantial input. Faced with a drastic cut in domestic military procurement and government allocation of funds, the defense industrial managers had to rely on arms sales abroad to make up the shortfall under a new interpretation of the guideline as *yijün yangjün*—to use sales of military products to maintain the military production capabilities.

In 1979 the Fifth Ministry of Machine Building later known as the Ministry of Ordnance set up China's first arms trading company, North Industrial Corporation (NORINCO), to market convention arms overseas. This approach quickly received the endorsement of the State Council and the CMC in 1980 in a joint document that for the first time legalized commercial arms sales abroad.⁵⁴ NORINCO became the model for other ministries of defense industries which one after another set up their respective trading companies: China National Nuclear Corp. under the Second MMB, China Aviation Industry Corp. under the Third MMB, China Space Industry Corp. under the Third and Seventh MMBs, and China Shipbuilding Industry Corp. under the Fourth MMB.

In a major reorganization of government agencies in 1982, the defence industrial ministries were respectively "civilianized" into the Ministry of Nuclear Industry, Ministry of Space and Aviation Industries, Ministry of Machinery and Electronic Industries. The Fifth MMB became the Ministry of Ordnance and the Sixth MMB was eliminated. By merging the Commission for National Defense Science and Technology, the Office of National Defense Industries and the CMC Science, Technology and Equipment Commission, COSTIND was established in 1982 under the dual leadership of the State Council and the CMC to supervise defense R&D and industries.⁵⁵ COSTIND first "incorporated" its foreign affairs office as *Xinshidai* (New Era) Corporation to supervise commercial arms sales abroad conducted by the defense industry corporations. Later New Era spinned off to become a separate corporation. In 1986 COSTIND was granted the authority to supervise and manage the trade in military products of the entire defense industry.⁵⁶

While arms sales abroad have attracted much of the international attention, COSTIND's role in importing military technologies and products and its impact on China's relations with an important country on the MFA's "sensitive" list remain almost unnoticed. If the impact of arms sales abroad on Chinese foreign relations has been mixed, that of the import of foreign military technologies and products has been largely positive.

The Import of Military Technologies and Products from Israel. Israel was one of the first countries to recognize the People's Republic of China. The official recognition came on January 9, 1950, three months after Mao announced the founding of the People's Republic.⁵⁷ After some bitter debate, the Israeli cabinet finally made a decision to establish diplomatic relations with Beijing on June 28, 1950. However because of the outbreak of the Korean War, the decision was kept secret and its implementation postponed.

In 1954 after the Geneva Conference, Beijing renewed its efforts to establish ties with Israel. Worried about a possible US reaction, however, the Israeli government failed to respond positively to the Chinese overture. With the convention of the Bandung Conference in April 1955, Beijing's diplomatic orientation decidedly switched in favor of the Arab states in the Middle East. Later Zhou Enlai summarized Beijing's strategic tilt in simple mathematical terms—as a choice between one hundred million (Arabs) and one million (Israelis).⁵⁸

Although the Israeli vote in 1971 to seat Beijing in the UN was viewed as a positive signal and became a much talked-about anecdote within the MFA in association with Beijing's victory at the UN, the real ease of Beijing's pro-Arab stance came in 1978 following Egyptian President Anwar Sadat's initiative to make peace with and recognize the Jewish state. The MFA officials began to argue that Beijing could not and should not be more "Arabic" than the Arabs themselves.

In the second half of 1981, Beijing began a comprehensive reorientation of its foreign policy, officially termed as foreign policy readjustment. One of the unpublicized long term goals was to normalize relations with Israel through a gradual process of policy readjustment so that it would not jeopardize Beijing's relations with the Arab world. The MFA was to control the pace and timing of a series of small steps when the occasion arose to ease the relations between the two countries.

Such an occasion came in 1982 when Austrian businessman Shaul Eisenberg, who had extensive business and family contacts in the Jewish state, approached the Chinese with an offer to sell Israeli military technologies and products. The PLA and COSTIND, which had watched with intense interest how Israeli technologies defeated modern Soviet weaponry in actual combats, were very enthusiastic. Although the revelation of Israeli-made tank cannons mounted on Chinese tanks during the 1984 National Day parade in Beijing received much of international attention, the first large deal between the Israeli defense industry and COSTIND involved air-to-air tactical missiles.[59]

The missile offered was Python III, a missile used for air combat similar to American Sidewinder but developed and tested based on Israeli technologies.[60] Under an arrangement between Eisenberg and COSTIND, a live missile test was organized in China and the PLA air force expressed satisfaction with the performance of the missile.[61]

An ensuing high level meeting was held by the CMC. Yang Shangkun, then Executive Vice-Chairman and Secretary General of the CMC who handled the day-to-day operations of the PLA, presided over the meeting. With the participation of officials from the PLA GSD, COSTIND and the PLA Air Force and the MFA, the meeting was to decide whether Beijing was to purchase the missile and what kind of deal to be worked out with the Israelis. It was decided that Beijing would negotiate an agreement that would enable it to make an off-the-shelf purchase of a few hundred Python IIIs and to co-produce the missile in China under Israeli licensing.

Because of the very "sensitive" nature of such deals, Eisenberg's company was designated as the only "window" for dealing with technological imports from Israel.[62] As the project would involve a large number of Israeli technicians and experts travelling back and forth between the two nations, Eisenberg's Austrian-registered company would provide the cover. To maintain deniability, most of the Israelis came as employees of the company with American or Austrian passports. In China COSTIND would become the lead organization in dealing with the Israelis and organize the production of the missiles while the MFA was responsible for the policy aspect in the implementation of the deal.

Although the decision was made as a strictly military one, it nevertheless represented a first step in Beijing's foreign policy adjustment toward Israel and opened the door and a channel for further exchanges and contacts between the two nations as cooperation extended from military to other fields like agriculture irrigation and the production of certain types of sophisticated batteries.

The exchanges also served to foster goodwill between the two sides separated for more than three decades. The MFA, in addition to facilitating the transactions, gradually (1) eased travel restrictions for those with Israeli passports visiting China in a group organized by a third country (1982), (2) permitted individual Israelis visiting China as tourists or attending international conferences (1985), (3) exchanged visits by non-official delegations (1985), (4) established "unofficial" representations in each other's capital (1989) and (5) finally normalized diplomatic relations (1992).

On the other hand, the MFA accompanied its moves by gradually toning down its official rhetoric with an aim to get the Arab nations—Beijing's traditional allies—accustomed to its change of position, a preparatory process known within the MFA as *xia maomao yü*—drizzling. As early as 1978, Beijing implicitly recognized Israel's right to existence but demanded that it withdraw from all Arab territories beyond the 1948 UN partition plan. In 1981 Beijing's official position shifted in that it demanded an Israeli withdrawal from territories seized since 1967. In 1986 Beijing stopped cosponsoring with Arab states a resolution that challenged Israeli's credentials at the UN. In 1991 Beijing officially stopped supporting a UN resolution that equates Zionism with racism.

In sum, COSTIND has been instrumental in providing an opportunity for Beijing to adjust its relations with Jerusalem in a gradual process, that looked, to the outsider, like a natural outgrowth of an evolving relationship. On the whole the process of policy readjustment has been well coordinated and very successful. Not only did Beijing acquire much needed technological knowhow,[63] it also managed to keep on good terms with its traditional Arab allies.[64]

Foreign Affairs Research Institutes

One of the characteristics of the Chinese system of political power is the cosmetic nature of "academic" research institutes that deal with political and security issues. This probably has been a legacy of Mao's distrust of intellectuals in institutions where the Party leadership is deemed weak.[65]

When Mao tried to mobilize Chinese intellectuals in 1957 to criticize his adversaries within the CPC in what was known as the "hundred flower" movement, some of them, to his great disappointment, turned to criticize him and the CPC. As a result he had to wage an Anti-Rightist Campaign to crack down on those "misguided" intellectuals. Although Deng, who ironically supervised Mao's Anti-Rightist Campaign in 1957, has come to understand the importance of intellectuals to his modernization program, he, like Mao, does not really trust the intellectuals, particularly those in the fields of social sciences including foreign affairs.

In general, foreign affairs research institutes have little relevance to the policy process. Within this context, among them, those foreign policy research institutions that are affiliated with government, party or military bureaucracies play a relatively more important role than those independent institutions such as the Chinese Academy of Social Sciences (CASS). This is largely because bureaucracy-affiliated institutions have better access—(a) to processed, often confidential information generated through the bureaucratic system such as diplomatic cables for the MFA affiliated institute, and (b) to top decision makers through the well-established bureaucratic channels.

Institute of International Studies (IIS) First established in 1956, the IIS is officially the research arm of the MFA, carrying out research on long term international issues as against the research on short-term issues conducted by the MFA inhouse departmental research units. In 1959 it started to publish the journal *Guoji Wenti Yanjiü—Journal on International Studies*. The institute was abolished in 1967 during the Cultural Revolution. Though it was reopened in 1973, *Journal on International Studies* did not reappear until 1981.

The nature of the Chinese bureaucracy dictates that the MFA leadership attaches more importance to casework than research, and more to short-term research by MFA departments than to long-term research by academic institutions. For a long time, the IIS has been used by the MFA as a place to dispose of the undesirable and untrustworthy elements from the MFA in a thinly veiled "internal exile." Their "sins," ranging from being politically incorrect to sexual indiscretion, are often considered serious enough for a slap on the wrist but not sufficient to warrant an outright expulsion from the MFA.[66]

As the MFA began to rectify the chronicle bias in favor of casework, the IIS has enjoyed a mini revival since the early 1980s. With a staff size of around 180, the institute is divided into five regional sections on the Americas, Russia and Eastern Europe, Western Europe, Middle East/Africa/South Asia, and Asia-Pacific, and two functional sections on international economy and comprehensive research. It comes under the direct supervision of a vice FM and its director is in most cases a former high ranking diplomat on the verge of retirement. The IIS has the bureaucratic rank of a department and thus receives diplomatic cables and MFA documents as a MFA department. It is therefore better informed of the operational side of the picture in China's foreign affairs than most other similar research institutions.

The MFA occasionally commissions specific research studies. Otherwise the research sections generate their own research plans and select their own research topics. Most of their research products are classified for the consumption of the MFA and central leadership. *Journal on International Studies* and *Shijie Zhishi*—a magazine published by the publishing house of the MFA—are the chief public outlets of their selected research products, the former catering to the professionals and the latter to the general public.[67]

Since the early 1980s, as part of the MFA internal reform program, a regular brainstorming session for researchers within the MFA system has been instituted. Presided over by the vice FM for research, the biweekly session, known as *shuangzhou xingshi wuxühui,* gathers all the representatives of the research units to discuss candidly preselected issues. Presentations by the IIS, the MFA Policy Research Office, and the ID4D, the three primary research units of the MFA, are in most cases mandatory. The relevant regional department is also required to present its own views. The Policy Research Office would afterwards summarize the discussion, which in most cases lasts one whole afternoon, and distribute it among ministerial leadership and relevant departments.

The IIS itself also convenes periodic conferences at which researchers and departmental chiefs of the MFA are invited to participate in discussing some major issues like the outlook of world economy, US presidential election, etc. These discussions serve as a forum for an exchange of information and ideas between those who have maintained operational contacts with foreign government officials and those who have been engaged in exchanges with foreign academics.

Some IIS researchers over the years have built up a substantial reputation for their expertise in a particular field that they on certain occasions are invited to sit in on discussions of the Central Foreign Affairs LSG. Sometimes they are entrusted with important assignments. For instance, when Washington and Moscow reached an agreement to eliminate medium range missiles from Europe and Asia and requested Beijing to send an observer to attend the ceremony for the destruction of the missiles, Zhuang Qübing of the IIS was the only Chinese representative to witness the exercise.[68]

The IIS's known affiliation with the MFA adds credibility to its views as reflecting semi-official thinking. However closer association with the

MFA could also prove a liability in that it makes its positions appear less flexible than some other research institutes. Starting in the early 1980s the MFA have been trying to encourage institutions such as IIS to deviate in tone but not in essence from the official line. However it has not been very successful in practice as diplomatic discipline is as rigorously enforced in the IIS as in any department of the MFA.

Most of the IIS staff rotate to take up assignments in MFA missions abroad. There are also some opportunities for its researchers to participate in international conferences and take up foreign scholarships. However to many of the new recruits the setting for academic research is considered less exciting than the day-to-day operations of the MFA.[69] The IIS is yet to rid itself of the stigma as a place for the MFA to dispose of its unwanted. Until then, most of its young researchers tend to opt for a permanent move to the MFA given the opportunity.

Institute for Contemporary International Relations (ICIR) The ICIR was originally the research arm of the Investigation Department of the CPC (*zhonggong zhongyang diaocha bu*)—then the closest Chinese equivalent of the CIA.[70] It began to assume a separate identity in 1965 when it acquired its current name, but would remain an affiliate of the Central Investigation Department. It was partially closed down during the Cultural Revolution but its functions were restored in 1969. By 1980 it became a full-fledged research institute.[71]

During the major reorganization of government and party bureaucracies in 1982, the CPC Central Investigation Department merged with counter-intelligence operations of the Ministry of Public Security of the government to form a new Ministry of State Security under the State Council. Since then the ICIR has come out of the shadow and begun to play an active role in exchanges with foreign academic institutions. Some of its research works are published in *Contemporary International Relations*.

With a research staff of around 300, the ICIR is divided into seven regional research divisions on North America, Latin America, Russia and Eastern Europe, Western Europe, South and Southeast Asia, East Asia and Pacific, West Asia (Middle East) and Africa, and one comprehensive research division. Some of its research projects are commissioned directly by the State Council through its Center for International Studies. Otherwise most of its research is self generated for internal bureaucratic consumption through its internal publication.

Its access to "processed" information generated outside the bureaucracy is limited, but to information generated inside the bureaucracy, its access is better than other institutions. As an information provider, its real impact on foreign policy decisionmakers is limited, as much of its research is thought to be based on foreign public sources, thus considered unreliable. Its research products almost never even make it to the desks of MFA leadership.

China Institute of International Strategic Studies (CIISS) Established in 1979 under the GSD, the CIISS is PLA's window on the world in that it provides a venue for the PLA GSD to carry out academic exchanges and interact with foreign military and security experts and scholars on an "unofficial" basis. It also serves as an institution for retired researchers of the Second Directorate of the GSD to use their expertise by continuing to work on international issues.

With a small research staff, most of whom are active service officers of the Second Directorate, its research works center mostly on strategic issues with an emphasis on the military aspects of these issues. Some of its works come out in its public journal *International Strategy*. Most of its research is channeled through the military system in the internal publications of the Second Directorate—*Jünqing*. Its access to "processed" information generated outside the military system is limited to those available to the Second Directorate but its access to information generated within the military system is second to none. The value of its work is to provide central foreign policy makers with a view of the military aspects of international security issues. However its real impact on decisionmaking is limited.

Chinese Academy of Social Sciences (CASS) CASS, like Xinhua News Agency, is an institution under the direct administrative control of the State Council. In the government system, it enjoys the bureaucratic ranking of a ministry. Of CASS's numerous institutes doing research on international affairs, the most important ones are the American Institute, Russian and East European Institute and the Institute of World Economy. The importance of these institutes is attributable to a number of experts well established through years of research in particular fields, like Li Shenzhi, Zi Zhongyün, former directors of the American Institutes, and Pu Shan, one of the Pu brothers with a Harvard PhD in economics, who served as the director of the Institute of World Economy.

For the Russian and East European Institute, its strength comes from its past affiliation with the CPC International Liaison Department. Before 1982, the Institute was part of the International Liaison Department specializing in the CPC's relations with communist countries. During the reorganization of 1982, the REEI together with the Latin American Institute was transferred to CASS. Its research on Russian and East European affairs is considered the best in the country, a legacy of the "Socialist Camp" days of the 1950s and early 1960s. It played an important role in changing the elite perception of the former Soviet Union in the early 1980s and paved the way for the eventual normalization of relations between the two countries.[72]

Generally speaking, however, CASS institutes' influence on foreign policy makers has been weaker than other institutes with strong bureaucratic affiliations. CASS's problems during each political turmoil further erode its credibility in the eyes of the central leadership.[73]

Conclusion In sum, academic institutes specializing in research on international issues play the role of an information provider. As institutions, they have little impact on foreign policy decisions. Several factors have contributed to their relative insignificance.

First the relatively high concentration of intellectuals in such institutions, where the party leadership has been traditionally regarded as weak, makes them politically unreliable. This view from the top and from bureaucracies is reinforced by the "political" problems they tend to have during almost each and every political movement. This gives rise to a vicious cycle in which, because of their problems, bureaucracies often use those affiliated with them as a place to "internally exile" their unwanted.

Second, the current Chinese political system is based on control of access to processed information. If the Chinese political power is structured like a pyramid, the access to information is an inverse one with the apex of the power pyramid having the widest access to information. The irony is that the higher the decisionmaker the less unprocessed information he directly consumes as his daily information supplies are simply overwhelming at these levels. Processed information generated by research institutes is often handicapped by their lengthy reasoning and arguments and less than concise assessment or clear-cut policy choices. Their limited access to classified processed information further undercuts the value of their research dealing with current issues.

Third, foreign affairs bureaucracies are structured to cope with current problems that demand quick assessment and immediate solution while research institutes are, on the other hand, structured to deal with long term issues with a historical perspective. Therefore foreign affairs bureaucracies find little interest or utility in the research products generated by research institutes unless they are commissioned by the bureaucracies for specific purposes.

Despite these problems with research institutes, individual scholars from these institutes with well established reputations for their expertise in some specific fields of study may have a greater impact on foreign policy decisionmakers depending on their individual access to the leadership.

Individual Bureaucrats and Researchers

In view of the highly centralized and personalized nature of foreign policy decisionmaking in China, one question must be asked: do working-level bureaucrats and researchers in the foreign policy establishment matter? Generally speaking, not much. The role of the individual is largely confined to processing information for foreign policy decisionmakers, correctly understanding foreign policy decisions and interpreting the intentions of the policy makers so as to ensure strict implementation of the decisions.

Although in processing information, the working level bureaucrat may have some indirect impact on policy decisionmaking by influencing the perception of the decisionmakers, it has always been more of an art to second guess the thinking of top decisionmakers given the limited access he has to the top leaders. Indeed during the Mao era, the over-politicization of the foreign affairs establishment in successive political movements virtually killed any real incentive for policy initiation and innovation on the part of working level bureaucrats. "Wrong" analyses or policy recommendations either contrary to or at variance with the thinking of the top leaders could exact a high personal cost.

The No. 153 Issue of **Xin Qingkuang**   From the second half of 1972, US-Soviet relations seemed to have entered a period of détente following Nixon's visit to Moscow in May 1972. There was an apparent general relaxation of tensions between the two old rivals following the signing of Strategic Arms Limitation Treaty (SALT I). This trend continued in early 1973 when the Paris Accord was signed ending the war in Vietnam, that marked the beginning of American disengagement from Southeast Asia. A series of bilateral agreements of cooperation was signed between the two superpowers during Brezhnev's visit to the U.S. in June 1993. By mid 1974 Washington and Moscow were close to a SALT II agreement. The Europeans meanwhile were busily preparing for the Helsinki Conference on European Security.

In view of this trend, the American Division of the MFA Department of American and Oceanian Affairs wrote an analysis for the ID4D internal publication *Xin Qingkuang* which came out as its 1973 No. 153 issue. The analysis argued that although the two superpowers "collude and contend with each other"—using Mao's official line, the superpower relationship for the time being was dominated by "collusion." It suggested implicitly that China should be prepared for the consequences of superpower détente.

This assessment might well be inaccurate as it indeed turned out that the two superpowers had their worst confrontation since the 1962 Cuban missile crisis when the 1973 October War broke out in the Middle East. However the political toll for an "incorrect" analysis was unnecessarily heavy. Mao personally repudiated the assessment and insisted that the nature of the US-Soviet relationship remain confrontational.[74] He criticized Ji Pengfei, the then Foreign Minister, for only being interested in foreign travel.[75] As a result Ji was replaced by Qiao Guanhua, and Zhang Wenjin, then Assistant Foreign Minister for American Affairs, was sent in diplomatic exile to Canada as Chinese ambassador to that country. Thanks to Zhou Enlai, the MFA officials fared relatively well under the circumstances. Ji Pengfei was "kicked upstairs" to the ceremonial post of Vice Chairman of the NPC Standing Committee.

Wang Shu and Diplomatic Recognition with West Germany As in many other businesses, the individual risk involved in taking personal initiative in foreign policy formulation is often proportionate to the opportunity of rewards it offers. The exchange of diplomatic recognition between Beijing and Bonn in 1972 offers one good example.

Until the late 1960s, Beijing's views of and policy toward the Federal Republic of Germany were largely shaped by those of the Soviet Union and Eastern bloc during the early years of the Cold War. West Germany, particularly West Berlin, was regarded as a bridgehead of the Western capitalist camp led by the U.S. against the socialist camp headed by the Soviet Union. Under active US support, claimed the Eastern bloc, there was a revival of militarism in West Germany. Despite the Sino-Soviet split in the early 1960s and close identification of the East German leadership with Moscow, the official Chinese position toward West Germany had not been altered. On the other hand, Bonn's China policy was also largely dictated by long-standing US hostility to Beijing.

France was the first major Western nation to break rank with the U.S. in exchanging diplomatic recognition with Beijing in 1964. However the internal strife initiated by Mao in the mid 1960s checked any possible momentum in the West to end Beijing's diplomatic isolation. The new initiative came in 1970 when Canada became the first Western country to normalized relations with Beijing as the Cultural Revolution was winding to a close. In 1971, Beijing and Washington began a process of rapprochement that culminated in Nixon's visit in early 1972.

Meanwhile in West Germany, the Social Democratic Party (SDP) won a historic victory in the general election held in late 1969 and formed a new government with the Free Democrats (FDP), thus ending the 20-year rule of the conservative Christian Democratic Union (CDU) and its Bavarian sister Christian Social Union (CSU). CDU and CSU for the first time since 1949 became an opposition party in the German *Bundestag*. The leader of the Social Democrats, Willy Brandt, became the new German Chancellor.

Soon after the election, the new German government initiated a new policy of détente toward the Soviet Union and Eastern Europe known as *Ostpolitik*.

Fearing a backlash that would jeopardize its new opening to the Soviets and East Europeans, the new German Socialist government was very cautious about relations with Beijing, unwilling to initiate any policy change. However following Kissinger's secret trip to Beijing and China's reentry into the UN in 1971, the wave of diplomatic recognition of Beijing by Western countries began to affect the politics of Bonn. Leaders of the opposition used the issue to criticize the government.

At the time, Beijing had only a correspondent of the Xinhua News Agency in Bonn named Wang Shu. Wang sensed that despite the international repercussions generated by Nixon's visit to China in early 1972, the Socialist government in Bonn had no intention of changing its priority of improving relations first with the Soviet Union and Eastern Europe while keeping the issue of China on the back burner. "The key to German unification can not be found on the Great Wall," claimed the social democrats. In order to change the situation, Beijing needed to play the opposition card. The opportunity came in late April when the Socialist government having barely survived a no-confidence vote in the parliament announced a new general election to be held in late 1974.

Wang met in early May 1972 Vice Chairman of the CDU Gerhard Schröder, who had been Foreign and Defense Minister in previous governments and was at the time Chairman of the Foreign Affairs Committee of the parliament. During two hours of talks, Schröder, who had previously expressed his desire to visit Beijing, raised the issue again and indicated that it take place during the summer recess. Within two weeks, an invitation was extended to him from the Chinese People's Institute of Foreign Affairs for him to visit China in July.[76]

Besides playing the role of a messenger, Wang wrote a series of articles on German foreign policy and the nature of the German society. The articles, which were published in Xinhua's *Guoji Neican*, argued, among other things, that the Federal Republic was not "reviving militarism," and that the strategic interest of the Soviet Union lay in Europe, which remained the main focus of Soviet global strategy. The implications that Beijing should abandon its outdated policy toward West Germany and seek instead a normalization of relations, and that an escalation of Soviet military pressure on Beijing would probably not happen, caught the attention of Mao.

Mao, never quite convinced that Moscow was willing to go to war with Beijing, eagerly endorsed Wang's argument that the Soviet Union's predominant strategic interest was in Europe and not in Asia. At the same time, encouraged by the diplomatic successes in relations with the U.S. and at the UN, Mao was planning major diplomatic breakthroughs in Western Europe not only for their own sake but also with an eye on a grander prize—Japan. Zhou Enlai believed that diplomatic recognition by West Germany would exert on a hesitant Japanese leadership necessary pressures that would force it to finally make up its mind and switch diplomatic recognition to Beijing.[77]

Schröder visited China between July 15 and 29, 1972 and during his visit indicated to the Chinese leaders that he would work to promote diplomatic recognition between the two countries. The MFA on the other hand drafted an RFI that proposed establishment of diplomatic relations with West Germany. Wang was summoned back to Beijing on July 20. He reported personally to Zhou Enlai on his view of the relationship. In the evening of the 24th, Wang was suddenly called to Mao's residence and had a 3-hour meeting with Mao. His ideas about Soviet strategy and West Germany received a full endorsement from Mao, who approved the MFA plan for opening negotiations with West Germany over an exchange of diplomatic recognition.[78]

By the time Wang flew back to Bonn on August 3, the German government was ready to negotiate an exchange of diplomatic recognition. In an extraordinary move, Wang, officially only a private Chinese citizen, was appointed the chief Chinese negotiator. After some 40 days of negotiations, the two sides reached an agreement on September 29. German Foreign Minister Walter Scheel visited Beijing on October 10 and official signature took place the next day. As a result, Wang Shu was transferred to the MFA and later became Chinese ambassador to Bonn.[79] Blessed by Mao, Wang's otherwise undistinguished career would continue to rise until he was appointed after the fall of the Gang of Four to the prestigious post of editor-in-chief of the CPC theoretical magazine *Red Flag* in January 1977.[80]

In this case Wang clearly played a significant role in changing China's policy toward the Federal Republic of Germany and was instrumental in altering Bonn's China policy. By farsightedness or opportunism, Wang's views conveniently provided the justification and basis for a major policy shift in Beijing foreign policy orientation engineered by Mao. Wang himself was rewarded as a result.

Hua Di and the Proposal for a Strategic Alliance with the U.S. Under normal circumstances, researchers associated with institutes of international studies are considered insignificant in the formulation of China's foreign policy. Their research products are routinely ignored by the central leadership and the foreign policy establishment as ill-informed and unreliable. However the case of Hua Di, a rocket propulsion engineer-turned researcher of CASS, who in 1984 submitted a formal proposal for China to enter into a strategic alliance with the U.S., had such an unusual impact on the top leaders and foreign policy establishment that it deserves a careful examination.[81]

After Nixon's historic visit to China in early 1972, relations between Beijing and Washington improved rapidly. However beginning in 1975 the relationship started to level off. The problem of Taiwan and leadership transition in China and leadership crisis in the U.S. stalled the momentum toward a full normalization of relations.

The election of Jimmy Carter as US President in 1976 and the rehabilitation of Deng Xiaoping in 1977 following the death of Mao and the fall of the Gang of Four stabilized the political leadership in the two capitals. The new leadership, again sought to revive the stalled normalization process. The successes of what was perceived as Soviet expansionism in the Third World from Angola to Vietnam and the renewed commitment by the new Chinese leadership to economic development gave new impetus to this process which culminated in the re-establishment of diplomatic relations between the two countries in January 1979.[82]

During his visit to the U.S. in January 1979, Deng Xiaoping called for the establishment of a strategic relationship between the two countries in what he called "a united front" that would include Western Europe and Japan, to check Soviet expansion. He also emphasized the need to "do a number of concrete things on a down-to-earth manner to counter hegemonism." To Beijing's foreign affairs establishment, this meant cooperation with the U.S. on the strategic and diplomatic fronts in specific projects like the agreement to set up joint SIGINT stations in western China to monitor Soviet missile tests.

Hua Di, a Russian-trained rocket engineer who later joined the CASS Institute of American Studies, had a broader interpretation and perhaps a closer reading of Deng's intention. In late 1978 after consolidating his power, Deng Xiaoping successfully engineered a fundamental reorientation of the focus of CPC work to economic development. To realize his goal, Deng knew that he had to rely on the West for much of the capital and technology needed for China's modernization.

Through much of the 1980s the top leadership had to grapple with the problems of shortages in foreign capital and Western restrictions on technology transfer to China. For some time it looked like these problems were intractable unless Beijing was willing to compromise its claim of sovereignty over Taiwan or forgo its communist system—issues that are considered fundamental to the Chinese leadership. The foreign policy establishment after a lengthy debate in 1981 concluded that Beijing gained little by maintaining a hardline stance toward the Soviet Union as there was a limit to the Western support for Beijing. It proposed a policy shift away from seeking a de facto strategic relationship with the U.S. and to gradually moderate China's policies toward Moscow in order to create a more peaceful environment for domestic economic development. This proposal was endorsed by Hu Yaobang and Zhao Ziyang, but accepted only reluctantly by Deng Xiaoping—for the lack of a better choice. It was officially unveiled in 1982 by Hu Yaobang at the 12th Party Congress as China's "independent foreign policy."

Hua Di, during his stay in the U.S. in 1980–82 as a visiting fellow of the Asia-US Forum on International Policy at Stanford University, came up with ideas for an alternative solution to Beijing's dilemma. Hua suggested that Beijing's dilemma could be resolved by entering into more substantial strategic cooperation with the U.S. instead of distancing itself from Washington as advocated by the foreign policy establishment. For instance, he proposed that Beijing should open up its port facilities and airports to the U.S. for refueling and services and allow the Pentagon to set up strategic reserves of ammunition and supply depots in Chinese territories. For these services, it was hoped that Beijing should be able to collect a substantial amount of fees, and because of the enhanced strategic role that Beijing played, the U.S. and the West would facilitate a greater infusion of capital into China to build up the infrastructures in China's interior and would relax the restrictions placed on technology transfer to China. In sum, Hua envisaged the generation of tens of billions of dollars in a period of ten years in exchange for strategic cooperation with the U.S.

Hua first floated his idea in 1981 at a Sino-US seminar organized by the Beijing Institute of International Strategic Studies. He continued to lobby to sell his idea to top policy makers through his personal connections.[83] He approached successively Zou Jiahua, current Vice Premier of the State Council, General Zhang Aiping, former Defense Minister and Wan Li, former Vice Premier. None of them had foreign affairs expertise and declined to voice an opinion. Song Jian, China's science czar, suggested that in order to gain more credibility and access to the top leadership, Hua should co-author an article with a foreign scholar. Hua approached Professor Victor Li of Stanford University who declined to get involved. Finally Hua found a sympathetic audience in, of all places, the MFA. The Vice Foreign Minister for American affairs, Zhang Wenjin, invited him to make a presentation at his home and seemed fascinated by the idea. Although Zhang had the session taped, in the end nothing came out of it.

Hua was persistent. In 1984 following his official transfer from the Ministry of Space and Aviation Industries to the CASS Institute of American Studies, he wrote a formal policy proposal and submitted it to CPC

General Secretary Hu Yaobang through Zhang Yün, a CPC veteran to whom Hua was related. Hu turned it over to Deng Xiaoping. The view apparently struck the right chord with Deng, who had a deeper conviction of the wisdom of a pro-American tilt. Deng enthusiastically embraced the strategic thinking without explicitly endorsing the proposal and instructed to have the author put to better use.

Hu had Wei Jianxing, Head of the CPC Central Organizational Department, initiate a background check in preparation for enlisting Hua into the ranks of the "third echelon"—a new generation of future CPC leaders. The policy side was left to Zhao Ziyang who sent the proposal to the MFA for further studies and comments. Zhao apparently was not enthusiastic about the idea. Without commenting on the merit of the proposal, Zhao's secretary told Hua that it was at least too late. As early as in October 1981 at the summit meeting between Zhao and Reagan in Cancún, Mexico, Zhao had already told Reagan of Beijing's new "independent foreign policy."

The proposal created an uproar in the MFA which was never known to be open to ideas from other foreign affairs bureaucracies to say nothing of anything from outside the foreign affairs establishment. It was rejected as totally unrealistic and as unrequited wishful thinking. However to show its respect for Deng, the MFA would arrange to have the Chinese People's Institute of Foreign Affairs under former Vice Foreign Minister Han Nianlong call a meeting with the participation of the main institutions of Beijing's foreign affairs establishment to discuss the proposal before an official repudiation was submitted by the MFA to Zhao. No policy changes were initiated as a result.

The idea by 1984 was indeed outdated. Beijing and Washington, after an initial period of stormy relations after Reagan took office, stabilized their relationship and lowered their mutual expectations by downplaying the strategic factors in the relationship. One can only speculate on the impact on the foreign policy orientation it could have had if the proposal had reached Deng in 1980–81. If adopted then, the whole outlook of Beijing's foreign policy throughout the 1980s could have been significantly different. On the other hand, one can also surmise that had Hua Di had no personal connections that provided access to the highest authority, the proposal, however well reasoned, might never have been noticed at all.

The examples given above represent exceptions rather than the rule. Generally speaking working-level bureaucrats of Beijing's foreign affairs establishment had little incentive to put forward policy initiatives that may be at variance with the view of the central leadership. In the pervasive atmosphere of mediocrity and conformity within Chinese bureaucracies, any unauthorized personal initiative tends to be viewed unfavorably by colleagues and the superior as a demonstration of unwarranted personal ambition. Outside the foreign affairs establishment, the problem is largely one of access. The central political leadership has never believed in the utility of "think tanks" in the fields of politics and international affairs. For the foreign affairs establishment, any foreign policy initiative of an extra-establishment origin tends to be viewed as an encroachment on its own turf and thus dismissed out of hand without a careful study of its own merits. Unless one has access to the central leadership bypassing the establishment, individual initiatives are not likely to be noticed either by the leadership of foreign affairs bureaucracies or by the central leadership.

Notes

1. *Zhonghua Renmin Gongheguo Jingji Guanli Dashiji* (The Chronicles of Major Events in Economic Management of the People's Republic of China) (Beijing: Zhongguo Jingji Chubanshe, 1986), p.#106.

2. Xü Jiatun, *Xü Jiatun Xianggang Huiyilu I* (Xü Jiatun's Hong Kong Memoirs I) (Hong Kong: Lianhe Bao, 1993), p.#17. Jiang Weiwen, "*Zhonggong Gaoceng Jigou Gaige Fang'an da Pilu: Zhonggong Gaoceng Renshi da Tiaozheng* (A Big Exposé of the Reform Plan for High Level CPC Organs: A Big Reshuffle of High Ranking CPC Officials)," *Guangjiaojing* (Wide Angle), January 16, 1988 p.#8.

3. Jiang Weiwen, p.#8.

4. Si Maqian, "*Zhonggong Waishi Xiaozu Qüanmian Gaizu: Li Peng Kaishi Zhangguan Zhongguo Waijiao* (A Comprehensive Reorganization of the CPC Foreign Affairs LSG: Li Peng Begins to Control Chinese Diplomacy)," *Guangjiaojing* (Wide Angle), January 16, 1988, p.#11.

5. Guojia Jigou Bianzhi Weiyüanhui (Office of the State Organ Staff Sizing Committee) (ed.), *Zhongguo Zhengfu Jigou 1991* (China Government Organization 1991) (Beijing: Zhongguo Renshi Chubanshe, 1991), p.#397.

6. In Chinese, "deplore" is translated as "regret."

7. Personal recollections.

8. Although Beijing and the Vatican have been conducting secret talks on the normalization of relations, there is no real incentive for Beijing to compromise. Thus far Beijing has been insisting on a normalization based on its own terms: the Vatican must sever official ties with Taiwan (that is easy) and recognize the official independent church in China (that is hard).

9. For details of central document types and their respective functions, see Yan Huai, "*Zhongguo Mimi Wenjian Gaiyao* (A Survey of China's Secret Documents)" *Papers of the Center for Modern China,* Vol. IV, No. 22, December 1993, pp.#3–9.

10. Despite widespread Western reports to the contrary, with few exceptions, there were no direct Chinese exports of arms to Iran and Iraq during the Iran-Iraq War. The repeated Chinese denials of such arms sales to Iran and Iraq were technically correct, since almost all sales were made and shipped to Jordan, which sided with Iraq, and Syria, which supported Iran. However the quantities of the sales made it clear that they were intended for Iran or Iraq. In order to maintain strict deniability, the MFA insisted that China could only accept arms purchase delegations from Jordan and Syria. As a result all members of the Iraqi delega-

tions held Jordanian passports. There were however a few exceptions involving the sales of Chinese surface-to-air missiles. Although the sales were made to Hong Kong or Singapore companies, they were shipped directly from China to Iran and Chinese technicians as employees of these companies provided training for the local personnel to operate the systems.

11. The Chinese never subscribed to the argument, since they were told by the Iranians that unlike Iraq which had oil pipelines to Turkey, Iran was almost completely dependent on shipping through the Gulf for its oil exports. The closing of shipping would have been devastating to the Iranian economy. The Chinese reasoned that only under one condition that the Iranians would try to close the Gulf oil shipping—they wanted to end the war since it would mean a cutoff of its main source to finance the war—oil exports. Ending the war was exactly the declared American objective.

12. Yan Kong, "China's Arms Trade Bureaucracy," *Jane's Intelligence Review,* February 1994, p.#80.

13. For the Saudi side of the story, see HRH General Khaled Bin Sultan, "Chapter X: Capturing the East Wind" in *Desert Warrior: A Personal View of the Gulf War by the Joint Forces Commander* (New York: HarperCollins Publishers, 1995), pp.#137–152.

14. Xinhua, November 19, 1985, *BBC SWB-FE/8118/A4/1,* November 26, 1985.

15. Xinhua, December 3, 1985, *BBC SWF-FE/8133/A4/2,* December 13, 1985.

16. Xinhua, December 22, 1985, *BBC SWB-FE/8144/A4/1,* December 31, 1985.

17. According to General Khaled Bin Sultan, former Saudi air force and strategic missile force commander, another reason for seeking to acquire surface-to-surface missiles was to counter a perceived threat from Israel, which had developed nuclear weapons and the delivery systems such as long-range strike aircraft and ballistic missiles—the Jericho. For a fuller account of the Saudi rationale, see Khaled Bin Sultan, pp.#142–145.

18. *The Washington Post (WP),* March 29, 1988, p.#A13.

19. The Saudi decision to acquire surface-to-surface missiles was not an idea of Saudi military commanders, but was made personally by Saudi King Fahd, who sent Bandar to approach Beijing because the Saudis believed that Beijing was "the country able to supply such a weapon at speed and without constraining conditions." Khaled Bin Sultan, pp.#138, 145.

20. For details about the missile and its launch procedures, see Hua Di, "China's Case: Ballistic Missile Proliferation" in William C. Potter and Harlan W. Jencks (eds.), *The International Missile Bazaar: The New Suppliers' Network* (Boulder: Westview Press, 1994), p.#170, and Shichor Yitzhak, *East Wind over Arabia: Origins and Implications of the Sino-Saudi Missile Deal* (Berkeley: Institute of East Asian Studies, 1989), pp.#29–30.

21. The same line was apparently resold to General Khaled Bin Sultan who later took over the negotiations and was shown a Chinese missile base. Khaled Bin Sultan, p.#141.

22. General Khaled Bin Sultan, in his four trips to China negotiating the deal, would fly in his own private jet with his regular American crew. The Saudis, as a cover, would tell Washington, and Britain, that they were travelling to China, a country with which they had no diplomatic relations, to purchase small arms in

the hope of dissuading the Chinese from selling arms to Iran. They apparently played the game with great success. Ibid, p.#139.

23. The claim that the MFA objected to the sale and the objection was overruled by Deng Xiaoping (see John W. Lewis, Hua Di and Xüe Litai, "Beijing's Defence Establishment," *International Security*, 15:4, 1991, p.96) was erroneous. Neither did the MFA object to nor was Deng Xiaoping personally involved in the decision.

24. The DF–3s are said to have a life span of 14 years. Since the first generation of DF–3s were deployed in May 1971, most of the missiles sold to Saudi Arabia would have to be decommissioned by the end of the century. Hua Di, p.#170.

25. Cash payment was Saudi's trump card in the negotiations. Khaled Bin Sultan, p.#141.

26. Khaled Bin Sultan, p.#138.

27. Yan Kong, p.#82.

28. *WP*, March 29, 1988, p.#A1. Both the Chinese and the Saudis were surprised that the secret over the purchase was kept for so long. Khaled bin Sultan, p.#150.

29. For the critical role the missile sales played in the establishment of diplomatic links, see Khaled bin Sultan, pp.#151–152.

30. *China Government Organization*, p.#328.

31. The publication used to come out twice a day with a morning and an after edition. Since 1983 it has become a daily publication.

32. Yan Huai, "Confidential Documents," pp.#12–13.

33. For this and other examples, see Wang Shu, "*Kaizhan tong Sahara yi nan Feizhou Geguo de Guanxi* (Developing Relations with Sub-Sahara African Countries)," Pei Jianzhang et al. (eds.), *Xin Zhongguo Waijiao Fengyün II* (New China Diplomacy II), p.#64–69.

34. *China Government Organization*, p.515.

35. Jeffrey T. Richelson, *Foreign Intelligence Organizations* (Cambridge: Ballinger Publishing Co., 1988), pp.#291–292.

36. Chen Xiaolu, *Jinian Chen Yi* (In Memory of Chen Yi) (Beijing: Wenwu Chubanshe, 1991), #497. Fan Shuo, *Ye Jianying zai 1976* (Ye Jianying in 1976) (Beijing: Zhongyang Dangxiao Chubanshe, 1990), p.#71.

37. The merger of the two bureaucracies resulted in so much infighting that in the end the central leadership had to separate the two again. Personal recollections.

38. David L. Shambaugh, "China's National Security Research Bureaucracy," *The China Quarterly*, No. 110, June 1987, pp.#296–299.

39. John Lewis et al, p.#93.

40. Zheng Xiaoguo and Nan Dongfeng, (eds.), *Wo shi Zhongguo Renmin de Erzi: Deng Xiaoping 1977–1992 nian Huodong Shilu* (I Am a Son of the Chinese People: A Chronicle of Deng Xiaoping's Activities in 1977–1992) (Beijing: Zhongguo Guoji Guangbo Dianshi Chubanshe, 1993), pp.#175–184.

41. Often COSTIND would accuse Poly Technologies of violating the original rule for its entry into the market. Instead of selling only the surplus in the PLA inventory created as a result of the downsizing, COSTIND would charge, Poly Technologies would disguise its purchases of new weapon systems from COSTIND corporations under its procurement programs for the PLA so as to take advantage of the low prices fixed by the Government for such procurement, and

would later resell them on the international markets in what was perceived as "unfair" direct competition with their producers.

There is a myth perpetuated in the Western defense analyst community that both COSTIND and Poly Technologies serve the interest of the PLA. This is true only to the extent that Boeing's military-related researches benefit the Pentagon. Otherwise COSTIND in the field of arms sales only looks after the interest of the Chinese defense industries—the producer, and Poly Technologies that of the PLA—the consumer. To assume that the profits generated by COSTIND corporations will automatically flow into the PLA coffer is unrealistic at a time when the defense industries on the whole are losing money because of the PLA downsizing and are forced to convert to civilian production.

The Chinese themselves are partly to blame for the perpetuation of this myth since when COSTIND was created in 1982, it was decided that its leadership and staff members of its headquarters would wear PLA uniforms and later have military ranks. But to those familiar with the history of Chinese politics, wearing PLA uniforms is not necessarily a sure identification of PLA interest. During the Cultural Revolution, for instance, even Peking Opera singers and ballet dancers wore PLA uniforms.

42. Ren Mingyang, "*Zhonggong dui Tai Gongzuo Guanjian Renwu Yang Side Shengping da Pilu* (A Big Exposé of Yang Side, A Key Figure in the Taiwanese Work of the CPC)," *Guangjiaojing* (Wide Angle), 1988, pp.#8–11.

43. Personal communications, August 1994.

44. Contrary to some portrayals of a methodological push by Beijing in the South China Sea (John Garver, "China's Push Through the South China Sea: the Interaction of Bureaucratic and National Interests," *The China Quarterly*, No. 132, December 1992), the PLAN was totally unprepared for the Battle of the Paracels. For a detailed account and analysis of the Battle of the Paracels, see Lu Ning, *Flashpoint Spratlys* (Singapore: Dolphin Books, 1995), Chapter Three.

45. Hu Yaobang was not in Beijing at the time. Hu Qili was in charge of the Secretariat during his absence. Personal recollections.

46. *The New York Times*, March 23, 1985.

47. *Facts on File 1985*.

48. *Dangdai Zhongguo Haijün* (The Contemporary Chinese Navy) (Beijing: Zhongguo Shehui Kexüe Chubanshe, 1987), pp.#324–325.

49. Song Shuren and Chen Zhibai, "Hurrah, No. 502 Formation" in Lin Daoyüan, (ed.), *Nansha Gaosu Women* (What the Spratlys tell Us) (Beijing: Haijün Chubanshe, 1988), pp.#25–26.

50. For details about the skirmish, see Lu Ning.

51. Interview with a senior PLAN officer, January 1995.

52. Yang Shangkun, Executive Vice Chairman of the CMC in charge of the day-to-day operations of the PLA, reportedly told the PLAN: "Don't carry out your troop training in the South China Sea." Interview with a retired senior PLA expert on the South China Sea, September 1995.

53. They were the First Ministry of Machine Building (MMB) responsible for industrial machinery production, the Second MMB for nuclear weapon research and production, the Third MMB for military aircraft, the Fourth MMB for electronics, the Fifth MMB for conventional arms, the Sixth MMB for naval ships, the

Seventh MMB for strategic guided missiles and the Eighth MMB for agricultural machinery.

54. Yan Kong, p.#80.

55. While the CMC provides professional leadership, it is under the administrative control of the State Council.

56. Yan Kong, p.#80.

57. Israeli Foreign Minister Moshe Sharett cabled Zhou Enlai, the new PRC Foreign Minister, informing him of Israel's *de jure* recognition of the new Chinese government. Yossi Melman and Ruth Sinai, "Israeli-Chinese Relations and Their Future Prospects: From Shadow to Sunlight," *Asian Survey*, Vol. XXVII, No. 4, April 1987, p.#398.

58. Personal recollections. For details about this policy choice, see Wu Chuwen, *"Shi Lun Zhou Enlai guanyü Zhongdong Gongzuo de Waijiao Sixiang yü Shijian* (A Tentative Study of Zhou Enlai's Diplomatic Thought and Practice in Regard to the Middle East Work)," in Pei Jianzhang (ed.), *Yanjiü Zhou Enlai Waijiao Sixiang yü Shijian* (A Study of Zhou Enlai's Diplomatic Thoughts and Practice) (Beijing: Shijie Zhishi Chubanshe, 1989), p.#135.

59. There were initial concerns whether the PLA should parade its T–79 tank with its tell-tale Israeli 105mm L–7 tank cannon that features advanced thermal-insulation casing. Hu Yaobang dismissed those concerns and included the tanks in the parade which served to publicly confirm for the first time Beijing's secret dealings with Israel in military technologies.

60. William C. Potter and Harlan W. Jencks, *The International Missile Bazaar: The New Suppliers' Network* (Boulder: Westview, 1994), p.#244.

61. Python III is a third generation short range air-to-air missile similar in appearance to but slightly larger than the US AIM–9 Sidewinder. Unlike the tail-aspect engagement only systems of the first and second generations, Python III is reportedly an all-aspect infrared seeker with a countermeasures capability equivalent to AIM–9M Sidewinders. It entered service with the Israeli Air Force in 1982 and was credited with about 50 kills in the Bekaa Valley conflict with Syria that year. Duncan Lennox and Arthur Rees (eds.), *Jane's Air-Launched Weapons (JALW)* (Alexandria, VA: Jane's Information Group Inc., 1990), Issue 10.

62. A variety of sources had approached Beijing for sales of Israeli technologies and products. For some time, all these offers were turned down.

63. COSTIND would later try to turn the deal into a much more profitable one by marketing the missile on international markets. In March 1991, at the Defence Asia Exhibition in Singapore, it unveiled the missile designated PL–8H in a new missile/gun air defense system, thus providing direct evidence of military cooperation between Beijing and Tel Aviv. *JALW-ISSUE 10*.

64. Privately Palestinian Liberation Organization (PLO) officials would confide to MFA officials that they were aware of what was going on between Beijing and the Jewish state, but were willing to look the other way.

65. These institutions were defined by Mao derogatorily as *"zhishi fenzi cheng dui de difang* (places where intellectuals congregate)."

66. Over the years, the ranks of the IIS have included such researchers as Zhuang Qübing, a leading American affairs expert who as a former KMT diplomat has never been fully trusted, Qian Dayong, a former Counselor in the

Chinese Liaison Office in Washington who was "exiled" because of his association with the Young Mistress Faction (see Chapter 3), and Yao Wei, a former chief of the 1st Division of the Information Department who had irked Qian Qichen by bypassing Qian in taking up a visiting scholarship in the U.S. in the early 1980s (see Chapter 3).

67. David L. Shambaugh, "China's National Security Research Bureaucracy," *The China Quarterly*, No. 110, June 1987, p.#291–294.

68. Personal communications with Zhuang, January 1991.

69. Most of the fresh college graduates start out by doing newspaper and *Reference Material* clippings—"with a bottle of glue and a pair of scissors" as it is known.

70. Contrary to some of the Western literature on the subject, e.g. Nicholas Eftimiades, *Chinese Intelligence Operations* (Annapolis: Naval Institute Press, 1994), the Chinese intelligence operations are nothing, both in terms of their scale and resources, when compared to the CIA and KGB. This is partly because the top leadership has always put a premium on the strategic intent of its adversaries rather than the technical capabilities. For instance with few exceptions (one of them being Hong Kong), Chinese diplomatic missions abroad are forbidden to engage in intelligence operations according to the CPC Central Committee regulations. Xü Jiatun, I, p.#52.

71. Shambaugh, pp.#288–289.

72. For a detailed study of the Institute's work during the period, see Gilbert Rozman, *The Chinese Debate about Soviet Socialism, 1978–1985* (Princeton: Princeton University Press, 1987).

73. For instance, after the military crackdown in June 1989, CASS was identified as one of the "heavy disaster areas" by the central leadership.

74. On July 4, 1993, Mao summoned Zhang Chunqiao and Wang Hongwen to discuss the political report of the coming CPC 10th National Congress and the proposed revision of the CPC party constitution. He instead lashed out at the MFA's analysis of US-Soviet relations as a "bullshit document" that he never cared to read, "including premier's speech." He criticized Zhou Enlai and the MFA for "not discussing major issues while forwarding small cases to (him) everyday." "If this is not changed," he warned, "they would inevitably become revisionists." He urged Zhang and Wang: "You are still not too old, therefore should study a little foreign languages, so as not to be mislead by those lords (at the MFA) and jump on board (with them)." *Zhongguo Gongchandang Zhizheng Sishi Nian* (The CPC's Forty Years in Power) (Beijing: Zhonggong Dangshi Ziliao Chubanshe, 1989).

75. Mao referred to Ji's visit to Britain, France, Iran and Pakistan between June 7 and 19, 1993.

76. Wang Shu, "*Wo Guo tong Lianbang Deguo Jianjiao de Qianhou Jingguo* (Events Surrounding China's Establishment of Diplomatic Relations with Federal Republic of Germany)," *New China Diplomacy I*, pp.#109–121.

77. Ibid., p.#118.

78. Almost dragged off Beijing street, a totally unprepared Wang was so overwhelmed by the experience that he could not control his excitement and started to cry when he saw Mao. Mao offered him a cigarette to calm him down. Ibid.

79. Ibid.

80. Wang's rise would end in May 1978 when *Red Flag* under his editorship dutifully pushed the line of Party Chairman Hua Guofeng, known as "whateverism," which was opposed by Deng Xiaoping. Wang would return to the MFA and served in several ambassadorial assignments before taking up the directorship of the Institute of International Studies.

81. This part is largely based on author's personal interview with Mr. Hua Di conducted on April 3, 1995 and on some personal recollections.

82. For details of Sino-US relations during this period, see Robert G. Sutter, *The China Quandary: Domestic Determinants of U.S. China Policy, 1972–1982* (Boulder: Westview Press, 1983).

83. Hua Di is the son of a high ranking official and has extensive personal and family connections in the CPC hierarchy. Personal communication, April 3, 1995.

6

Changing Dynamics in Foreign Policy Decisionmaking

The dominant role of the CPC leading nucleus in the making of China's foreign policy decisions has been one of the most important characteristics in the formulation of China's foreign policies. Although there have been repeated attempts to officially define the roles of the different components of the central leadership and the bureaucratic institutions of the foreign affairs establishment in the foreign policy formulation, the making of foreign policies has been a dynamic process. Leadership change, domestic political and economic transformation, and changes in the external environment can influence the dynamics of the process and the relative balance of the actors in the policy formulation.

Foreign Policy Decisionmaking in the Era of Mao

On the eve of communist victory, Mao personally formulated the three main components of the foreign policy of the new regime. Although the five-men CPC Secretariat, which was equivalent to the present-day Standing Committee of the Politburo, held discussions over this new policy orientation, its true role was to lend legitimacy to a major policy decision made personally by Mao which was to be ratified later at the 2nd Plenum of the 7th Party Congress in early 1949.

Mao would soon discover however that his lack of foreign affairs experience made it difficult for him to move independently beyond setting policy orientation and guidelines for the new regime. Mao realized that he needed a manager to conduct foreign affairs and this manager would be Zhou Enlai.

Mao travelled to the Soviet Union in December 1949, his first trip ever beyond the Chinese borders. In his initial talks with Stalin, Mao found it impossible to communicate with the Russian leader. While Mao, coming from a traditional Chinese cultural background, deemed it proper for the

Russian leader to voluntarily offer his assistance to the new communist regime, Stalin on the other hand was anxious to learn from Mao what he wanted. Mao's reply that he wanted something that "not only looks nice but also tastes good" puzzled his hosts. After a dozen days or so that Mao and Stalin spoke past each other, Mao finally decided to call to his rescue Zhou Enlai who helped bridge the gap between Mao and Stalin and negotiate the Treaty of Sino-Soviet Alliance.[1]

The Korean War represented the first major test of his foreign policy decision. As the decision could determine the life or death of the new communist regime, Mao was not confident enough to make it alone. He needed to convene a series of enlarged Politburo meetings to help him weigh the pros and cons of a Chinese intervention so as to arrive at a sound judgement. Once he made up his mind, these meetings were used to overcome opposition and reservation on the part of the majority of the participants in order to build a consensus to ensure implementation of his decision. While Mao concentrated on military strategy, implementation details of his decision were delegated to Zhou Enlai for diplomacy, Gao Gang for logistic support and Peng Dehuai for military operations.

Later as State President, Mao would learn more about diplomacy. He was never comfortable in dealing with foreigners on a ceremonial basis and was happy to leave the management of foreign affairs in the hands of Zhou Enlai while he concentrated on main policy issues. In early 1953 Mao began to stress party leadership in government operations and abolished the General Party Group of the State Council under Zhou Enlai. The government ministries would report directly to Mao through eight comprehensive sectors. Zhou Enlai was deprived of much of the economic portfolio and left in charge of only one sector—the foreign affairs.[2]

In 1954, with the creation of a permanent CPC Secretary-General Work Conference and the Central Military Commission under the CPC Secretariat,[3] the current political power structure was institutionalized. Under this structure, the CPC leading nucleus and nuclear circle would exercise overall leadership and control over the party, the government and the military through the Secretary-General Work Conference which would later become the Secretariat at the 8th Party Congress in 1956, the State Council, and the Central Military Commission respectively.[4] Foreign affairs however would remain in the hands of Mao and Zhou.

1956 marked a turning point. Mao would further concentrate decision-making power in his own hands and his decisions would become increasingly arbitrary. Several events had contributed to Mao's increased suspicion and turn to autocracy. In February 1956, Soviet leader N. Khrushchev made his famous secret speech repudiating Stalin on the 20th Congress of the Soviet Communist Party. In September the CPC convened its 8th Party Congress and made an important decision that stressed collective leadership against personality cult.⁵ Also at the 8th Party Congress, Zhou's effort to rein in reckless pursuit of high production targets in the economy, an endeavor which was later known as *fan maojin*—"anti rash advance," was ratified. Mao, who had earlier called for accelerated economic development, harbored deep reservations about the cautious approach to economic development.

Mao counter-attacked. Through a series of meetings between September 1957 and May 1958, Mao repudiated Zhou Enlai and Chen Yün for the anti rash advance program as conservative that dampened the enthusiasm of the masses. Mao also attempted to weaken Zhou's position by relieving him of the foreign affairs portfolio. In February 1958, he appointed Chen Yi to succeed Zhou as Foreign Minister. In March the CPC Central Committee and the State Council issued a joint circular announcing the establishment of the CPC Central Foreign Affairs Small Group and the Foreign Affairs Office of the State Council. Chen Yi was appointed Head of the Foreign Affairs Small Group in charge of the overall foreign affairs work.⁶ Zhou had to cut the size of the Premier's Office in half from 17 secretaries to eight, with some of his foreign affairs secretaries reassigned to the newly created Foreign Affairs Office of the State Council.⁷

Mao's increasing totalitarian rule was also reflected in his handling of the offshore island crisis of 1958, a high drama that he orchestrated almost single-handedly.

The Artillery Shelling of Quemoy. In August 1958, Mao ordered a massive artillery bombardment of Nationalist held offshore islands of Jinmen (Quemoy) and created a crisis. In 1957 Mao approved a large scale demobilization of the PLA. In 1958 the size of the PLA was reduced to 2.4 million—its lowest level since 1949. Mao was launching the "Great Leap Forward" and organizing rural "people's communes," and therefore was anxious to find out the bottom line of the mutual defense treaty between the U.S. and Taiwan.

The Middle East crisis in July gave Mao an opportunity. On July 15, US marines landed in Lebanon and US forces in the Far East went on alert. Two days later, the Nationalist forces in Taiwan, which had been sending reinforcement to Jinmen, were also put on a special alert and started military exercises.⁸ Mao on July 17 instructed Defense Minister Peng Dehuai to prepare for a blockade of Jinmen islands.⁹ On July 18, Mao summoned his generals and told them to prepare mainly for an artillery campaign that would last two or three months. The subsequent CMC meeting set the date for July 25. However on July 27 Mao decided to postpone the campaign.

Soviet leader Khrushchev visited Beijing between July 31 and August 3. Mao and Khrushchev clashed over the Soviet proposal to set up joint long wave communication stations and a joint naval fleet. The confrontation with Khrushchev seemed to strengthen Mao's resolve to demonstrate his independence. At the end of an enlarged Politburo meeting in late August in which two key decisions were adopted concerning the establishment of the people's commune and militia systems, Mao decided on August 20 to launch his campaign. The artillery bombardment started on August 23. After 10 days of blockade, the supplies to the 88,500 Nationalist troops on the islands were reduced to a trickle—about 5.5% of their normal level.[10] As his frontline commanders waited anxiously for his order to launch an amphibious assault on the islands,[11] Mao, to the surprise of almost everyone, suddenly ordered a halt to artillery bombardment and gradually loosened the stranglehold on the islands out of a concern that taking the islands would sever Taiwan's link with the mainland and drive Taiwan to declare independence.[12] Once Mao found out the defensive nature of the US-Taiwan mutual defense treaty, he was able to further reduce the size of the military and the level of defense spending.[13]

Throughout the crisis, Mao personally made all the decisions with little consultation with his Politburo. Zhou Enlai however would manage the details of the diplomatic exchanges with the U.S., and the MFA under Zhou would draw up the negotiation plan for the Sino-U.S. ambassadorial talks in Warsaw.[14]

Chen Yi however would never be able to replace Zhou as the general manager of China's foreign affairs. This was partly due to his unfamiliarity with foreign affairs but also to the meticulous style of Zhou Enlai who would insist on micro-managing Beijing's relations with the outside world.[15]

In 1957 Mao's effort to mobilize Chinese intellectuals to attack his political enemies within the CPC backfired. The subsequent anti-rightist campaign successfully silenced his critics in society. In 1959 at the 8th Plenum of the 8th Party Congress, Mao also managed to silence dissent within the CPC leadership by purging Peng Dehuai who voiced open opposition to his Great Leap Forward Movement. From then on, Mao became increasingly autocratic. He alone would make all the major foreign policy decisions. The Politburo became a rubber stamp routinely ratifying his decisions even though some of its members had different opinions. For instance on such an important question as the Sino-Soviet split, although Lin Biao, then one of the seven Standing Committee members of the Politburo, privately believed that Mao's decision to break with the Russians was extreme and excessive, publicly he would support Mao's decision.[16]

The failure of the Great Leap Forward forced Mao to retreat by giving up his title of State President in 1959. Although Liü Shaoqi, who became the new President, began to take over most of the ceremonial part of the work associated with the job, the part that Mao did not like anyway, Mao remained the ultimate decisionmaker in foreign affairs.

Starting from 1960 Mao believed that the Soviet Union became "revisionist"—a term Mao used to refer to what he considered deviations from orthodox Marxism. At the 10th Plenum of the 8th Party Congress held in 1962, Mao mounted a comeback from his temporary retreat in 1959 by re-emphasizing "class struggle" and "fight against revisionism" in China. The Sino-Soviet split and polemic debate in the early 1960s aggravated Mao's paranoia that within the CPC central leadership there were "Chinese Khrushchevs" conspiring against him. As he built up a personality cult, political power began to further concentrate in his own hands. This finally culminated in 1966 when Mao launched the Cultural Revolution to bring down his political enemies and establish his ultimate power.

Since the 8th Party Congress, the Politburo and its Standing Committee had proven ineffective bodies to manage day-to-day operations. Of the seven members of the Standing Committee of the Politburo—Mao Zedong, Liü Shaoqi, Zhou Enlai, Zhu De, Chen Yün, Lin Biao and Deng Xiaoping, Zhu was semi-retired due to advanced age, Lin was on long-term sick leave and Chen was on the sideline from time to time because of his "right" tendencies. Similarly the Politburo was handicapped by the advanced age of some its members and the fact that many were based outside Beijing. The locus of decisionmaking on issues of CPC's day-to-day operations shifted from the Politburo to the Secretariat headed by Deng Xiaoping. Its members, like Peng Zhen, took charge of party affairs, Lo Ruiqing military affairs and Lu Dingyi culture and arts and propaganda.[17]

Foreign affairs however was an exception. Most of the decisions of secondary importance were made by Zhou with Mao's approval. Unless called upon, other members of the Politburo and the Secretariat with the exception of Chen Yi would not venture into this domain considered exclusive to Mao and Zhou.

The Secretariat ironically because of its role in managing the day-to-day operations of the CPC became the first casualty of the Cultural Revolution. In late 1965 and early 1966, members of the Secretariat, Peng Zhen, Lo Ruiqing, Lu Dingyi and Yang Shangkun would be the first to fall in the central leadership, all branded members of an "anti-Party clique." Deng Xiaoping, its General Secretary, would follow in 1967. The Secretariat was subsequently disbanded. Its power was taken over by the newly created CPC Central Committee Cultural Revolution Small Group (SG).[18] Of the seven members of the Standing Committee of the Politburo, only Mao Zedong, Lin Biao and Zhou Enlai remained untouched. Together with Kang Sheng and Chen Boda—advisor and Head of the Central Cultural Revolution SG they would become the *de facto* Standing

Committee of the Politburo during the Cultural Revolution making most of the decisions. This composition of the new Standing Committee was officially ratified at the 9th Party Congress in 1969.

Foreign affairs would remain in the hands of Mao and Zhou. This was mainly due to Mao's firm grip on foreign and military affairs decisions, but also partly because of Lin Biao's disinterest in foreign affairs and the Cultural Revolution SG's preoccupation with the political movement.[19] Attempts by certain members of the Cultural Revolution SG to seize power in the foreign affairs establishment in summer 1967 were firmly rebuked by Zhou with Mao's support. This led to the subsequent downfall of Wang Li, a leading member of the Cultural Revolution SG. With Chen Yi purged in 1969 and most of the members of the Foreign Affairs LSG in disgrace, the Foreign Affairs LSG ceased to exist. In the same year, its staff office—the State Council Foreign Affairs Office—was eliminated together with other staff offices. Its staff was transferred to the MFA and many ended up in "May 4 Cadres' Schools" doing farm work.[20] The MFA's day-to-day operations were again back under the direct control of Zhou, whose position was further strengthened after the fall of Lin Biao in late 1971.

This arrangement whereby Mao would make all the important policy decision and Zhou would manage the day-to-day operations and the implementation of policy decisions would continue until 1974 when Zhou had to check into the hospital for cancer treatment and Deng Xiaoping took over the day-to-day operations of the government. With both Mao's and Zhou's health deteriorating rapidly, Beijing was in leadership transition. No major foreign policy decisions were initiated. Factional infighting intensified that led to Deng's loss of Mao's favor in his last days. In January 1976 shortly after the death of Zhou, Deng had to give up most of his power to Hua Guofeng and retained only the foreign affairs portfolio.[21] By early April Deng again was expelled from the central leadership. Mao would soon die in September that year.

From Deng's second exile until 1978, Beijing's diplomacy lacked clear direction under Hua Guofeng, who had been an official of an inland province through much of his career and had no foreign affairs experience. Li Xiannian, the Vice Premier most experienced in foreign affairs in the new leading nuclear circle, took charge of foreign affairs as the Head of the Central Foreign Affairs Small Group.[22] With the central leadership's inexperience in foreign affairs and its preoccupation with domestic power transition, Beijing's foreign relations were put on autopilot with the foreign affairs bureaucracies following the previously established policy guidelines.

China's foreign policy has always been dictated by twin sources: the nation's physical security and the nation's economic development.

Throughout the Mao era, the nation's physical security was the primary concern. Incessant wars and the threats to Beijing's security on its periphery from Korea to Taiwan to Indochina to India to the Sino-Soviet border led Mao to believe that a major war was inevitable and imminent. Diplomacy as a result was used as one important instrument to contain the perceived threats to its security. Economic development was subordinate to the paramount concern of securing the nation's physical security.

As a result, Beijing's foreign trade and foreign aid were required to serve the political objectives of its foreign relations. Thus not only did Beijing devote a disproportionately large amount of its resources to foreign aid, but much of it including military assistance was provided with no or low interest loans or for gratis. Foreign trade was conducted sometimes at a loss. In the foreign affairs establishment, the MFA under Zhou Enlai dominated the decisionmaking in the implementation of foreign policies. The International Liaison Department whose primary responsibility was to handle CPC's relations with other communist parties played a prominent role in Beijing's relations with the Soviet Union, East European countries and Korea, Vietnam and Cuba, countries with communist parties as ruling parties. However its influence began to wane following the Sino-Soviet split in the early 1960s. Through this period, the military, except in a few cases that involved military operations like in Korea, Vietnam and the Sino-Indian border, played no policy role in foreign affairs. It served strictly as an instrument of Mao's foreign policy.

Foreign Policy Decisionmaking in the Deng Era

The Central Leadership

Deng Xiaoping returned to the center of power on the 3rd Plenum of the 10th Party Congress held in July 1977. He took over the portfolios of military and foreign affairs. At the 11th Party Congress held one month later, Hua Guofeng was elected Chairman, and Deng Xiaoping, Ye Jianying, Li Xiannian and Wang Dongxing Vice Chairmen of the CPC. The five of them also formed the Standing Committee of the Politburo.

Deng began a well orchestrated campaign to out-manoeuvre his rivals. At the 3rd Plenum of the 11th Party Congress in late 1978, Deng managed to have Chen Yün elected Vice Chairman of the Standing Committee and member of the Standing Committee. At the same time, to circumvent the Politburo which was then still dominated by holdovers from the Cultural Revolution period, Deng created the position of *zhonggong zhongyang mishuzhang*—Secretary-General of the CPC Central Committee—and named Hu Yaobang to the post. Hu Qiaomu and Yao Yilin were appointed Deputy Secretary-Generals. Thus with his allies outnumbering his rivals in the central leadership, Deng was able to reestablish himself as the leading nucleus of the CPC even though Hua Guofeng would remain Chairman of the CPC until June 1981.

At the 5th Plenum of the 11th Party Congress in February 1980, Deng's chief lieutenants Hu Yaobang and Zhao Ziyang were elected members of the Standing Committee, and his opponents Wang Dongxing, Wu De and Chen Xilian were stripped of their posts. Hua Guofeng, though retaining his CPC chairmanship, became isolated and was forced to give up the premiership under the name of "separating the party from the governmental functions." The Secretariat was recreated and became Deng's chief instrument to carry out his reform program. With Hu Yaobang as its General Secretary, it consisted of 11 members. It took over the day-to-day operations of the CPC.

Noteworthy in the newly created Secretariat was the inclusion of Yang Dezhi, a professional soldier. For the first time since the fall of Luo Ruiqing, Secretary-General of the CMC, in 1965, the Secretariat resumed charge of the day-to-day operations of the PLA. However it was not responsible for foreign affairs. Standing Committee member Li Xiannian, who was relieved of his economic responsibilities after taking blame for the failed massive import program known as *yang maojin* (rash foreign advance) in 1978, was left with the portfolio of foreign affairs. However Li's position was weak, foreign affairs was in fact in the hands of Deng who launched a series of new initiatives in foreign affairs: the signing of the Sino-Japanese peace treaty in 1978, the normalization of relations with the U.S. in 1979 and the border war with Vietnam in spring 1979.

Deng's rush to normalization of relations with the U.S. however was based on a false premise: In the face of aggressive Soviet actions around the world in the late 1970s, Washington would forsake its ties with Taibei in exchange for strategic cooperation with Beijing, and it would come up with substantial financial and technological support for Beijing. The Taiwan Relations Act and the unsatisfactory outcome of the border war with Vietnam during which the West, including the U.S., gave no support called into question Deng's judgement in foreign affairs. Deng, like Mao in the face of policy failures, would retreat from the front line of foreign affairs.

With the election of Zhao Ziyang as Premier of the State Council in 1980 and Hu Yaobang as CPC Chairman in 1981 (he would later become General Secretary in 1982), a new leading nuclear circle consisting of Deng, Chen Yün, Hu and Zhao began to emerge. It was officially ratified at the 12th Party Congress in 1982.[23]

Hu and Zhao, who came to the front lines of CPC and government operations in 1980, were relatively inactive in foreign affairs due to a lack of experience. Li Xiannian headed the Central Foreign Affairs LSG who appointed former FM Ji Pengfei Director of the State Council's FAO. The reorientation of China's domestic agenda toward economic development and Deng's slogan of "emancipating the mind" encouraged the foreign affairs establishment to rethink Beijing's international posture. Disillusionment with the lukewarm support from the West for Beijing modernization programs, as reflected in the low level of capital inflow and slow pace of technology transfer, was exacerbated by the election in late 1980 of Ronald Reagan, well known for his pro-Taiwan stance. A consensus began to emerge in the foreign affairs establishment that a major foreign policy adjustment was needed to reduce tension with the Soviet Union which by then was bogged down in the Afghanistan quagmire, and to draw a distance from the U.S.

Hu and Zhao compelled by the need to create a peaceful environment for the domestic agenda signed on to the concept. Initially Deng was cool to the idea. Knowing full well that Beijing had to rely on the West for much of its capital and technology needs, Deng feared that such a strategy could trigger a backlash in the West. However Zhao managed to persuade him that with careful management Beijing could have the best of both worlds. Deng finally signed on to the idea with reservations. This policy initiative was officially unveiled as "independent foreign policy" at the 12th Party Congress by Hu Yaobang in 1982.

Hu and Zhao would quickly become familiarized with foreign affairs and began to take command of major decisionmaking. Hu, impressed by the Japanese miracle after a trip to that country in late 1983, became deeply involved in policies toward Japan. On the other hand, Zhao, who became Deputy Head of the Central Foreign Affairs LSG, took the lead in handling Beijing's relations with Washington. Deng remained the ultimate decisionmaker but retreated to the second line, essentially letting Hu and Zhao run the show. However on some crucial decisions including some over tactics, Deng would get personally involved either on his own initiative or under solicitation by Hu or Zhao.[24] Of the other two active members of the Standing Committee, Chen Yün seldom voiced his opinion on foreign policy issues, but when he did, it carried a lot of weight given the senior positions he had held within the CPC and his reputation of high personal integrity. Li Xiannian served largely as a senior advisor to the leading triumvirate. His uninterrupted service in the State Council and familiarity with the foreign policy establishment lent him an influential voice in important appointments to senior positions in the foreign affairs bureaucracies.[25]

By mid 1986 Deng had become increasingly dissatisfied with Hu's performance mainly in handling domestic issues, but also over certain foreign affairs matters.[26] The student demonstration in Shanghai later that year provided an excuse to dismiss Hu as the General Secretary of the CPC. Zhao became most important on the front line managing foreign affairs.

On the 13th Party Congress in 1987, a younger looking team emerged for the Politburo Standing Committee now consisting of Zhao Ziyang as General Secretary, Li Peng as Premier, Qiao Shi, Hu Qili and Yao Yilin. The Secretariat in contrast was reduced from 12 members to six because of its association with Hu. The political reform plan unveiled on the Congress focused on separating the Party from the government. The Secretariat's functions were also conveniently restricted to managing only Party affairs. There was no longer military representation in the body. The locus of decisionmaking shifted to the Politburo Standing Committee.

The new Standing Committee, more than any of its predecessors, was better qualified to handle foreign affairs decisions. Besides Zhao and Li, other members all shared personal interest and had substantial experience in foreign affairs. For instance, Yao Yilin had long been an expert on foreign trade through his years with the Ministry of Foreign Trade and Qiao Shi built his career in the corridors of the International Liaison Department.

Significant personnel changes also took place in the foreign affairs team. Li Peng took over the Central Foreign Affairs LSG from Li Xiannian who relinquished his last official post of State President to Yang Shangkun and fully retired. In the Politburo Standing Committee, Li Peng now is in charge of the foreign affairs sector.

However the most significant change in the 13th Party Congress was Deng's voluntary retirement from all party posts retaining only that of the Chairman of the CMC (both party and state). Although the 1st Plenum of the 13th Party Congress adopted a secret resolution that for those most critical decisions, Deng was accorded the power to convene Politburo Standing Committee meetings and make the ultimate call, Deng insisted that he not be concerned with most of the decisions except for the most critical ones over which, when his opinion was solicited, he would always be supportive to the collective decisions or sign on to the majority opinion of the Politburo Standing Committee.[27] Therefore Zhao Ziyang and Li Peng would make most of the foreign policy decisions. Wu Xüeqian who became Vice Premier and Deputy Head of the Central Foreign Affairs LSG was their senior advisor in foreign affairs.

This new lineup however was short-lived as the events in May and June 1989 precipitated a new round of reshuffling of the CPC leadership. Zhao Ziyang was dismissed as General Secretary. Jiang Zemin, former Party Secretary of Shanghai, took over the post. On the 5th Plenum of the 13th Party Congress, Deng relinquished his last official position—Chairman of the CMC—and retreated into full retirement. Jiang's initial lack of foreign affairs experience and of a non-Party title restricted him to handling, with Qiao Shi's assistance, foreign relations of the CPC. Li Peng assisted by Qian Qichen oversaw the foreign affairs of the government and state.[28] Foreign affairs were not entirely new to Jiang however. Having served as Director of the Foreign Affairs Bureau of the First Ministry of Machine Building and the Mayor of Shanghai, Jiang would soon come out of the learning curve and took full control of major foreign policy decisionmaking as he acquired the State Presidency after Yang Shangkun's retirement in March 1993.

The 14th Party Congress in October 1992 continued the practice of the previous Congress to have a "weak" Secretariat restricted to Party affairs.[29] With the departure of Yang Baibing, who had become a member of the Secretariat since the 5th Plenum of the 13th Party Congress in November 1989, the Secretariat is again excluded from military affairs. The tradition that the State Council under its Premier not the CPC Secretariat plays the role of the chief executive body of the Politburo Standing Committee in foreign affairs has not changed.

Although Deng officially retired in 1989, the historical change in post-War world structure in the early 1990s and the diplomatic dilemma Beijing faced after June 1989 have presented a new challenge to its foreign policy. Some critical decisions would determine its basic post-Cold War orientation and could have a lasting impact on the fate of the nation. On such issues Jiang and the rest of the central leadership had no choice but to solicit Deng's judgement. For instance, after the June 4, 89 crackdown that precipitated sanctions by Western powers, Deng gave a 16-character instruction that set the basic tone of China's diplomacy in the current post-Cold War environment.[30] Following the disintegration of the Soviet Union, Deng specifically admonished that Beijing must resist the temptation to assume the role of "the standard-bearer of socialism."[31] Similarly the MFA's original proposal to retaliate openly against Bush's decision to sell 150 F–16 advanced fighter aircraft to Taiwan during the US presidential election campaign in late 1992 was overruled by Deng.[32]

As noted above, Li Xiannian took over the portfolio of foreign affairs after the fall of the Gang of Four. His association with Hua Guofeng in the 1978 misadventure of massive importation of foreign plants and technologies cost him the portfolio of economic affairs. Although he would remain the Head of the Central Foreign Affairs LSG till 1987, he was soon overshadowed by his deputy of the LSG—Premier Zhao Ziyang—who by then became a member of the leading nuclear circle.[33]

At the 13th Party Congress, Zhao was elevated to become CPC General Secretary. Li Peng as the new Premier of the State Council began to head the Central Foreign Affairs LSG. Wu Xüeqian as Vice Premier was appointed Deputy Head of the LSG. He represented the most senior bureaucrat in charge of the foreign affairs sector. His predecessor Ji Pengfei would remain an advisor of the LSG. Having lost his post as the Head of the Central Foreign Affairs Propaganda LSG due to the decision to eliminate it, Zhu Muzhi became the other advisor of the Central Foreign Affairs LSG.

Most significant in the new composition of the Foreign Affairs LSG was that for the first time in its history it included Qin Jiwei, Minister of Defense, pointing to the emergence of the PLA as a bureaucratic interest in foreign policy formulation and the need for better coordination between the military system and the party and government systems.[34] The foreign affairs subsectors were condensed and consolidated from the original six at the time of its establishment in 1958 to five with each member of the LSG heading one subsector: Qian Qichen—foreign political relations, Zheng Tuobing—foreign economic relations, Zhu Liang—CPC external relations, Qin Jiwei—foreign military relations, and Qian Liren—foreign cultural relations and propaganda.

The Foreign Affairs Office of the State Council which serves as the staff office of the Foreign Affairs LSG became a powerful institution under Ji Pengfei, who, as one of the longest serving former Vice Foreign Ministers, commanded a strong following in the MFA and controlled some key MFA appointments. Although Ji was old and in poor health, the FAO remained powerful under his deputy Chen Chu, another MFA veteran who had served as Chinese ambassador to Japan and the UN. However following the takeover by Wu Xüeqian in late 1988, the FAO was considerably weakened when Wu's position was seriously compromised after the arrest of his son for his role during the June 4, 89 military crackdown.[35] The office would remain weak in recent years as Qian Qichen holds concurrently the post of Vice Premier in charge of foreign affairs and the post of Foreign Minister. Sandwiched between the two, the Director of the FAO can no longer play any policy role but acts like a secretariat shuffling papers around. Because of its ministerial ranking, the directorship of the FAO has also become a position for Qian to "kick upstairs" the Vice Foreign Ministers positioned, though deemed unsuited, by Qian to succeed him as Foreign Minister. First it was Qi Huaiyüan. More recently it is Liü Huaqiü. However there is good reason to believe that once Qian relinquishes the post of Foreign Minister, the FAO's fortune may turn around.

Emerging Trends

The most fundamental to the change in dynamics of foreign policy decisionmaking has been the shift of focus on the part of the central leadership since 1978 from the nation's physical security to the nation's economic development. Although the Vietnamese invasion of Cambodia and the Soviet invasion of Afghanistan caused considerable concern over China's security, it soon became clear to Beijing that Moscow's and Hanoi's overseas misadventures were such a painful drain on the resources of the two adversaries that any threats they posed to Beijing were manageable. By the early 1980s, the leadership in Beijing reached a consensus that although the Soviet forces and proxies around China still posed security concerns, they were no longer a threat for the lack of intent and resources. Deng would invent "the three main obstacles" to the normalization of relations between Moscow and Beijing mainly to control the domestic pressure to trade with Moscow so as not to create a backlash in the West.

The impact of this shift in focus on the dynamics of foreign policy decisionmaking is the emergence of some significant trends. One is the gradual erosion of the preponderant role of the paramount leader or CPC leading nucleus in favor of the leading nuclear circle in the making of foreign policy decisions. Deng Xiaoping as the nucleus of the second generation of CPC leadership has retreated first from active involvement in the decisions ranging from normalization of relations with the U.S. to the invasion of Vietnam in the late 1970s, to the second line through much of the 80s by letting Zhao Ziyang and Hu Yaobang make most of the important decisions and intervening only occasionally, and again to the third line since late 1989 intervening rarely and only when solicited.

This shift has come both as a matter of objective necessity and subjective limitations, as well as personal style. One of the main characteristics of Beijing's relations with the outside world was its growing complexity. For more than 20 years Beijing was largely isolated from the rest of the world. Following the Sino-US rapprochement in the early 1970s Beijing gingerly opened its door to the West. The open door policy of the 1980s has ushered in a new era of Chinese interaction with the rest of the world. Currently Beijing maintains diplomatic relations with some 160 countries and conducts US$280 billion (1995) in trade relations with the rest of the world. To retain the same high level of concentration of decisionmaking power as during the Mao era is no longer possible. To manage such an extensive and complex relationship requires technical expertise for which Deng's generation of leaders is ill-equipped.

Furthermore, Deng does not possess the absolute authority that Mao once commanded. Deng alone cannot dictate every major decision if they are under serious challenge within the central leadership. It is necessary for him to build consensus. Further, Deng's personal work style has never been that of a micro-manager like Zhou Enlai. While keeping the most critical of all decisions firmly in his own hands, Deng believes in the delegation of powers and places his chief lieutenants in the front line of decisionmaking. Unless he believes it is imperative, Deng would refrain from intervening in most foreign policy decisions.

The emergence of Jiang Zemin and Li Peng at the center of political power represents a transition of the Chinese political leadership from a generation of revolutionary politicians to a generation of technocrat politicians. This new group of technocrat politicians is characterized by their lack of absolute authority based on charisma and prestige established through decades of wars and construction, and by their respective small, narrowly confined power base. No single leader can command unquestioned authority simultaneously in the three major systems of China's political power—the party, the government and the military. This will lead to a more collectivized decisionmaking process with checks and balances reflected in the structure and composition of the Politburo Standing Committee which begins to represent more of bureaucratic interests.

Another trend that emerges from the shift of focus to economic development is the centrality of the economic factor in the making of foreign policy decisions. During the Mao era, because the focus was centered on national security, Beijing's political consideration dominated foreign policy decisionmaking. Foreign trade and economic aid were but instruments serving its international political objectives. By 1980, this was reversed: China's diplomacy was required to serve the nation's paramount interest of economic development. Since the late 70s, the driving force behind major Chinese foreign policies was economic development.

Examples of this abound. When Beijing announced its "independent foreign policy," it was mainly aimed at reducing tension between Beijing and Moscow so that it could devote more resources to economic development. And it was out of a concern that the new policy could backfire and endanger Beijing's opening to the West—its main source of supply of capital and technology—that it was decided to make the policy change gradual and incremental. The adjustment of Beijing's policies toward South Korea and Israel shared the same motivation to attract capital and technology. Similarly the decision to allow defense industries and the PLA to enter international arms markets came as a result of a domestic economic need to sustain the industries in a process of conversion and maintain the military in the face of drastic defense budget cuts. When faced with choices, the decisionmakers in the central leadership, particularly the Premier, under great pressures to deliver economically, tend to have a bias in favor of economic interest.

As a result of this economic bias, the third trend in the dynamics in foreign policy decisions is the decentralization of decisionmaking power (1) in favor of foreign affairs establishment at the expense of the central leadership, (2) in favor of other bureaucracies at the expense of the MFA, (3) in favor of trade corporations and local authorities at the expense of the MOFTEC.

The subtle shift of dynamics from the central political leadership toward the foreign affairs establishment is driven by the same forces that are responsible for the erosion of the power of the leading nucleus in favor of the leading nuclear circle. In addition, the fluidity of the leading nuclear circle has also contributed to the process. The leadership turnover at this level has been fairly frequent. Between 1976 and 1989, there had been four Party Chairmen and General Secretaries and three Premiers compared to only three US Presidencies. The political leadership at this level, due to relative inexperience, has to rely more heavily on professional bureaucrats to reach foreign policy decisions. The bureaucratic institutions, on the other hand, have become more assertive and occasionally resisted some ill-conceived policy initiatives by members of the leading nuclear circle.[36] As an indication of this trend, Foreign Minister Qian Qichen and Minister of MOFTEC Li Lanqing, both career bureaucrats, were elevated to members of the Politburo at the 14th Party Congress in late 1992 and later made Vice Premiers.

The gradual erosion of the MFA's predominant role in the management of China's foreign affairs is primarily due to the CPC's reorientation of its focus on economic development. As the bureaucratic institution primarily responsible for the conduct of the nation's diplomacy, the MFA is required by the central leadership to serve the nation's economic interest. Although since the early 1980s there has been an emphasis on economic diplomacy within the MFA, old habits die hard. The MFA has an institutional interest in maintaining good relations with other countries and derives little material benefit from controversial issues like arms sales abroad. As a result, it has been charged by other bureaucracies for its alleged tendency to argue for the case of foreign countries. The second reason for this shift has been the rapid expansion of Beijing's relations with the rest of the world and their growing complexity. Ironically the MFA has fallen victim to its own success as it spearheads an expansion that would overwhelm it. A good example of this is the control of issuing passports. The MFA had long been designated the only institution in China that had the authority to issue PRC passports. By the mid-1980s, the Department of Consular Affairs was overwhelmed by the workload. Many young recruits who started out as passport/visa officers complained that they had spent the initial two or three years of what was supposed to be an exciting career doing nothing but processing passports. The MFA had no choice but to delegate to local public security bureaux the authority to issue ordinary passports. The third factor in the MFA's decline is attributable to the loss of its chief patron—Zhou Enlai. Zhou who served as its first Minister had supervised every stage of its growth and viewed the MFA as his own baby. As Premier of the State Council, Zhou had always put the interest of foreign affairs above those of other bureaucracies. After Zhou's death, the MFA, although as first among equals it still commands great trust, has lost the exclusiveness of its access to the central leadership. More frequently, it has to compete for their hearts and minds with an increasing number of bureaucracies with vested interests that have entered the field of foreign affairs.

MOFTEC's growing influence is a contributing factor to the erosion of the MFA's power. It however itself is losing some of its own decision-making powers in the conduct of Beijing's foreign economic and trade relations. This has mainly come as a logical result of the economic reform program that emphasizes decentralization of economic decisionmaking power from central to local authorities and from administrative bureaucracies to corporations and enterprises. In the 1985 reform of foreign trade structure, the MOFTEC eased its oversight of the business management of the 16 foreign trade corporations which till then had been under its direct control. In the meantime various ministries of the central bureaucracy have set up their own corporations to conduct trade independent of the MOFTEC. Similarly, MOFTEC has to yield more powers to trade departments in the provinces to allow them to conduct trade negotiations independently with foreign concerns.

In the shift of balance in the central foreign affairs establishment, the emergence of the PLA in foreign affairs has caught much of the attention in the West. Although the opening of the PLA since the early 1980s to the outside world has been unprecedented, the perception that the PLA has become an independent force in foreign policy decisionmaking is ill-founded. Arms sales abroad are a domestic economic decision, not an attempt by the PLA to extend influence abroad or to encroach on foreign policy formulation. As noted earlier in the book, the sale of sensitive arms or to sensitive regions has been firmly under the control of established guidelines formulated by the civilian central leadership not the CMC. In this regard the PLA represents but one of the many interest groups that have emerged in the field of foreign affairs with a primary focus on business rather than politico-military issues. However the PLAN with the extension of its range of operations may add new dynamics to the PLA's role in foreign policy in the future.

The biggest loser in the changing fortunes of the bureaucratic institutions in the traditional foreign affairs establishment has been the International Liaison Department of the CPC. The International Liaison Department more than any other foreign affairs institution has been susceptible to the changes in external environment beyond China's control. Its tentative revival in the late 1970s and 80s, when Beijing began to mend its fences with the Soviet Union and East European nations where Communist parties still dominated, would soon fall victim to the fall of Communist regimes in Eastern Europe and the disintegration of the former Soviet Union in 1989–1991. With the Khmer Rouge fading into oblivion and North Korea and Cuba struggling to survive, it is doubtful if the International

Liaison Department can ever regain the influence it once wielded in the foreign policy decisionmaking concerning socialist countries.

A final note on the changing dynamics concerns the foreign policy research institutes. As noted early in the book, the central leadership has traditionally distrusted such academic institutes and never found a need for think-tanks in the formulation of foreign policies. However when Zhao Ziyang became Premier, he created a number of institutes under the jurisdiction of the State Council mainly to provide fresh ideas and views on systemic reform independent of vested bureaucratic interests.[37] One of the institutes is the Center for International Studies under the veteran diplomat, Ambassador Huan Xiang. For a time Huan sat in some Central Foreign Affairs LSG meetings and the Center seemed to have carved out a think tank role for itself, serving as an institutional "backdoor" to Zhao for second opinions. However with the fall of Zhao Ziyang in May 1989 and the death of Huan Xiang, the whole dynamics changed. Today the Center is struggling to remain relevant as Li Peng views these creatures of Zhao with suspicion and distrust. For the moment its prospect looks bleak as it is degenerating into a body whose main function, it seems, is to provide a soft landing for former senior Chinese diplomats.

Notes

1. Shi Zhe, "*Mao Zedong Zhuxi Diyici Fangwen Sulian Jingguo* (Chairman Mao Zedong's First Visit to the Soviet Union)," Pei Jianzhang et al (eds.), *Xin Zhongguo Waijiao Fengyün I* (New China Diplomacy I) (Beijing: Shijie Zhishi Chubanshe, 1990), pp.#3–9.

2. The eight sectors and their managers were: foreign affairs—Zhou Enlai, planning and industry—Gao Gang, Li Fuchun and Jia Tuofu, internal security and judiciary—Dong Biwu, Peng Zhen and Luo Ruiqing, finance and commerce—Chen Yün, Bo Yibo, Zeng Shan and Ye Jizhuang, railway, transportation and post and communication—Deng Xiaoping, agriculture and forestry—Deng Zihui, labor—Rao Shushi, and culture and education—Xi Zhongxün. Bo Yibo, *Ruogan Zhongda Jüece yü Shijian de Huigu* (A Reminiscence on Some Major Decisions and Events) (Beijing: Zhongyang Dangxiao Chubanshe, 1991), pp.#309–310.

3. The CPC Secretariat at the time represented the CPC leadership core that was equivalent to the present day CPC Standing Committee of the Politburo. It consisted of Mao Zedong, Liü Shaoqi, Zhou Enlai, Zhu De, and Ren Bishi.

4. Pang Song and Han Gang, "*Dang he Guojia Lingdao Tizhi de Lishi Kaocha yü Gaige Zhanwang* (A Historical Study and Reform Prospect of the Party and State Leadership Systems)," *Zhongguo Shehui Kexüe* (China Social Sciences), Issue 48, No. 6, 1987, p.#7.

5. Li Zhisui, Mao's personal physician, believed that the origins of Mao's eventual split with Liu Shaoqi and Deng Xiaoping in the mid 1960s could be traced back to the 8th Party Congress, see Li Zhisui, *Mao Zedong Siren Yisheng Huiyilu* (The Private Life of Chairman Mao) (Taipei: China Times Publishing Company,

1994), p.#174. However Li's allegations are challenged by Lin Ke, Mao's personal secretary, and some newly released material. For instance, Mao was deeply involved in the decisions that stressed collective leadership against personality cult. The creation of the post of honorary chairman of the Party in the revised Party constitution was suggested by Mao. See Lin Ke, Xü Tao and Wu Xüjün, *Lishi de Zhenshi* (The True Life of Mao Zedong) (Hongkong: Liwen Chubanshe, 1995), pp.#40–54, and Zheng Qian and Han Gang, *Wannian Suiyue: 1956 Nian hou de Mao Zedong* (The Late Years: Mao Zedong after 1956) (Beijing: Zhongguo Qingnian Chubanshe, 1993), pp.#29–30.

6. *Zhonghua Renmin Gongheguo Jingji Guanli Dashiji* (Chronicle of the Economic Management of the People's Republic of China) (Beijing: China Economics Publishers, 1986), p.#106.

7. Five of his secretaries would leave the State Council. Of the eight secretaries who stayed until 1965, Ma Lie and Pu Shouchang would be in charge of foreign affairs. Ma Lie, "*Dang Fanyi Kake de Shihou* (When the Interpreter Stammers)," Chen Hao, "*Danxin yi Pian, Hongtu Wanjüan* (A Loyal Heart, Many Grand Plans)" in Cheng Hua (ed.), *Zhou Enlai he ta de Mishumen* (Zhou Enlai and his Secretaries) (Beijing: Zhongguo Guangbo Dianshi Chubanshe, 1992), p.#198, 233.

8. A number of Chinese sources claim that Mao's decision on July 18 was a direct response to the alert of the Taiwanese forces on July 17. Zhong Zhaoyün, "*Liü Yalou yü Zhongguo Kongjün* (Liü Yalou and the Chinese Air Force)," *Wen Wei Po*, March 28, 1996. Mao told a Politburo Standing Committee meeting on August 23, 1958—the day he launched the artillery bombardment—that the alert of the Taiwanese forces showed that Jiang's army was going to make some moves soon. He also mentioned a statement (around August 6) by the chief of staff of the US Navy claiming that the American armed forces were ready anytime for a landing campaign in the Taiwan Straits just as they did in Lebanon. For a more detailed account of Mao's speeches at the time, see Wu Lengxi (director of Xinhua News Agency and editor-in-chief of *Renmin Ribao* in 1958), "Inside Story of the Decisionmaking during the Shelling of Jinmen," *Zhuanji Wenxue* (Biographical Literature), No. 1, 1994, pp.#5–11. Lin Ke, who was serving as Mao's international affairs secretary, also names the following as important factors for Mao's decision: the consolidation of 17 US agencies in Taiwan into a single, unified military command in May 1958, Washington's refusal to respond to China's request made on June 30, 1958 for resumption of Sino-US ambassadorial talks in Warsaw, a State Department memorandum of August 11 on non-recognition of the PRC government, and US announcement of sending six warships and two thousand soldiers to Singapore. Lin Ke et al, pp.#276–277.

9. The original initiative was said to have come from local officials. In 1957 during the Great Leap Forward, the Fujian Party Committee submitted a report to Beijing that requested permission to take the Jinmen islands by force so that the province could develop its economy like the rest of China. Mao agreed in principle, but later, after soliciting opinions from others, decided not to physically capture the islands to prevent Taiwan from declaring independence. Huang Wenfang (former head of the Taiwanese Affairs Department of Xinhua News Agency in Hongkong), "*Jiang Zemin ti 'Batiao' Yi zhai Shuangfei* (Jiang Zemin Put Forward 'Eight Points' for Win-win)," *Hongkong Economic Times,* March 23, 1996.

10. Xü Yan, *Jinmen zih Zhan* (The Battle of Quemoy) (Beijing: Zhongguo Guangbo Dianshi Chubanshe, 1992), p.#239.

11. Ye Fei, the frontline commander of PLA forces, writes in his memoir: "If our forces launched a landing (assault) at this time, Jinmen would have fallen into our hands easily (*chuishou kede*). Thus all of us at the Fujian frontline were waiting anxiously for Mao's order. We could not figure out what Mao's intentions were for the next step?". *Ye Fei Huiyi Lu* (Memoirs of Ye Fei) (Beijing: Jiefangjün Chubanshe, 1988), p.#666.

12. Unlike popular assumptions in the West, available Chinese and Russian sources show that attacking Taiwan was never in Mao's cards. Whether to capture Jinmen or not also depended on how the events would unfold. For more detailed accounts of Mao's objectives, see *CWIHP Bulletin,* Issue 5, Winter 1995/1996, pp.#208–231, Lin Ke et al, pp.#267–286, Li Zhisui, p.#252, 260.

13. In analyses of the US strategy on September 5 and 8, Mao concluded that the U.S. was mainly interested in occupying the "middle grounds" and that unless socialist countries were in great turmoil and on the verge of disintegration, the U.S. would not launch an invasion. Mao's "Speech at the 15th Meeting of the Supreme State Council" on September 5 and 8, 1958, *Mao Zedong Waijiao Wenxuan* (Selected Diplomatic Papers of Mao Zedong) (Beijing: Zhongyang Lishi Wenxian Chubanshe, 1994), pp.#341–348, 348–352. According to Mao's international affairs secretary, Lin Ke, Mao concluded that (1) the US-Taiwan defense treaty was defensive in nature, intended to leash rather than unleash Jiang Jeshi; (2) the US would not risk a direct military conflict with China and therefore a Sino-US war would be unlikely; (3) US policies moved toward disengaging from the offshore islands. Lin Ke, pp.#278–279. As a result of this conclusion, the size of the PLA in 1958–1959 was reduced to its smallest since 1949 and defense spending to its lowest level in 1949–1984. Xü Yan, p.#253.

14. Wang Bingnan, *Zhong Mei Huitan Jiünian Huigu* (Memoir of Nine Years of Sino-U.S. Talks) (Beijing: Shijie Zhishi Chubanshe, 1985), pp.#70–79.

15. Li Yan, "*Zuji Bian Tianya, Chun Feng Song Wanjia,*" Cheng Hua, p.#99–100.

16. Zhang Yünsheng, *Lin Biao Mishu Huiyi: Maojiawan Jishi* (Lin Biao Secretary's Memoir: A Record of Events at Maojiawan) (Hong Kong: Cunzhen Chubanshe, 1987).

17. Yan Huai, "*Zhongguo Dalu Zhengzhi Tizhi Qianlun* (Understanding the Political System of Contemporary China)," *Papers of the Center for Modern China,* No. 10, August 1991, p.#19. Li Zhisui, p.#422.

18. The Cultural Revolution SG was headed by Chen Boda, Mao's former secretary. Jiang Qing, Wang Renzhong, Liü Zhijian and Zhang Chunqiao were deputy group leaders. Its members included Wang Li, Guan Feng, Qi Benyü and Yao Wenyüan. Kang Sheng and Tao Zhu were its advisors. Wang Renzhong, Tao Zhu, Liü Zhijian, and Wang Li, Guan Feng and Qi Benyü would fall in the course of the Cultural Revolution. Lin Ke et al, pp.#32–33. Li Zhisui, p.#440.

19. There is a widely held belief that Lin Biao represented the pro-Russian faction within the Chinese leadership and that he and the Chinese military were opposed to Mao and Zhou's opening to the West (see Thomas M. Gottlieb, *Chinese Foreign Policy Factionalism and the Origins of the Strategic Triangle* [Santa Monica: Rand Corp., 1977]). This belief is a misconception based on speculations: Lin's

split with Mao had nothing to do with foreign policy even though Lin privately believed that Mao's actions toward Moscow were excessive. In fact, according to Zhang Yünsheng—Lin's secretary of the period, Lin had no expertise and little interest in foreign affairs. Zhang could only remember two things Lin did in foreign affairs during his four years with Lin, both ceremonial in his capacity as Defense Minister. One was a meeting with Vietnamese Premier Pham Van Dong and Defense Minister Vo Nguyen Giap during which Lin counselled that *endurance* would be the key to Vietnamese victory. The other was a meeting with Albanian Defense Minister Balluku. After the 4–5 minute meeting at the insistence of the Albanian, Lin would exclaim with great relief: "It's really so unbearable dealing with foreigners!" Zhang Yünsheng, pp.#261–262. As a matter of fact, it was four PLA marshals that first presented Mao with the policy recommendation for seeking rapprochement with the US. Chen Xiaolu, *Jinian Chen Yi* (In Memory of Chen Yi) (Beijing: Wenwu Chubanshe, 1991), #497. Fan Shuo, *Ye Jianying zai 1976* (Ye Jianying in 1976) (Beijing: Zhongyang Dangxiao Chubanshe, 1990), p.#71.

20. Ma Lie, p.#237.

21. Fan Shuo, *Ye Jianying zai 1976* (Ye Jianying in 1976) (Beijing: Zhongyang Dangxiao Chubanshe, 1990), p.#65.

22. Chen Youwei, "*Qiao Guanhua Gaiguan Shinian reng wei Dinglun* (The Verdict is Still Out Ten Years After Qiao Guanhua's Death)," *Shijie Zhoukan* (World Journal Weekly), October 10, 1993, p.#S–3.

23. The 12th Party Congress elected Deng, Hu, Zhao, Ye Jianying, Li Xiannian, Chen Yün members of the Politburo Standing Committee. Hu became General Secretary after the post of Party Chairman was abolished. Deng held the post of CMC Chairman. As Ye was in poor health and Li was not in favor, the real leading nuclear circle consisted of Deng, Chen, Hu and Zhao with the last two in the front line.

24. For instance, when it embarked on economic reform, Beijing's past differences with the Soviet Union over domestic policies became irrelevant. The Soviet Union bogged down in Afghanistan and with a failing economy was no longer considered a security threat by the Chinese leadership. However the announcement of policy adjustment toward Moscow created a stampede among Beijing's bureaucracies and provinces to restore relations and exchanges with the former enemy. Deng invented the "three major obstacles"—Soviet forces on the border, Afghanistan and Cambodia—mainly as speed bumps to slow down the normalization process so as not to jeopardize Beijing's relations with the West.

25. Li was instrumental in appointing Ji Pengfei to head the Foreign Affairs Office of the State Council in 1982 and the Hong Kong Macao Office in 1983 after the death of Liao Chengzhi, Beijing's foremost manager of overseas Chinese affairs. Xü Jiatun, Vol. I, pp.#16–18.

26. One involved the invitation extended by Hu Yaobang to 3,000 Japanese youth to visit China, expenses paid, in 1984. The invitation caused widespread public resentment. When Hu again extended an invitation in summer 1986 to visiting Japanese Prime Minister Yasuhiro Nakasone for another 3,000 Japanese youth to visit China, Deng, commenting on the issue of the MFA's *Waijiaobu Jianbao*, criticized him implicitly for being carried away by the Japanese and for making

such decisions without prior consultation with or consent by members of the leading nuclear circle.

27. Zhao Ziyang, "Speech on the 4th Plenum of the 13th Party Congress," *Xinbao* (Hongkong), June 4, 1994. Deng Xiaoping, "Letter of Resignation," *Renmin Ribao,* November 10, 1989.

28. He Zi, "*Zhonggong Tuozhan Zhengdang Waijiao* (The CPC Develops its Diplomacy with Political Parties)," *Zhonguo Shibao Zhoukan* (China Times Weekly), No. 67, April 11–17, 1993, p.#21.

29. The new Secretariat consists of Hu Jintao, Ding Guangen, Wei Jianxing, Wen Jiabao and Ren Jianxin, none of whom has any experience in foreign affairs.

30. The 16-character guideline by Deng is *lengjing guancha, taoguang yanghui, zhanwen jiaogen, chenzhuo yingfu*—observe (the situation) with a sobre mind, keep a low profile and bide time, maintain a firm footing, meet the challenges calmly. Chen Youwei, "*Deng Xiaoping Waijiao Zhanlüe ji qi zhihou de Waijiao* (Deng Xiaoping's Diplomatic Strategy and post-Deng Diplomacy)" presented at the East Asia Forum, Yale University, February 7, 1995.

31. In Chinese: *shehuizhuyi de da qi women buyao kang.*

32. Personal communications with MFA officials. Doug Paal, February 14, 1995.

33. It was not clear when the Central Foreign Affairs LSG was reinstituted after the Cultural Revolution. It should be between 1978 and 1980 when most of the LSGs, such as the Political and Legal Affairs LSG and the powerful Finance and Economic LSG, were reinstituted. Zheng Qian, Pang Song, Han Gang and Zhang Zhanwu, *Dangdai Zhongguo Zhengzhi Tizhi Fazhan Gaiyao* (An Outline of the Evolution of the Contemporary Chinese Political System) (Beijing: Zhonggong Dangshi Ziliao Chubanshe, 1988), p.#219.

34. Other members of the Central Foreign Affairs LSG were Foreign Minister Qian Qichen, Minister of Foreign Trade and Economic Cooperation Zheng Tuobin, Head of the CPC International Liaison Department Zhu Liang, and President of *Renmin Ribao* Qian Liren. Jiang Weiwen, *Wide Angle,* January 16, 1988, pp.#12–13.

35. Wu's son as editor on duty that fateful night was accused of endorsing a radio broadcast condemning the military crackdown.

36. For example, in the mid 1980s, Hu Yaobang was so frustrated by the poor performance of the Khmer Rouge and other Cambodian resistance that he suggested direct Chinese military intervention in Cambodia. The MFA and the PLA GSD, both appalled by the diplomatic and logistic implications of such a move, argued strongly for the continuation of the existing policy of "bleeding the Vietnamese dry" and prevailed. Hu would later claim that he only meant to stimulate the bureaucracies to come up with some new ideas.

37. Ironically, after the crackdown in June 1989, Zhao flatly denied the existence of any personal "think tank," claiming that he only occasionally invited some academics to discuss issues with him, while many dissidents who fled abroad including some who had never been members of these institutes would all claim to be Zhao's "advisors." See Zhao Ziyang, "Speech on the 4th Plenum of the 13th Party Congress."

7

Western Theories and Chinese Practices

Since the Second World War, interest has increased in the study of decisionmaking which has come to be considered a central element in the political process and a focal point for study by political and social scientists. In conjunction with the study of decisionmaking in political, psychological, economic and business fields, there has also been a relatively extensive and rich literature in the West on foreign policy decisionmaking with a number of theoretical models advanced in this subfield of study.

The post-War period also saw the birth of a new field of study devoted exclusively to China known as Sinology, which in turn has spawned a subfield of inquiry centered on the study of contemporary Chinese foreign policy. Since the 1950s particularly since the 1970s, the study of contemporary Chinese foreign policy has developed into a significant discipline of scholarship with a number of competing schools in interpreting Chinese foreign policy behavior. It is not the purpose of this author to advance any original theoretical framework for the study of Chinese foreign policy decisionmaking. Rather it is hoped that some new thoughts could be provoked through an examination of some of the existing Western theories in decisionmaking against the current Chinese practices, which in turn, it is hoped, would lead to a renewed endeavor to construct a meaningful theoretical framework for the study of Chinese foreign policy formulation and decisionmaking as well as their dynamics.

The Classical School[1]

Classical theories of foreign policy decisionmaking contend that foreign policy decisionmaking is the *rational choice* among possible alternatives made by nation-states as basic actors within the international system to maximize utility within a total, perceived environment that includes their national political system as well as the international system as a whole—an internal environment as well as an external environment.

Within this classical school, some theorists diverge from the traditional political analyses that reify or personify nation-states as the basic actors. Instead of directing attention to metaphysical abstractions of the state, the government or broadly labelled institutions as "the Executive," they narrow the subjects of their inquiry from a larger collectivity to a smaller unit of identifiable persons responsible for making decisions, or to the specific human decisionmakers who actually shape state or government policies. As Richard Snyder, H.W. Bruck and Burton Sapin put it:

> It is one of our basic methodological choices to define the state as its official decision-makers—those whose authoritative acts are, for all intents and purposes, the acts of the state. State action is the action taken by those acting in the name of the state.[2]

As a logical further step, an emphasis is placed on the study of motivation and characteristics of decisionmakers, for motives of states, it is argued, are really not separable from the motives of individual decisionmakers who speak on behalf of states and rationalize their policy actions. In the study of decisionmakers, a useful distinction is drawn between two types of motivation—"in-order-to" motives and "because-of" motives. The first type represents the conscious and is verbalizable: the decisions are made by the individual decisionmaker(s) in order to accomplish certain particular objectives of the state that they serve. The second type, on the other hand, is based on the unconscious or semiconscious, motives that have arisen out of the previous life experience of the decisionmaker, and which predispose or impel them toward certain kinds of policy orientations for private psychological reasons.[3]

Scholars of this school differ over the emphasis they place on the significance of different decisionmaking determinants. Some focus on the study of the decision *situation* which encompasses the total "external setting" and "internal setting" in which the choice must be made. The external setting includes the state's geopolitical position within the global system and regional balance of power as well as its relationship with relevant individual powers. As for the internal setting, two crucially important variables are the state's military and economic capabilities which set limits to what the government can do. The internal setting also includes the domestic systemic environment and the structure of the political system in which decision-makers must operate. In sum they believe the *objective* constitutes the critical determinants.

Other scholars assign perception a central place in foreign policy decisionmaking. They regard the world as viewed *subjectively* by decisionmakers to be more important than objective reality. Thereby a distinction is drawn between the "psychomilieu" and the "operational environment."

"The operational environment affects the results or outcome of decisions directly," they argue, "but influences the choice among policy options, that is, the decisions themselves, only as it is filtered through the images of decisionmakers."[4]

In line with this classical school in the study of foreign policy decisionmaking, there are three traditional schools that for some time dominated the study of contemporary Chinese foreign policy: the *traditional/historical*, the *Maoist/communist ideology*, and the *realist/rational actor*.[5]

The first school of scholarship as represented by such eminent China scholars as the late John K. Fairbank emphasizes China's uniqueness.[6] Most of its proponents historian, it argues that China's foreign policy behavior can only be understood on the basis of its historical and cultural legacy of the past. The foreign policy under the Communist regime represents a continuation of the practice of traditional Sinocentrism according to which the world as perceived by the Chinese rulers is not one based on the concept of sovereign equality of nation/states, but one structured in hierarchical terms. Under such a world system as perceived by the Chinese rulers, China—the "Middle Kingdom"—is the preeminent power that maintains a suzerain-tributary relationship with the rest of the world. A nation's status within this system depends on its level of sinicization. Thus the primary sources of Chinese foreign policy are to be found in such traditional philosophies as Confucianism, Taoism, and Buddhism.

This school that emphasizes China's uniqueness is challenged by the Maoist/communist ideology school of the early 1950s, coinciding with the onset of the politics of the Cold War and American military involvement in Asia. The historical and cultural legacy of the past, the ideology school argues, is less relevant than the principles of orthodox Marxism-Leninism and its Chinese derivative—Maoism—in understanding contemporary Chinese foreign policy behavior. It suggests that China interacts with the rest of the world based largely on the ideological belief of its elite as personified in Mao Zedong, some of whose ideas often appear antithetical to Chinese tradition.[7]

While both the traditional and ideological schools stress the significance of the subjective "psychomilieu" of China's power elite in the formulation of the nation's foreign policy, the realist/rational actor school focuses its attention on the objective "operational environment."[8] In his landmark study *China Crosses the Yalu: The Decision to Enter the Korean War*, Allen Whiting is able to reconstruct the events that led to the Chinese decision to intervene in the Korean War. By carefully analyzing US intelligence information and sifting through Beijing's public pronouncements at the time, Whiting concludes that the Chinese action was largely reactive, for the purpose of self-defense. Its explanation therefore does not lie in an aggressive communist ideology or a traditional impulse to pacify its periphery, but in realism to be found in the mainstream Western theories on international relations. It debunks as a myth the notion of China's uniqueness. Given the operational environment, the realist/rational actor school argues, the Chinese foreign policy behavior is not much different from other countries. The Chinese foreign policy can be viewed in traditional Western paradigms of balance of power, national interests and domestic economic, military and systemic constraints.

Two other sub-branches concerning Chinese foreign policy behavior under this realist school have also emerged. Instead of looking at China as a *unitary* rational actor, the *factional* model places greater emphasis on the influences of some dynamic domestic variables like the factionalism in China's power elite in the formulation of its foreign policies.[9] In an era of open and fierce factional infighting during the late 1960s and early 1970s, it is only natural to assume that factions that differ in domestic policy orientations would have different approaches to foreign policy. It is therefore logical to study the possible impact of elite politics on foreign affairs.

Unlike the *factional* model that focuses on the internal setting within which decisionmakers have to operate, the *triangular* model that came in vogue in the early 1970s stresses the external environment, particularly foreign policy behaviors of the United States, the Soviet Union and China in relation to each other.[10] Instead of examining the broad operational environment, this approach believes that China's relationship with the other two key players in the so-called strategic triangle is most critical to understanding China's foreign policy behavior. Numerous theories have been advanced concerning what is essentially perceived as a three-power game.

Despite their differences in focus on different key variables, the theoretical frameworks established under the classical school attempt to explain state behavior in terms of a rational actor. Policy choices are viewed as the more or less purposive acts of a unified state (the winner in the factional model) based on logical means of achieving given objectives. The classical school assumes that decisionmakers strive to be consistent, to make optimal choices in narrowly constrained, neatly defined situations, and to rank and maximize values by choosing the most efficient alternative. It assumes that decisionmakers discern clearly their objectives, the options available, and the likely consequences of each alternative choice before making their decision.

In sum, the classical school stresses the rationality of decisionmaking, a reflection perhaps of the Western intellectual's faith in the essential rationality of human behavior inherited from the Enlightenment. However, with a gradual erosion of this faith in human rationality, attention has shifted in recent decades from decisionmaking as mere rational choice among possible maximum-utility alternatives to decisionmaking as an incremental process containing partial choices and compromises among competing organizational interests and bureaucratic pressures.

The Institutional School

The Institutional School emerges as a result of the inadequacies found in the rational actor model to explain foreign policy behaviors of nation-states. In addition to the rational actor model which is still deemed useful, the School offers two other frames of reference that focus on the governmental *machine* instead of nation-state actors sometimes personified by their supreme decision-makers: the *organizational process* model and the *bureaucratic politics* model.[11]

The *organizational process* model envisages governmental behavior less as a matter of deliberate *choice* and more as independent *outputs* of several large, key organizations, only partly coordinated by government leaders. The behavior of these organizations is primarily determined by standard or routine operating procedures with only gradual, incremental deviations.

The *bureaucratic politics* model, on the other hand, hypothesizes intense competition among decisionmaking units, and foreign policies are the *result* of bargaining among the different components of a bureaucracy. At times, the players are guided less by conceptions of national, or even bureaucratic and personal goals. Sometimes, it is a win-or-lose game, but more often the result is a decisional compromise, less than what is sought by any individual or group. The outcome thus depends not on the rational justification for the policy or on routine organizational procedure, but on the relative power and skill of the bargainers.[12]

Parallel to the advent of institutional models in decisionmaking theories, there has also been a shift in focus from the power elite to the bureaucratic institutions and structures that support political power in the field of China studies.[13] In his 1967 trail-blazing study *Cadres, Bureaucracy, and Political Power in Communist China*, A. Doak Barnett for the first time highlights the importance of bureaucratic institutions in China's domestic policy-making structure. Such early works rely heavily on official documents both public and internal and on interviews conducted with mainland refugees. Beginning in the early 1980s, as China embarked on a program of economic reform and opening to the outside world, Western scholars have gained increased access to the vast Chinese bureaucratic system hitherto closed to outsiders. This increased access has yielded a new crop of studies focusing on the bureaucratic institutions in the domestic policy process. Most of them are centered on a specific field in the economy or services where the interaction with the outside world has been relatively intensive, reflecting an uneven penetration of the Chinese system. Barnett's 1985 study of China's foreign policy establishment is the first successful attempt to examine in considerable detail a major sector of the Chinese *political* system. This was followed in 1988 by a much more comprehensive and indepth study of the whole policy-making structure conducted by Kenneth Lieberthal and Mike Oksenberg.

Despite China's opening, foreign affairs remains a field that is deliberately and carefully shielded from scrutiny by outsiders due to Chinese sensitivity over the formulation of the nation's foreign policies. Increased academic exchanges however have created many opportunities to penetrate China's institutes of international studies, which have proliferated and been increasingly active since the early 1980s.[14] As a result there have been a number of studies that focus on the perception not of the political leadership but of particular groups of Chinese foreign affairs experts on specific countries in an attempt to shed more light on China's policies toward major powers.[15] Like the Classical School, these studies focus on the problem of perception. However instead of examining the perception of the political leadership, the emphasis is on that of the institutions and key experts.

A number of paradigms have been developed in an attempt to capture the essence of the Chinese political and economic system. They range from *bureaucratic authoritarianism,* which emphasizes the rigidity of central control and party-dominated bureaucratic hierarchy, to *fragmented authoritarianism* that focuses on the centrifugal effects of the bureaucratic interactive bargaining process with the power elite and lower-level components of the system.[16]

In sum, the Institutional School believes that the rational actor model under the Classical School does not completely capture the whole picture of decisionmaking and all the forces that influence policy formulation. It points to organizational processes and bureaucratically based politics as significant factors affecting the final policy outcome.

Theory and Practice: A Summary

The examination of the roles of the top leadership, the foreign affairs establishment and the working-level bureaucrats and researchers in the previous chapters suggests that no single Western theoretical framework as presented above can readily capture the entirety of foreign policy decisionmaking in China as it is understood by the author. They are however useful and mostly relevant tools in the study of the formulation and making of China's foreign policy decisions. To make a better connection between the Western theories and the Chinese practice so as to show their relevance, it is important to establish two simple lenses which are not entirely appropriate but nevertheless are helpful to avoid falling into a quagmire of jargon.

The Elephant and the Blindmen The Chinese fable, the elephant and the blindmen—*mangren mo xiang*,[17] seems most apt in that it captures the dilemma in checking the existing Western theories as they are presented in this chapter against the Chinese realities depicted in previous chapters: For, with few exceptions, they individually are true in individual cases and at specific periods of time, but are largely false as the theory that captures the full picture.

The applicability and the relevance of the models to the Chinese case depend largely on the nature and the importance of the decision. A distinction must be drawn between decisions that have been regarded as vital, such as over military operations, top-level appointments, and foreign policy, and thus require a very high degree of centralization, and other decisions that have been regarded as less critical, such as in the case of most economic decisions. After his personal intervention produced some spectacular failures, Mao, even at the height of his dictatorial rule, left most economic decisions in the hands of experts such as Zhou Enlai, Chen Yün and Li Xiannian, admitting, though grudgingly, that he did not really understand economics. Even at the height of economic campaigns waged by Mao such as the Great Leap Forward, provincial leaders had demonstrated a high degree of autonomy in decisions in implementing Mao's directives. Thus studies done admirably by Lieberthal, Oksenberg, Lampton in such fields as water conservation, medicine and agriculture have very limited relevance to foreign policy decisions, as they simply do not belong on the same level of decisions. One, for instance, can never expect a major foreign policy to be openly debated and drag on for decades—through the era of Mao and that of Deng—as one witnessed the decision to build the Three Gorges Dam.

For those key decisions that are the prerogative of the top leadership, often with the paramount leader or leading nucleus as the ultimate arbiter, the models of the classical school seem more relevant—the top leadership making a rational choice among possible alternatives according to his/their perception of the environment, both internal and external, to maximize utility. Decisions of this nature include (1) decisions that would determine the fundamental orientation of the Chinese foreign policy, (2) decisions on the major foreign policy strategy, guidelines and principles, (3) decisions over military operations that involve actual or potential conflicts with foreign powers, (4) decisions in the formulation of regional policies and country policies toward key world powers such as the United States, Russia and Japan, (5) major decisions concerning the implementation of country policies toward the key world powers, and (6) decisions over policies on sensitive issues or toward sensitive countries.

In these decisions, ideology has not been a decisive factor: Mao did not embrace Nixon for ideological affinity, nor did Deng turned his gun on the Vietnamese comrades because of conflicting ideological convictions. Decisions are made as a rational choice to advance what is perceived as the nation's best interest. However ideology did play a limited part in coloring the perception of top decision makers, as in the Korean decision and in decisions to support Hanoi in the Vietnam War. But the impact of ideology is insignificant in shaping the perception of each individual leader compared to his personal education and experience. While Mao, with a classical Chinese education and limited exposure to the outside world appeared to be heavily influenced in his perception by Chinese history and traditions (e.g. Mao would use classic Chinese strategy of *yüan-jiao jingong* to describe his opening to the U.S.), Deng who had spent some youthful years in Paris and Moscow has consistently demonstrated a down-to-earth pragmatic realism (it doesn't matter, he once said, if a cat is black or white, so long as it catches mice).

In sum, during the Mao era, because of the high concentration of foreign policy decisionmaking power in the hands of one or two persons, the realist/rational actor model of the classical school is most applicable to most of the foreign policy decisions which were dominated by Mao and Zhou. Although neither the traditional/historical model nor the Maoist/communist ideological model itself was central to these decisions, they nevertheless played an indirect role by helping to shape the perception of key individual decisionmakers. Under the realist/rational actor model, the factional model though useful in explaining some of China's domestic policy decisions is largely irrelevant to the foreign policy process which was exclusive to Mao and Zhou. Neither Lin Biao nor the Gang of Four, the two major factions during the Mao era, was known to have encroached into this field. The fact that it was four PLA marshals who first suggested to Mao to seek a rapprochement with the US shows that the assertion that the PLA was opposed to Sino-US détente was but a myth.

This is also largely true for much of the Deng era during which foreign policy decisionmaking power was gradually transferred from the hands of one man—the leading nucleus of a small group—the leading nuclear circle.

The classical school however has its own limitations. It fails to capture the spontaneous and irrational or idiosyncratic elements that characterize some of the decisions. The fact that such a momentous foreign policy decision as the initial overture to the US was made when Mao was only semi-conscious on a dose of sleeping pills points to some of the pitfalls in the realist/rational actor model. One can only speculate what China's policy regarding foreign navy ships' visits would be like if Hu Yaobang had not planned a visit to the South Pacific that year, or if the New Zealand journalist had not asked him the question, or if David Lange had not won the general election in New Zealand. This question is particularly relevant when a decisionmaking process is characterized by a high degree of personalism as during the era of Mao and the early period of Deng.

For decisions of secondary importance and of a tactical nature, the role of the foreign affairs establishment becomes prominent. These decisions include (1) decisions over the interpretation of established foreign policy strategy, guidelines and principles, (2) decisions over the implementing details of established strategy, guidelines and principles, (3) decisions over the interpretation and implementation of regional policies, (4) decisions over the interpretation and implementation of policies toward key world powers in day-to-day operations, (5) formulation and implementation of country policies toward non-critical countries under established regional policy guidelines, and (6) decisions over the interpretation and implementation of policies on sensitive issues and toward sensitive countries.

In the case of these decisions of secondary importance, the model of bureaucratic politics of the Institutional School appears more applicable. Motivated by different institutional interests or simply some idiosyncratic personal goals of top bureaucrats, bureaucracies fight and bargain as well as cooperate with each other. The final decision is often in the form of a compromise. In foreign policy decisionmaking, however, the room that the top leadership allows bureaucratic debate is considerably narrower than in other areas of less vital concerns. Therefore, bureaucratic authoritarianism that stresses central control and discipline in the bureaucratic processes is more relevant than fragmented authoritarianism that emphasizes contention and conflict among bureaucratic interests.

For the most rudimentary decisions concerning the day-to-day operations of foreign affairs under well-established policy guidelines and with ample precedents, and decisions that fall within the competence of a single bureaucratic agency with no point of contention, the model of organizational process of the Institutional School offers the best explanation. A large number of such decisions are made every day under the established operational procedures of different bureaucracies in a process not much different from a manufacturing operation.

A Series of Motion Pictures Decisionmaking is a dynamic process. Western theories examined thus far are relevant and useful only in the study of specific single frames of what is essentially a series of motion pictures. The rational actor model, the bureaucratic politics model and organizational process model only capture parts of a dynamic process.

They provide useful lenses for a better understanding of some of the policy outcomes and a useful though not always reliable tool to make certain predictions, given numerous variables that are difficult to control. This is particularly true in the case of important decisions where the perception of top leadership is critical. A decision may also run through all the three models before it becomes final.

A dominant model may also change with domestic leadership transition and political transformation. In the early days of the People's Republic, Mao dominated but did not dictate. And it was reflected in some of the decisions with limited debates and dissent within the elite. This was replaced after 1957–59 by a "strongman" model that would dominate through the rest of the Mao era as Mao concentrated all political powers in his own hands. Even the highest decisionmaking body—the CPC Standing Committee of the Politburo—was reduced to a rubber stamp of Mao. During leadership transition from Mao to Deng, the bureaucratic politics model filled the vacuum before Deng consolidated his power and the dominant model reverted back to that of a "strongman." With the introduction of reforms that were based on decentralization of power, foreign policy decisionmaking power began to diffuse from the leading nucleus to the nuclear circle and the institutional model started its ascendancy.

With the death of Chen Yün and the decline of the health of Deng Xiaoping, the trend toward depersonalization of foreign policy decisionmaking and the gradual shift of the locus of decisionmaking power to institutions are more evident. The rise of a new generation of technocrats with narrow power bases as top leaders each in charge of a sector could mean the demise of China's long history of rule by a single charismatic leader and herald a new era of bureaucratic politics in decisionmaking at the apex of the political structure.

While the "strongman" model in the past proved both efficient and effective in terms of policy decisionmaking and implementation, it also demonstrated that it could be costly when personal perceptions of the ultimate decisionmaker were seriously flawed. The new model, on the other hand, may lack clear vision and may be more susceptible to domestic lobbying and foreign pressure. However, a more institutionalized decisionmaking process will lead to foreign policy decisions that are on the whole more rational and pragmatic, and more predictable. The biggest unknown, however, is whether it will be efficient and if it will be able to respond to a major foreign policy crisis, and how.

Notes

1. The author claims no originality nor authority in the following divisions of foreign policy decisionmaking theories and those concerning Chinese foreign

policy decisionmaking. They are both subjective and arbitrary—based on the author's limited understanding and knowledge of relevant theories. They are solely for the utilitarian purpose of establishing a framework of reference to facilitate the author's analyses.

2. Richard C. Snyder et al (eds.), *Foreign Policy Decision-Making* (New York: The Free Press, 1963), p.#65.

3. Ibid.

4. Michael Brecher, *The Foreign Policy System of Israel: Setting, Images, Process* (New Haven: Yale University Press, 1972), p.#4.

5. This author has made no original inquiry into the field of study of Chinese foreign policy, but relies largely on a comprehensive survey on the study of Chinese foreign policy conducted by Bin Yü in "The Study of Chinese Foreign Policy: Problems and Prospect," *World Politics* 46 (January 1994). For alternative surveys, see Samuel S. Kim, "China and the World in Theory and Practice" in Kim (ed.), *China and the World: Chinese Foreign Relations in the Post-Cold War Era* (Boulder: Westview Press, 1994), and James Rosenau, "China in a Bifurcated World: Competing Theoretical Perspectives" in Thomas Robinson and David Shambaugh (eds.), *Chinese Foreign policy: Theory and Practice* (New York: Oxford University Press, 1993).

6. A selected number of works in this school include: John K. Fairbank (ed.), *The Chinese World Order* (Cambridge: Harvard University Press, 1968), and "China's Foreign Policy in Historical Perspective," *Foreign Affairs* 47 (April 1969); C.P. Fitzgerald, *The Chinese View of Their Place in the World* (London: Faber and Faber, 1967); Chih-Yu Shih, *China's Just World: The Morality of Chinese Foreign Policy* (Boulder: Lynne Rienner, 1992), *The Spirit of Chinese Foreign Policy: A Psychocultural View*; Mark Mancall, *China at the Center: 300 Years of Foreign Policy* (New York: Free Press, 1984), "The Persistence of Tradition in Chinese Foreign Policy," *Annals of the American Academy of Political and Social Sciences* 349 (September 1963); Morris Rossabi, *China among Equals: The Middle Kingdom and Its Neighbors* (Berkeley: University of California Press, 1983); J. Cranmer-Byng, "The Chinese View of Their Place in the World: An Historical Perspective," *The China Quarterly*, no. 53 (January–March 1973); Michael H. Hunt, "Chinese Foreign Relations in Historical Perspective" in Harry Harding (ed.), *China's Foreign Relations in the 1980s* (New Haven: Yale University Press, 1984).

7. Among works of this school: Benjamin I. Schwartz, *Communism and China: Ideology in Flux* (Cambridge: Harvard University Press, 1968), "China and the West in the 'Thought of Mao Tse-tung'", in Ping-ti Ho and Tang Tsou (eds.), *China in Crisis*, vol. 1, book 1, (Chicago: University of Chicago Press, 1968); Harold C. Hinton, *China's Turbulent Quest* (Bloomington: Indiana University Press, 1972); John Gittings, *The World and China, 1922–1972* (New York: Harper and Row, 1974); Greg O'Leary, *The Shaping of Chinese Foreign Policy* (New York: St. Martin's Press, 1980); Peter Van Ness, *Revolution and Chinese Foreign Policy* (Berkeley: University of California Press, 1970); J.D. Armstrong, *Revolutionary Diplomacy: Chinese Foreign Policy and the United Front Doctrine* (Berkeley: University of California Press, 1977).

8. Some works of this school: Allen S. Whiting, *China Crosses the Yalu: The Decision to Enter the Korean War* (Stanford: Stanford University Press, 1960), *The Chinese Calculus of Deterrence* (Ann Arbor: University of Michigan Press, 1975), "The

Use of Force in Foreign Policy by the People's Republic of China," *Annals of the American Academy of Political and Social Science* 402 (July 1972), "New Light on Mao: Quemoy 1958: Mao's Miscalculations," *The China Quarterly,* no. 62 (June 1975); Jonathan Pollack, "Perception and Action in Chinese Foreign Policy: The Quemoy Decision," Ph.D dissertation, University of Michigan, 1976; Michael Yahuda, *China's Role in World Affairs* (New York: St. Martin's Press, 1978); Melvin Gurtov and Byong-moo Hwang, *China under Threat: The Politics of Strategy and Diplomacy* (Baltimore: Johns Hopkins University Press, 1980).

9. Works in this regard include: Andrew Nathans, "A Factionalism Model for CCP Politics," *The China Quarterly,* no. 53 (January–March 1973); Uri Ra'anan, "Peking's Foreign Policy 'Debate,' 1965–1966" in Tang Tsou (ed.), *China in Crisis,* vol. 2, (Chicago: Chicago University Press, 1968); Allen Whiting, *Chinese Domestic Politics and Foreign Policy in the 1970s* (Ann Arbor: Center for Chinese Studies, 1979); Michael Yahuda, "Kremlinology and the Chinese Strategic Debate, 1965–66," *The China Quarterly,* no. 49, January 1972; Thomas Gottlieb, *Chinese Foreign Policy Factionalism and the Origins of the Strategic Triangle* (Santa Monica: Rand Corporation, Report R–1902-NA, 1977); John Garver, *China's Decision for Rapprochement with the United States* (Boulder: Westview Press, 1982); Kenneth G. Lieberthal, "The Foreign policy Debate in Peking as Seen through Allegorical Articles, 1973–76," *The China Quarterly,* no. 71, September 1977; Jonathan D. Pollack, *The Sino-Soviet Rivalry and Chinese Security Debate* (Santa Monica: Rand Corporation, R–2907-AE, October 1982); Peter Van Ness, "Three Lines in Chinese Foreign Relations, 1950–1983: The Development imperative" in Dorothy Solinger (ed.), *Three Visions of Chinese Socialism* (Boulder: Westview Press, 1984).

10. Some of such works: Ilpyong Kim (ed.), *The Strategic Triangle: China, the United States and the Soviet Union* (New York: Paragon House, 1987); Gerald Segal, *The Great Power Triangle* (London: Macmillan Press, 1982); Douglas T. Stuart and William T. Tow (eds.), *China, the Soviet Union, and the West: Strategic and Political Dimensions in the 1980s* (Boulder: Westview Press, 1982); Strobe Talbott, "The Strategic Dimension of the Sino-American Relationship: Enemy of Our Enemy, or True Friend?" in Richard R. Solomon (ed.), *The China Factor* (Englewood Cliffs: Prentice-Hall, 1981); Lowell Dittmer, "The Strategic Triangle: An Elementary Game-Theoretical Analysis," *World Politics* 33, July 1981; Kenneth G. Lieberthal, *Sino-Soviet Conflict in the 1970s: Its Evolution and Implications for the Strategic Triangle* (Santa Monica: Rand Corporation, 1978); Min Chen, *The Strategic Triangle and Regional Conflicts: Lessons from the Indochina Wars* (Boulder: Lynne Rienner, 1991); Harvey W. Nelson, *Power and Insecurity: Beijing, Moscow, and Washington, 1949–1988* (Boulder: Lynne Rienner, 1989).

11. Graham T. Allison, *Essence of Decision* (Boston: Little, Brown and Company, 1971).

12. Ibid.

13. Such studies include: A. Doak Barnett, *Cadres, Bureaucracy, and Political Power in China* (New York: Columbia University Press, 1967), *The Making of Foreign Policy in China: Structure and Process* (Boulder: Westview Press, 1985); Nina Halpern, *Economic Specialists and the Making of Chinese Economic Policy, 1955–1983* (Ann Arbor: University of Michigan, 1985); Harry Harding, *Organizing China: The*

Problem of Bureaucracy, 1949–1976 (Stanford: Stanford University Press, 1981); David M. Lampton, *Health, Conflict, and the Chinese political System* (Ann Arbor: University of Michigan Center for Chinese Studies, 1974), *The Politics of Medicine in China: The Policy Process, 1949–1977* (Boulder: Westview Press, 1975), *Policy Implementation in the People's Republic of China* (Berkeley: University of California Press, 1987); John Wilson Lewis and Xüe Litai, *China Builds the Bomb* (Stanford: Stanford University Press, 1988); Kenneth G. Lieberthal and David M. Lampton (eds.), *Bureaucracy, Politics, and Decision Making in Post-Mao China* (Berkeley: University of California Press, 1992); Michel Oksenberg and Kenneth G. Lieberthal, *Policy Making in China: Leaders, Structures, and Processes* (Princeton: Princeton University Press, 1988), Oksenberg, "Methods of Communication Within the Chinese Bureaucracy," *The China Quarterly*, no. 57, January–March 1974; Benedict Stavis, *The Politics of Agricultural Mechanization in China* (Ithaca: Cornell University Press, 1978); John W. Garver, "China's Push through the South China Sea: The Interaction of Bureaucratic and National interest," *The China Quarterly*, no. 132, December 1992.

14. Works devoted to the study of the works and structures of Chinese institutes of international studies include: David L. Shambaugh, "China's National Security Research Bureaucracy," *The China Quarterly*, no. 110, June 1987, Shambaugh and Wang Jisi, "Research on International Studies in the People's Republic of China," *PS*, 17, Fall 1984; Douglas Murray, *International Relations Research and Training in the People's Republic of China*, Stanford: Northeast Asia-United States Forum on International Policy, 1982.

15. Examples of this: David L. Shambaugh, "China's American Watchers," *Problems of Communism* 37, May—August 1988, "Anti-Americanism in China," *Annals of the American Academy of Political and Social Sciences*, 497, May 1988, *Beautiful Imperialist: China Perceives America, 1972–1990* (Princeton: Princeton University Press, 1991); Gilbert Rozman, "China Soviet Watchers in the 1980s: A New Era in Scholarship," *World Politics*, 37, July 1985, *The Chinese Debate about Soviet Socialism, 1978–1985* (Princeton: Princeton University Press, 1987); Allen S. Whiting, *China Eyes Japan* (Berkeley: University of California Press, 1989); Harish Kapur (ed.), *As China Sees the World: Perceptions of Chinese Scholars* (London: Frances Pinter Publishers, 1987).

16. For a brief description of these and other paradigms, see Carol Lee Hamrin and Suisheng Zhao, "Introduction: Core Issues in Understanding the Decision Process" in Hamrin and Zhao (eds.), *Decision-Making in Deng's China* (Armonk: M.E. Sharpe, 1995); Kenneth G. Lieberthal, "Introduction: The 'Fragmented Authoritarianism' Model and Its Limitations" in Lieberthal and David M. Lampton (eds.), *Bureaucracy, Politics, and Decision Making in Post-Mao China* (Berkeley: University of California Press, 1992).

17. The fable may be attributable to *Nirvana Sutra*, a classical work on the Buddhist faith. It describes how four blindmen trying to identify an elephant by touching different parts of the animal come up with vastly different ideas about what the animal is actually like. For instance, it is said to be like a stick (the tusk), a rope (the tail), a column (the leg), and a fan (the ear).

Appendix I: Foreign Policy Decision Making Structure

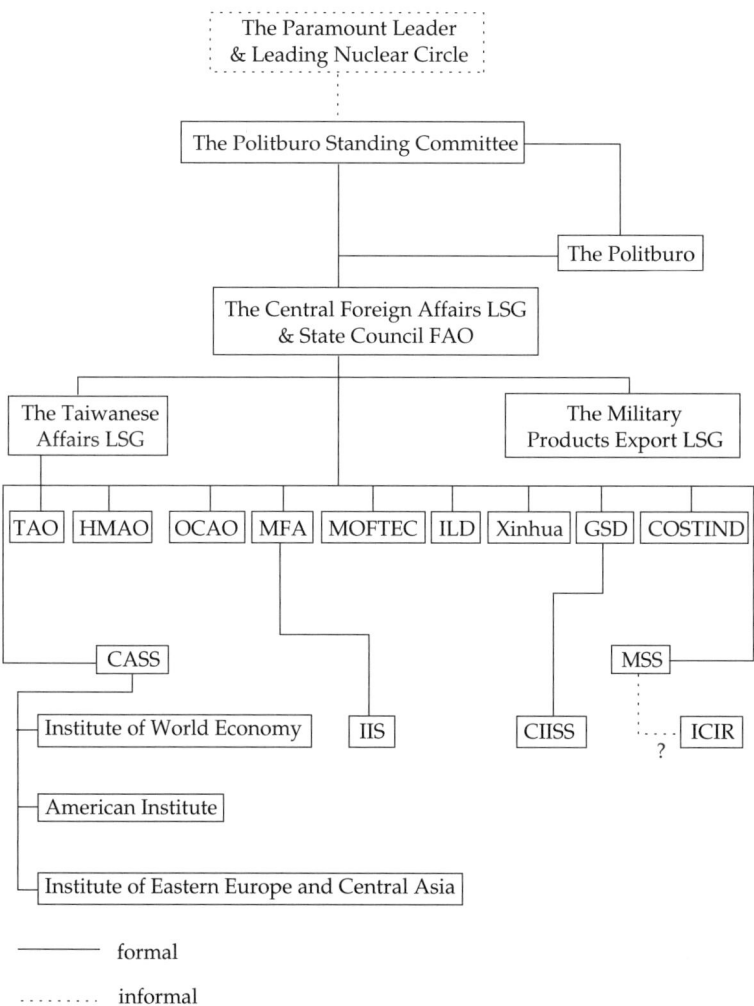

Appendix II:
The Foreign Affairs Office of the State Council*

Address & Telephone Number

Zhongnanhai Bei Qü
Beijing, PRC
Postal Code 100017
Situation Room: 3098375

Staff Size: 20

Main Functions

1) To conduct research and investigation on the relevant problems in the implementation of foreign policies and in foreign affairs management, and to put forward its recommendations.

2) To draft and revise national legislative documents on foreign affairs, to examine some important foreign affairs rules and regulations formulated by the departments of the Center and by the provinces, prefectures and cities.

3) To be responsible for the administrative and professional work in external propaganda, to coordinate and examine and approve funds for specific projects in external propaganda and to coordinate matters that need to be submitted to the State Council for approval.

4) To undertake the organization of the plenary meetings of the Central Foreign Affairs LSG and its work meetings, and to press for the implementation of decisions reached on these meetings.

5) To process the foreign affairs RFIs and reports submitted to the State Council and the Central Foreign Affairs LSG by the various departments of the Center and provinces, prefectures and cities.

6) To undertake matters consigned by the Center and State Council.

---

*As a result of the 1982–84 reform of the government and party bureaucracies, the functions and sizes of these bureaucracies have been officially established. The following Appendixes are based on Guojia Jigou Bianzhi Weiyuanhui Bangongshi, *Zhongguo Zhengfu Jigou* (China Government Organization), (Beijing: Zhongguo Renshi Chubanshe, 1991).

Appendix III: The Ministry of Foreign Affairs

Telephone Numbers

225 Chaoyangmen Nei Da Jie
Beijing, PRC
Postal Code 100701
Operator: 5135566
Situation Room: 555323

Staff Size: 2341

Main Functions

The Ministry of Foreign Affairs is the main functional organ of the State Council in charge of diplomatic work. Its main tasks are to assist the CPC Central Committee (hereafter referred to as the Center) and the State Council to exercise unified control over diplomatic affairs and to formulate and to carry out and implement on behalf of the State and Government China's foreign policy, and to coordinate on behalf of the State Council the implementation of guidelines and policies in external relations. Its main functions are:

1) To conduct research and study on international situation and the situations of foreign countries, to constantly keep abreast of major new developments, and to provide information and recommendations to the Center for its formulation of diplomatic strategy, guidelines, policy and tactics.

2) To conduct diplomatic affairs on behalf of the State and the Government.

3) Exercise sectoral management of related external affairs on behalf of the State Council or according to authorization.

4) To conduct research and study on world economic situation and to be up to date with major international economic information, and to serve China's socialist economic construction and reform, and its opening to the outside world.

5) To carry out in its diplomacy the guidelines and policies of the Center regarding Hong Kong and Macau, and the resolution of the Taiwan question, and to promote the peaceful reunification of the motherland.

6) To exercise leadership over Chinese embassies, consulates and other related representations abroad.

7) To exercise leadership over organs directly subordinate to the MFA; to manage in an acting capacity the foreign affairs of the Chinese People's Association for Friendship with Foreign Countries, the Red Cross and the Soong Ching Ling Foundation; to exercise professional leadership in coordination with provinces and cities over local foreign affairs offices.

8) To take charge of the building of the cadres' corps and its ideological and political work; to recommend the appointment and dismissal of major diplomatic and consular officials of the MFA and of embassies, consulates and other related representations abroad; to exercise sectoral management of size of embassies, consulates and other related representations abroad.

9) To undertake other matters consigned by the Party Center and the State Council.

Appendix IV:
The Ministry of Foreign Trade and Economic Cooperation (MOFTEC)

Address & Telephone Numbers

2 Dong Changan Jie
Beijing, PRC
Postal Code 100731
Operator: 5126644
Situation Room: 5198368

Staff Size: 937

Main Functions

The MOFTEC's main tasks are: in accordance with the strategic aims for China's economic and social development formulated by the Party Center and the State Council, to draw up in conjunction with other relevant organs development strategies and plans for China's foreign economic cooperation and trade, to study and carry out the guidelines and policies in foreign economic cooperation and trade, to exercise macro control over and economic adjustment in the foreign economic cooperation and trade of the whole country, to strengthen organizational coordination and supervision and oversight, to improve legislation and service, and to ensure the smooth development of China's foreign economic and trade enterprise. Its main functions are:

1) To study and formulate strategic guidelines, planning and country policy and other related policies in foreign economic cooperation and trade, and to be responsible for the organization of their implementation after their approval by the State Council.

2) To be responsible, under the guidance of the unified State plan, for the collection and compilation or the participation in the compilation of related medium and long term and yearly foreign economic and trade plans, to be responsible for the supervision, management and data collection in foreign economic and trade businesses, to organize the construction of export commodity production bases, and to provide guidance to foreign economic and trade enterprises in the management and financial accounting.

3) To be responsible for the organization of inter-governmental economic and trade negotiations and joint committee meetings, under the authorization of the State Council, to enter into multilateral, bilateral governmental economic and trade treaties and agreements on behalf of China, and to be responsible for organizing and supervising their implementation. To provide coordination and guidance to regions and departments in their economic and trade cooperation with CIS and Eastern Europe.

4) To be responsible for the formulation of related rules and regulations in the management of foreign economic cooperation and trade, and to organize and supervise their implementation.

5) To study and formulate in conjunction with other related organs systemic reform plans and related measures in foreign economic cooperation and trade, and to organize their implementation after their approval by the State Council.

6) In accordance with the State plan, to be responsible for the organization and coordination in managing the negotiation and signing of foreign governmental loans, foreign business investments, technology imports and exports, and the import of complete plants, to examine and approve agreements and contracts concerning major projects utilizing foreign capital and technology.

7) To exercise sectoral management in foreign aid, to formulate country aid plans, and to organize the implementation of foreign economic aid projects and technical cooperation.

8) To exercise sectoral management in overseas projects involving contractual construction, labor export and overseas economic cooperation.

9) To exercise sectoral management of economic and technical cooperation and exchange with United Nations organization and other related international organizations, and to be responsible to receive and manage economic and technical aid from overseas.

10) To exercise sectoral management of import/export licenses and export quota system. To exercise sectoral examination of the setting up of foreign economic and trade enterprises at home and abroad. To exercise sectoral management of MOFTEC commercial offices, economic counsellor's offices in embassies and consulates abroad and its overseas enterprises. According to the regulations, to examine foreign business representations in China.

11) To participate in the study and formulation of the overall tariff rate, tariff structure, exchange rates and other regulating measures in external economic relations.

12) To exercise sectoral management of the business of international shipping agencies.

13) To organize research and study on international economic and trade situation and markets, and to keep abreast of international economic and trade information.

14) In accordance with the cadres' management regulations, to manage the personnel, labor and compensation work of MOFTEC cadres and cadres of its

subordinate organs. To exercise sectoral management of MOFTEC subordinate colleges and schools and the training of senior management personnel.

15) In accordance with the unified State policy, to provide guidance to organs attached to MOFTEC, and to provide guidance and organization and coordination to the economic and trade of different regions and organs.

16) To undertake matters consigned by the State Council.

Appendix V: The Hong Kong and Macau Affairs Office of the State Council (HMAO)

Address & Telephone Number

12 Baiwanzhuang Nan Jie
Beijing, PRC
Postal Code 100037
Situation Room: 8315014

Staff Size: 89

Main Functions

The HMAO is the functional organ of the State Council responsible for the control and process of Hong Kong and Macau affairs. Its main functions are:

1) To study and formulate the Chinese government's guidelines and policies regarding the restoration of its sovereignty over Hong Kong and Macau, and the realization of a smooth transition of power.

2) To be responsible for drafting the basic law for the two special administrative zones of Hong Kong and Macau.

3) To plan and arrange works during Hong Kong and Macau's transitional periods.

4) To control and manage in conjunction with the MFA the foreign affairs work in relation to Hong Kong and Macau, and to participate in the work of the Sino-British and Sino-Portuguese joint liaison groups and the land committee.

5) To formulate and implement guidelines and policies governing the exchanges between the mainland and Hong Kong and Macau regions in political, economic, cultural, social and other fields, and to coordinate various regions and departments to fully utilize Hong Kong and Macau to serve the four modernization of the mainland.

6) To conduct research and investigation, to be up to date about information and development in the politics, economy, culture and society of the Hong Kong and Macau regions, and to provided timely reports to the Center and the State Council.

7) To do a good job in conjunction with various regions and departments in the reception of, and united front and propaganda work toward people from various walks of life of Hong Kong and Macau visiting the mainland.

8) To examine and approve the setting up of organs in and dispatch of personnel to Hong Kong and Macau by various regions and departments; to provide its recommendation to the State Council regarding permission of visits to Hong Kong and Macau by cadres of and above vice ministerial/governatorial rank.

Appendix VI:
The Taiwan Affairs Office of the State Council (TAO)

Address & Telephone Number

13 Wenjin Jie, Xicheng Qü
Beijing, PRC
Postal Code 100017
Situation Room: 3098946

Staff Size: 45

Main Functions

1) To carry out and implement the guidelines and policies of the Center toward Taiwan, to put into effect telecommunications, postal and transport service between the mainland and Taiwan, and to develop personnel exchanges and economic and trade relations.

2) To supervise and examine the implementation of the guidelines and policies of the Center and the State Council toward Taiwan by various State Council organs and provinces, autonomous regions and municipalities under the direct jurisdiction of the Center. To process the RFI submitted by relevant departments and provinces, autonomous regions and municipalities under the direct jurisdiction of the Center to the State Council regarding Taiwanese affairs.

3) To be well informed of important domestic and overseas information regarding Taiwanese affairs, and to report timely to the Center and the State Council and to inform the relevant departments.

4) To conduct research and study on questions and problems in Taiwanese affairs work, and to organize relevant departments to put forward detailed policy regulations regarding Taiwanese work and their opinion on the conduct of Taiwanese work.

5) To provide overall planning and guidance in economic cooperation with Taiwan, in construction and development projects and in utilizing Taiwanese capital, technologies and market; to coordinate exchanges in education, science and technology, culture, health, sports and other fields.

6) To do a good job in conjunction with other relevant organs in the reception of people from various walks of life in Taiwan and other well-known personages.

7) To be responsible to make official statements in Taiwanese affairs.

8) To undertake matters consigned by the Central and State Council leading comrades.

Appendix VII:
The Overseas Chinese Affairs Office of the State Council (OCAO)

Address & Telephone Number

1 Beixinqiao Santiao, Dongcheng Qü
Beijing, PRC
Postal Code 100710
Situation Room: 4015683

Staff Size: 230

Main Functions

The main tasks of the OCAO of the State Council are: to assist the Party Center and the State Council in formulating guidelines and policies regarding overseas Chinese affairs, to coordinate overseas Chinese affairs work, and to supervise and examine the implementation of the guidelines and policies. To protect the just and legitimate rights and interests of overseas Chinese, returnees and their relatives, to promote the relative feelings with ethnic Chinese with foreign nationalities, to unite broadly with overseas Chinese, returnees and their relatives, and to contribute to the renewal of the Chinese nation, the reunification of the motherland and to the development of unity, friendship and cooperation with peoples of various countries. Its main functions are:

1) To conduct research and study on domestic and overseas situation in overseas Chinese work, and to provide the Party Center and the State Council with overseas Chinese affairs information.

2) To assist the Party Center and the State Council in formulating guidelines, policies and regulations and legislation regarding overseas Chinese affairs, to protect the just rights and interests of overseas Chinese, to protect the legitimate rights and interests of returned overseas Chinese and relatives of overseas Chinese, and to be responsible for the supervision and examination of their implementation; to conduct propaganda on overseas Chinese policies.

3) To provide necessary overall planning and coordination over relevant policies formulated by relevant organs that involve overseas Chinese, ethnic Chinese of foreign nationality, returnees, and their relatives, and over their work on

overseas Chinese and ethnic Chinese of foreign nationality, particularly on key persons.

4) To formulate long term development plans and yearly plans for overseas Chinese work, and to provide guidance to the work of local overseas Chinese affairs offices.

5) To draft in conjunction with the MFA guidelines and policies regarding overseas Chinese and ethnic Chinese of foreign nationality work, to provide guidance to Chinese embassies, consulates and other overseas institutions in carrying out work among overseas Chinese, ethnic Chinese of foreign nationality and their organizations; to provide overseas Chinese affairs cadres to key embassies and consulates, to set up private institutions in key countries and regions and to organize delegations and groups to visit abroad when necessary.

6) To carry out unity and friendship work with overseas Chinese, ethnic Chinese of foreign nationality and their organizations; to support relevant organs in introducing capital, technology and human resources from overseas Chinese and Chinese of foreign nationality.

7) To draft the guidelines and policies regarding propaganda work among overseas Chinese and Chinese of foreign nationality, and to maintain contact with and support in an appropriate manner media operations run by overseas Chinese and Chinese of foreign nationality.

8) To support relevant organs in Taiwanese work through overseas Chinese channels.

9) To study and draft the guidelines and policies regarding overseas Chinese donation, remittance, capital inflow and overseas Chinese enterprises; to provide necessary guidance and assistance to local state-run overseas Chinese farms in their economic systemic reforms.

10) To carry out work with returned overseas Chinese and overseas Chinese relatives, to support relevant organs to make appropriate appointments and arrangements for the representatives of returnees and overseas Chinese relatives.

11) To manage the settlement of returned overseas Chinese; to support local governments in providing assistance and relief to poor returnees and overseas Chinese relatives; to assist the State Council HMAO in making a good arrangement of settlement of Hong Kong and Macau compatriots on the mainland and in work in regard to their relatives.

12) To assist relevant organs to study and resolve relevant policy issues concerning the exit of overseas Chinese, returnees, and their relatives.

13) To exercise leadership over Jinan University, Overseas Chinese University and Beijing Overseas Chinese Practical School, and to provide guidance to relevant local overseas Chinese organs to do a good job in running Guangzhou and Jimei Overseas Chinese Practical School; to keep in touch and support Chinese language schools run by overseas Chinese and Chinese of foreign nationality.

14) To exercise leadership over China News Agency, and to do a good job in written, pictorial, audio and visual propaganda to overseas Chinese, Hong Kong and Macau compatriots, Taiwan compatriots, and ethnic Chinese of foreign nationality.

15) To exercise leadership over the General Office of China Travel Agency (China Overseas Chinese Travel Agency), and do a good job in the reception of

and service for overseas Chinese, Hong Kong and Macau compatriots, Taiwan compatriots, and Chinese of foreign nationality.

16) To exercise leadership over Hua Sheng newspaper, propagate the accomplishments of China's four modernization programs and the guidelines and policies regarding overseas Chinese work.

17) To exercise leadership over and manage overseas Chinese cadre schools.

18) To exercise leadership over and manage its Hong Kong and other overseas institutions.

19) To exercise leadership over the Overseas Chinese City in the Shenzhen Special Economic Zone, and to authorize Hong Kong China Travel Agency Group for its development and construction under the guidance of the municipal government of Shenzhen.

20) To undertake matters consigned by the State Council.

Appendix VIII: Xinhua News Agency

Address & Telephone Numbers

57 Xuanwumen Xi Da Jie
Beijing, PRC
Operator: 3071114
Situation Room: 3073741

Staff Size: 5788

Main Functions

1) Under the authorization of the Party and the State, to centralize the release of important documents, communiqués of the party and the State, and of important news; to collect and release news stories, pictures, to provide information to domestic and overseas news agencies, newspapers and periodicals, radios, television stations and other press agencies, to play the roles of a mouthpiece of the Party and the State and of an important front in propaganda and mass media.

2) To collect widely information on new domestic and overseas developments in politics, economy, culture and education, military, social life and other fields, including reception, processing, utilization and storage of various dispatches by foreign news agencies under the authorization of the State and in agreement with the agencies; to provide the Center in a timely, comprehensive and accurate manner various reference material for its decision making, to play well the role of ears and eyes of the Center.

3) To release news stories on a world scale, to give full coverage of important events in countries of the world, to fully reflect in particular the aspirations, demands of the third world and the positions and views of China; to further occupy the front of world mass media and to accelerate the construction of a world class news agency.

4) To develop various information materials, to gradually build an authoritative information center open to domestic and overseas concerns and serving the whole society and an information service network, to provide a channel for domestic and overseas information interchange serving the cause of reform and opening to the world and of the four modernizations, to contribute to the development of China's information industry, professional personnel and technologies,

and to actively develop various enterprises related to the news business; in the meantime to increase revenues in order to lessen the financial burden on the State.

5) To compile and publish internal publications for leading cadres; to compile and publish *Cankao Xiaoxi* (daily newspaper), *Jingji Cankao* (daily newspaper), the domestic and overseas editions of *Liaowang* (weekly periodical), *Banyue Tan*, *Huanqiu* (monthly periodical), *Xin Zhongguo Jikan* (English edition), and other newspapers and periodicals and books.

6) Under the authorization of the Party and the State, to develop relations and sign agreements with overseas official information and propaganda agencies and international organizations. To develop and strengthen in accordance with China's diplomatic strategies, guidelines and policies the friendship and exchanges with media of various countries of the world, to participate in the beneficial activities of the international media, to actively support the media enterprises of the third world, to greatly develop China's overseas media business, to expand China's influence, and to contribute to the mutual understanding between China and countries of the world, and to the development of China's independent diplomacy for peace.

7) To do a good job in running the China Pictorial Archive, to collect, sort, manage and keep on behalf of the Party and the State important domestic and overseas historical pictorial files; to do a good job in running the Information Research Institute and China Information College, to contribute to the study and development of information theories and to the training of senior information personnel for the Party and the State, and to train at the same time some information personnel for third world countries.

8) To exercise centralized management of domestic and overseas branch offices, and to create necessary working conditions for the branch offices and journalists.

9) To undertake other tasks consigned by the Party and the State.

Bibliography

Books

Allison, Graham T., *Essence of Decision: Explaining the Cuban Missile Crisis*, (Boston: Little, Brown, 1971)

Bachman, David, *To Leap Forward: Chinese Policy-making, 1956–1957*, (Stanford: Stanford University, 1984)

Barnett, A. Doak, *Cadres, Bureaucracy, and Political Power in China*, (New York: Columbia University Press, 1967)

———. *The Making of Foreign Policy in China: Structure and Process*, (Boulder: Westview Press, 1985)

———. *China and the Major Powers in East Asia* (Washington, DC: The Brookings Institution, 1977)

Bo Yibo, *Ruogan Zhongda Jüece yü Shijian de Huigu* (A Reminiscence on Some Major Decisions and Events), (Beijing: Zhongyang Dangxiao Chubanshe, 1991)

Cao Runfang and Pan Xianying (eds.), *Zhongguo Gongchandang Jiguan Fazhan Shi* (A History of the Evolution of CPC Organs), (Beijing: Dangan Chubanshe, 1988)

Chai Chengwen and Zhao *Yütian, Banmendian Tanpan* (The Panmunjom Negotiations), (Beijing: Jiefangjün Chubanshe, 1992)

Chen Xiaolu, *Jinian Chen Yi* (In Memory of Chen Yi), (Beijing: Wenwu Chubanshe, 1991)

Cheng Hua (ed.), *Zhou Enlai he ta de Mishumen* (Zhou Enlai and his Secretaries), (Beijing: Zhongguo Guangbo Dianshi Chubanshe, 1992)

Crozier, Michel, *The Bureaucratic Phenomenon*, (Chicago: University of Chicago Press, 1960)

Cyert, Richard M., and March, James G., *A Behavioral Theory of the Firm*, (Eaglewood Cliffs, N.J.: Prentice-Hall, 1963)

Dial, Roger L., (ed.), *Advancing and Contending Approaches to the Study of Chinese Foreign Policy*, (Halifax, N.S.: Centre for Foreign Policy Studies, Dalhouseie University, 1974)

Dome, Jurgen, *The Government and Politics of the PRC: A Time of Transition*, (Boulder: Westview Press, 1985)

Eftimiades, Nicholas, *Chinese Intelligence Operations*, (Annapolis: Naval Institute Press, 1994)

Fan Shuo, *Ye Jianying zai 1976* (Ye Jianying in 1976), (Beijing: Zhonggong Dangxiao Chubanshe, 1990)

Gottlieb, Thomas M., *Chinese Foreign Policy Factionalism and the Origins of the Strategic Triangle*, (Santa Monica: Rand Corp., 1977)

Guojia Jigou Bianzhi Wenyüanhui, (ed.), *Zhongguo Zhengfu Jigou* (China Government Organization) (Beijing: Zhongguo Renshi Chubanshe, 1991)

Halpern, Nina, *Economic Specialists and the Making of Chinese Economic Policy, 1955–1983*, (Ann Arbor: University of Michigan, 1985)

Hamrin, Carol Lee, and Suisheng Zhao (eds.), *Decision Making in Deng's China*, (Armonk: M.E. Sharpe, 1995)

Hao, Yüfan, and Huan, Guocang, (eds.), *The Chinese View of the World*, (New York: Pantheon Books, 1989)

Harding, Harry, *A Fragile Relationship: the United States and China Since 1972*, (Washington, D.C.: Brookings Institution, 1992)

Harding, Harry, (ed.), *China's Foreign Relations in the 1980s*, (New Haven: Yale University Press, 1984)

———. *Organizing China: the Problem of Bureaucracy, 1949–1976*, (Stanford: Stanford University Press, 1981)

———. *Maoist Theories of Policy-making and Organization* (Santa Monica: Rand, 1969)

Harding, Harry, and Yuan, Ming, (ed.), *Sino-American Relations, 1945–1955*, (Wilmington: SR Books, 1989)

Hoxha, Enver, *Reflections on China: Extracts from the Political Diary*, (Tirana: Nentori Publishing House, 1979)

Khaled Bin Sultan, *Desert Warrior: A Personal View of the Gulf War by the Joint Forces Commander*, (New York: HarperCollins Publishers, 1995)

Kleist, Anna von, *Ich Kämpfte Für Mao*, (Hamburg: Holsten Verlag, 1973).

Lampton, David M., *Health, Conflict, and the Chinese Political System*, (Ann Arbor: University of Michigan's Center for Chinese Studies, 1974)

———. *The Politics of Medicine in China: The Policy Process, 1949–1977*, (Boulder: Westview Press, 1975)

———. *Policy Implementation in the People's Republic of China*, (Berkeley: University of California Press, 1987)

Lee, Hong Yung, *From Revolutionary Cadres to Party Technocrats in Socialist China*, (Berkeley: University of California Press, 1991)

Lewis, John Wilson, and Xüe, Litai, *China Builds the Bomb*, (Stanford: Stanford University Press, 1988)

Li Zhisui, *Mao Zedong Siren Yisheng Huiyilu* (The Private Life of Chairman Mao) (Taipei: China Times Publishing Company, 1994)

Lieberthal, Kenneth G., and Lampton, David M., (eds), *Bureaucracy, Politics, and Decision Making in Post-Mao China*, (Berkeley: University of California Press, 1992)

Lin Ke, Xü Tao and Wu Xüjün, *Lishi de Zhenshi* (The True Life of Mao Zedong) (Hongkong: Liwen Chubanshe, 1995)

Lovejoy, Charles, and Watson, Bruce W., (eds.), *China's Military Reforms: International and Domestic Implications*, (Boulder: Westview Press, 1986)

Lu Ning, *Flashpoint Spratlys*, (Singapore: Dolphin Books, 1995)

Maomao, *Wode Fuqin Deng Xiaoping* (My Father Deng Xiaoping) (Beijing: Zhongyang Wenxian Chubanshe, 1993)

March, James G., and Simon, Herbert A., *Organizations* (New York: John Wiley, 1958)
Nie Rongzhen, *Nie Rongzhen Huiyilu* (Nie Rongzhen Memoirs) (Beijing: Jiefangjün Chubanshe, 1984)
Oksenberg, Michel, and Lieberthal, Kenneth, *Policy Making in China: Leaders, Structures, and Processes*, (Princeton: Princeton University Press, 1988)
Pei Jianzhang (ed.), *Yanjiü Zhou Enlai Waijiao Sixiang yü Shijian* (A Study of Zhou Enlai's Diplomatic Thoughts and Practice) (Beijing: Shijie Zhishi Chubanshe, 1989)
Pei Jianzhang et al (eds.), *Xin Zhongguo Waijiao Fengyün* (New China Diplomacy) (Beijing: Shijie Zhishi Chubanshe, 1989)
Peng, Dehuai, *Memoirs of a Chinese Marshal*, (Beijing: Foreign Language Press, 1984)
Pye, Lucian, *The Spirit of Chinese Politics*, (Cambridge, Mass.: MIT Press, 1968)
Quan Yanchi, *Zouxia Shengtan de Zhou Enlai* (Zhou Enlai Desanctified) (Beijing: Zhonggong Zhongyang Dangxiao Chubanshe, 1994)
Rourke, John T., *Making Foreign Policy: United States, Soviet Union, China*, (Pacific Grove, Calif.: Brooks/Cole Publishing Co., 1990)
Rozman, Gilbert, *The Chinese Debate about Soviet Socialism, 1978–1985* (Princeton: Princeton University Press, 1987)
Salisbury, Harrison, *The New Emperors: China in the Era of Mao and Deng*, (Boston: Little, Brown & Company, 1992)
———. *The Long March: the Untold Story*, (Franklin Center, Pa.: Franklin Library, 1985)
Scalapino, Robert A., (ed.), *Elites in the People's Republic of China*, (Seattle: University of Washington Press, 1972)
Schurman, Franz, *Ideology and Organization in Communist China*, (Berkeley: University of California Press, 1967)
Shi Zhe, *Zai Lishi Jüren Shenbian: Shi Zhe Huiyilu* (By the Side of Historical Colossi: Shi Zhe's Memoirs) (Beijing: Zhongyang Wenxian Chubanshe, 1991)
Shih, Chih-yu, *The Spirit of Chinese Foreign Policy: A Psychocultural View*, (Houdmills: Macmillan, 1990)
Simon, Herbert A., *Administrative Behavior*, (New York: Macmillan, 1957)
Snyder, Richard C., et al, (eds), *Foreign Policy Decision-making*, (New York: The Free Press, 1963)
Solinger, Dorothy, *Chinese Business Under Socialism*, (Berkeley: University of California, 1984)
Solomon, Richard H., *Chinese Political Negotiating Behavior: A Briefing Analysis*, (Santa Monica: Rand, 1985)
———. *Mao's Revolution and the Chinese Political Culture*, (Berkeley and LA: University of California Press, 1971)
Stavis, Benedict, *The Politics of Agricultural Mechanization in China*, (Ithaca: Cornell University Press, 1978)
Steinbruner, John D., *The Cybernetic Theory of Decisions of Political Analysis*, (Princeton: Princeton University Press, 1974)
Sutter, Robert G., *East Asia and the Pacific: Challenges for U.S. Policy*, (Boulder: Westview Press, 1992)

———. *Chinese Foreign Policy: Developments After Mao*, (New York: Praeger, 1986)

———. *Chinese Foreign Policy After the Cultural Revolution, 1966–1977*, (Boulder: Westview Press, 1978)

Waijiaobu (Ministry of Foreign Affairs), *Dangdai Zhongguo Waijiao* (Contemporary Chinese Diplomacy)

Wang, Bingnan, *Zhongmei Huitan Jiünian Huigu* (Nine Years of Sino-US Talks Remembered) (Beijing: Shijie Zhishi Chubanshe, 1985)

Wang Li, *Xianchang Lishi: Wenhua Dageming Jishi* (Eyewitness to History: A Record of Events in the Great Cultural Revolution), (Oxford: Oxford University Press, 1993)

Wang, Yan, *China and Disarmament, 1980–1986*, (Geneva: Institut Universitaire de Hautes Etudes Internationales, 1990)

Whiting, Allen Suess, *China Crosses the Yalu: The Decision to Enter the Korean War*, (Stanford: Stanford University Press, 1968)

Whitson, William W., *The Chinese High Command: A History of Communist Military Politics, 1927–71*, (New York: Praeger, 1973)

Wilhelm, Alfred D., *The Chinese at the Negotiating Table: Style and Characteristics*, (Washington, D.C.: National Defense University Press, 1991)

Wu, Hsiu-chuan, *Eight Years in the Ministry of Foreign Affairs: Memoirs of a Diplomat*, (Beijing: New World Press, 1985)

Xü Jiatun, *Xü Jiatun Xianggang Huiyilu* (Xü Jiatun's Hong Kong Memoirs), (Hong Kong: H.K. Lianhebao Youxian Gongsi, 1993)

Xü, Yan, *Diyici Jiaoliang: Kangmeiyuanchao Zhanzheng de Lishi Huigu he Fansi* (The First Trial: the War of Resistance Against the United States and Aiding Korea: A Historical Review and Reflection), (Beijing: Zhongguo Guangbodianshi Chubanshe, 1990)

———. *Jinmen zhi Zhan* (The Battle of Kinmen), (Beijing: Zhongguo Guangbodianshi Chubanshe, 1992)

Ye Fei, *Ye Fei Huiyilu* (Ye Fei's Memoirs), (Beijing: Jiefangjün Chubanshe, 1988)

Ye Yonglie, *Jiang Qing Zhuan* (A Biography of Jiang Qing), (Beijing: Zuojia Chubanshe, 1993) Zhang Hanzhi, *Wo yü Qiao Guanhua* (Qiao Guanhua and I), (Beijing: Zhongguo Qingnian Chubanshe, 1994)

Zhang Hanzhi, *Wo yü Qiao Guanhua* (Qiao Guanhua and I), (Beijing: Zhongguo Qingnian Chubanshe, 1994)

Zhang Yünsheng, *Lin Biao Mishu Huiyilu: Maojiawan Jishi* (The Memoirs of Lin Biao's Secretary: A Record of Events at Maojiawan), (Hong Kong: Cunzhen Chubanshe, 1988)

Zheng Qian and Han Gang, *Wannian Suiyüe: 1956 Nian hou de Mao Zedong* (The Late Years: Mao Zedong After 1956), (Beijing: Zhongguo Qingnian Chubanshe, 1993)

Zheng Qian, Pang Song, Han Gang and Zhang Zhanbin, *Dangdai Zhongguo Zhengzhi Tizhi Fazhan Gaiyao* (An Outline of the Evolution of the Contemporary Chinese Political System), (Beijing: Zhonggong Dangshi Ziliao Chubanshe, 1988)

Zhongguo Gongchandang Zhisheng Sishi Nian (The CPC's Forty Years in Power) (Beijing: Zhonggong Dangshi Ziliao Chubanshe, 1989)

Zhu Lin, *Dashi Furen Huiyilu* (Memoirs of An Ambassador's Wife), (Beijing: Shijie Zhishi Chubanshe, 1991)

Articles

Bin Yü, "The Study of Chinese Foreign Policy: Problems and Prospects," *World Politics*, 46, January 1994.

Chen, Qimao, "New Approaches in China's Foreign Policy," *Asian Survey*, V. 33, March 1993

Chen Youwei, "*Qiao Guanhua Gaiguan Shinian reng wei Lunding* (The Verdict is Still Out Ten Years After Qiao Guanhua's Death)," *Shijie Zhoukan* (World Journal Weekly), October 3, 1993.

Christensen, Thomas J., "Threats, Assurances, and the Last Chance for Peace," *International Security*, V. 17, Summer 1992.

Cold War International History Project Bulletin, Washington: Woodrow Wilson International Center for Scholars, various issues.

Garver, John W., "China's Push through the South China Sea: The Interaction of Bureaucratic and National Interest," *The China Quarterly*, No. 132, December 1992.

Ge Ai, "*Zhonggong Duitai Gongzuo Xinbushu* (CPC's New Arrangement for its Taiwanese Work)," *Guangjiaojing* (Wide Angle), December 1988.

Gurtov, Melvin, "The Foreign Ministry and Foreign Affairs During the Cultural Revolution" in *The China Quarterly*, Oct–Dec 1969.

Hua Di, "China's Case: Ballistic Missile Proliferation" in William C. Potter and Harlan W. Jencks (eds.), *The International Missile Bazaar: The New Suppliers' Network*, (Boulder: Westview Press, 1994)

Hunt, Michael H., "Beijing and the Korean Crisis, June 1950–June 1951," *Political Science Quarterly*, V. 107, Fall 1992.

Jan, George P., "The Ministry of Foreign Affairs in China Since the Cultural Revolution," *Asian Survey*, V. 17, June 1977.

Jiang Weiwen, "*Zhonggong Gaoceng Gaige Da Pilu: Zhonggong Gaoceng Renshi Da Tiaozheng* (A Big Exposé of the Reform Plan for High Level CPC Bodies: A Big Reshuffle of High Ranking CPC Officials), *Guangjiaojing* (Wide Angle), No. 184, January 16, 1988.

Kim, Samuel K., "China and the World in Theory and Practice" in Kim (ed.), *China and the World: Chinese Foreign Relations in the Post-Cold War Era*, (Boulder: Westview Press, 1994)

Klein, Donald W., "The Management of Foreign Affairs in Communist China" in John Lindbeck (ed.), *China: Management of a Revolutionary Society*, (Seattle: University of Washington Press, 1971)

Lewis, John, Hua Di and Xüe Litai, "Beijing's Defence Establishment," *International Security*, 15:4, 1991.

Linblom, Charles E., "The Science of Muddling Through," *Public Administration Review*, Spring 1959

March, James G., "Bounded Rationality, Ambiguity, and the Engineering of Choice," *Bell Journal of Economics*, Autumn 1978.

Oksenberg, Michel, "Methods of Communication Within the Chinese Bureaucracy," *The China Quarterly*, No. 57, Jan.–Mar. 1974.

Pang Song and Han Gang, "*Dang he Guojia Lingdao Tizhi de Lishi Kaocha yü Gaige Zhanwang* (A Historical Review and Reform Outlook of the Party and State Leadership System)," *Zhongguo Shehui Kexüe*, No. 6, November 10, 1987.

Rosenau, James, "China in a Bifurcated World: Competing Theoretical Perspectives" in Thomas Robinson and David Shambaugh (eds.), *Chinese Foreign Policy: Theory and Practice*, (New York: Oxford University Press, 1993)

Shambaugh, David L., "China's National Security Research Bureaucracy," *The China Quarterly*, No. 110, June 1987,

Si Maqian, "*Zhonggong Waishi Xiaozu Qüanmian Gaizu: Li Peng Kaishi Zhangguan Zhongguo Waijiao* (A Comprehensive Reorganization of the CPC Foreign Affairs LSG: Li Peng Begins to Control Chinese Diplomacy)," *Guangjiaojing* (Wide Angle), January 16, 1988.

Simon, Herbert A., "A Behavioral Model of Rational Choice," *Models of Man: Social and Rational*, (New York: John Wiley, 1958)

Yan Huai, "*Zhongguo Dalu Zhengzhi Tizhi Qianlun* (Understanding the Political System of Contemporary China)," *Papers of the Center for Modern China*, No. 10, August 1991.

———. "*Zhongguo Mimi Wenjian Gaiyao* (Notes on China's Confidential Documents)," *Paper of the Center for Modern China*, No. 12, December 1993.

Yan Kong, "China's Arms Trade Bureaucracy," *Jane's Intelligence Review*, February 1994.

Yitzhak, Shichor, *East Wind Over Arabia: Origins and Implications of the Sino-Saudi Missile Deal* (Berkeley: Institute of East Asian Studies, 1989)

Zhao, Quansheng, "Domestic Factors of Chinese Foreign Policy: From Vertical to Horizontal Authoritarianism," China's Foreign Relations, *Annals of the American Academy of Political and Social Sciences*, V. 519, 1992.

About the Book and Author

Drawing on archival materials, interviews, and personal experiences, Lu Ning, former assistant to a vice-foreign minister of China, provides unique insights into the key players and the formal as well as informal structures, processes, mechanisms, and dynamics of foreign-policy decisionmaking in Beijing. Lu sheds light on such controversial decisions as China's entering the Korean War, selling DF–3 missiles to Saudi Arabia in 1986, and cooperating with the Israeli defense establishment.

Offering an insightful view of the inner workings of Beijing's foreign ministry, Lu introduces new Chinese language sources and presents a series of case studies that challenge existing Western theoretical analysis of Chinese policymaking. Based on his examination of the past forty years, Lu makes predictions about likely changes in Beijing's leadership and in its foreign-policy decisionmaking process. This accessibly written, incisive book will be invaluable to anyone interested in Sinology, Chinese foreign policy, comparative foreign policy, and contemporary international relations of East Asia.

Lu Ning, formerly a Chinese career foreign service officer, is a correspondent for *The Business Times* in Singapore.

Index

Africa, 112, 120
   and diplomatic recognition, 47
   South, relations with, 111, 112
Anti-Rightist Campaign, 2, 48, 131, 153
Arab countries, 112, 113, 128, 129, 130
Arms exports, 111, 113, 127, 128, 165.
   See also Iran-Iraq War
Atomic bomb, 92

Braun, Otto, 41, 60
Brezhnev, Leonid, 83
Bureaucracies
   central, 13–15
   and foreign affairs, 3, 179, 180
   shift in power of, 175
Bush, George, 89, 160

Cable News Network (CNN), 24, 25
Cadres' corps. *See* Ministry of Foreign Affairs
CASS. *See* Chinese Academy of Social Sciences
Central Intelligence Agency (U.S.), 120, 121
Chen Yi, 55, 107, 152, 153, 155
   as foreign minister, 54
   See also Third Field Army Group
Chen Yun, 10, 152, 156, 157
   death of, 180
   and decisionmaking, 158, 177
Chiang Kai-shek. *See* Jiang Jieshi
China Institute of International Strategic Studies (CIIS), 51, 134
Chinese Academy of Social Sciences (CASS), 134, 140
Chinese civil war, 43, 44, 77, 78
   and Korea, 79
   See also United States, intervention in
Chongqing Group, 60, 61
Cold War
   changes afterwards, 4
   and international relations, 1
Comintern, 41, 60, 61
   See also Communist Party of China
Commission for External Cultural Liaison, 13
Commission for Overseas Chinese Affairs, 13
Commission of Science, Technology and Industry for National Defense (COSTIND), 14, 123
   function of, 127–130
   and information flow, 32
   and warhead design, 115, 116
   See also Israel
Communist Party of China (CPC), 2, 7, 9, 10
   as apex, 8

213

and Comintern, 40
and Cultural Revolution, 55
and democratic centralism, 16
and information flow, 29
pre-revolution years, 41–42
role of leader vs. nuclear circle, 162
See also International Liaison Department; Mao Zedong; Politboro Standing Committee
Confidential Communications Bureau, 21
and information flow, 29
Confidential Traffic Division, 21
and information flow, 29
COSTIND. *See* Commission of Science, Technology and Industry for National Defense
Cultural Revolution, 10, 11, 107, 154, 155, 156
aftermath of, 62–64
and dismantling of institutions, 50
factionalism during, 54–59
and foreign relations, 49
and language schools, 49, 51

Deng Xiaoping, 8, 9, 10, 54
and decisionmaking, 88, 94, 155
and "emancipation of the mind" campaign, 26, 88, 158
and foreign policy initiation, 33, 35
health of, 58, 180
leadership style, 178
and reform, 2
and relations with the U.S., 88, 89, 140, 141, 142, 157
retirement, 7, 159
and Secretariat, 11
See also Gang of Four
Dixie mission, 42

Economic development, 155, 161–166

Foreign Affairs Leading Small Group, 13, 34, 90, 152, 159
cessation of, 154
changing composition of, 161
function of, 11, 12, 107, 108

and information flow, 33
and Ministry of Foreign Affairs, 20
and Peoples Liberation Army, 123
Foreign Affairs Office, 12, 13, 34, 152, 161
elimination of, 155
and General Office, 21
main functions of, 187
structure of, 107, 108
Foreign Language School, 43, 121
See also University of Foreign Studies
Foreign Ministry Bulletin, 28
France, 137
and diplomatic recognition, 47

Gang of Four, 53, 107
and battle with Deng Xiaoping, 57
See also Qiao Guanhua
General Office
function of, 27, 28
and information flow, 30
structure of, 21
General Staff Department, 20, 106
and missile development, 116
role of, 120–123
Germany, West, 137–139
Gorbachev, Mikhail, 93
Great Leap Forward, 152, 153
Grenada, 109
U.S. invasion of, 110
Gross national product, 1

Hong Kong, 2
Hua Di, 139–143
Hua Guofeng, 10, 87
as leader, 58, 155, 156, 157
Hu Yaobang, 9, 10, 11, 157, 158, 179

Information Department, Fourth Division, 23, 30, 132, 136
and Grenada invasion, 110
structure of, 24–27
Institute for Contemporary International Relations, 133
Institute of International Studies, 22
function of, 131–132

Index 215

International Liaison Department, 14,
    20, 106
  changing role, 165
  function of, 118, 156
  and information flow, 32
International relations
  institutes of, 122. *See also* specific
    institutes
  and political system, 2
  shift of focus in, 1
Iran-Iraq War, 112, 113, 123
Israel, 111, 112, 115, 121, 163
  military imports from, 128–130

Japan, 111, 139, 158
  army of, 42
  peace treaty of *1978*, 157
Jiang Jieshi (Chiang Kai-shek), 40, 81
Jiang Zemin, 8, 9, 10
  and decisionmaking, 160
  as General Secretary, 159, 162
Ji Pengfei, 52, 57, 60, 107, 137, 157
  as ambassador, 45
  and Cultural Revolution, 54,
    55
  leadership of, 161
  position in party, 160
  See also Third Field Army Group
Johnson Reef, 126
Journal on International Studies, 131–132

Ke Bainian, 44
  and Americans, 42
  and Marshall mission, 43
  See also Chongqing Group
Khrushchev, 151
  and Beijing visit, 152, 153
Kim Il Sung, 79, 81, 82, 83
Kissinger, Henry, 56, 57
  Beijing visit, 138
  and Chinese rapprochement with
    the U.S., 85, 86
Korea, 118, 178
  Chinese intervention in, 79–83, 151
  South, relations with, 111, 112,
    125–126, 163
  war of *1950*, 2, 3, 47, 128, 173

Leading small groups, function of, 12
Lin Biao, 9, 51, 56, 153
  fall of, 155
  and opposition to Korean
    intervention, 82
  and Sino-Soviet relations, 84
Li Peng, 8, 9, 10, 159, 160, 166
  and political leadership, 162
Liü Shaoqi, 9, 54, 78, 153
Li Xiannian, 10, 155, 156, 157, 158, 159,
    160
  and decisionmaking, 177
Local foreign affairs
  office, 43
  structure, 15–16
Long March, 3, 41, 43, 60
Lushan Conference, 2

MacArthur, Douglas, 81, 82
Mali, 119–120
Mao Zedong, 8, 9, 137
  deteriorating health, 56, 87
  distrust of intellectuals, 130
  early years of the People's Republic
    of China, 2
  era of, 17, 136
  and foreign policy initiation, 33, 35
  leadership style, 178
  opposition to, 60//
  and power structure, 7
  and radicals, 55, 59
  role in decisionmaking, 77–79, 94,
    177
  and Secretariat, 11//
  and Sino-Soviet relations, 83, 84,
    150, 151, 154
  "starting a new kitchen" policy, 45
  See also Anti-Rightist Campaign;
    Korea, Chinese intervention in
Marshall mission, 43
Middle East, 113, 114, 115, 136, 152
  oil imports from, 2
Mikoyan, Anastas, 78
Military program, 1
  control of, 9
  reduction of, 127

Ministry of Defense, 13
Ministry of Foreign Affairs (MFA), 4, 13, 20, 106, 142, 160, 161
  cadres' corps, 47//
  and decisionmaking, 111, 163
  erosion of role, 164
  formal structure of, 21, 108
  formative years, 44–47
  and information flow, 23–33, 117. *See also* specific media
  and Israel, 130
  main functions of, 189
  and missile sales, 115
  and nuclear ship visits, 92
  and patron-client relationship, 60, 65
  and policy control, 111–113
  pre-revolution years, 40–44
  and public news briefings, 22
  radicalism within, 55, 59
  and Standing Committee, 20
  subsidiary institutions, 22–23
  See also Peking Foreign Language Institute
Ministry of Foreign Trade and Economic Cooperation (MOFTEC), 13, 20, 106
  function of, 117–118, 163, 191
  growing influence, 165
  and information flow, 32
Missiles, 115–117
  ballistic, 112
  export of, 112
  surface-to-surface, 113, 114
  See also People's Liberation Army, PLA Navy; Trade//
MOFTEC. *See* Ministry of Foreign Trade and Economic Cooperation

Nationalists, 40, 43, 77, 78
  See also Quemoy
New Development Division. *See* Information Department, Fourth Division
New Zealand, 90, 91
Nixon, Richard, 83, 84, 86, 136, 178
  visit to China, 87, 137, 140

NORINCO (North Industrial Corporation). *See* Arms exports
Nuclear circle
  importance of, 9
  decisionmaking within, 16
Nuclear ship visits, 92

Oil imports, 2
Open door policy, 162, 163

Peking Foreign Language Institute (PFLI), 49, 51
  and Ministry of Foreign Affairs, 48
  rebels within, 54, 59
  See also University of Foreign Studies
People's Liberation Army (PLA), 3, 14, 84, 107, 161
  and arms market, 122, 123
  and Cultural Revolution, 55
  and Korean War, 80
  and missile talks, 114//
  and nuclear ship visits, 92
  PLA Navy (PLAN), 124–127
  reduction of, 123
  role in foreign affairs, 165, 178
  See also General Staff Development; Israel; Quemoy
Personnel Department, 21–22
PFLI. *See* Peking Foreign Language Institute
Physical security, 155, 156
PLA Navy (PLAN). *See* People's Liberation Army, PLA Navy
Politboro Standing Committee, 8, 11, 34, 79, 86, 88, 156
  communication within, 33
  decisionmaking in, 16, 93, 150
  function and importance of, 9–10, 12, 76, 160, 163, 180
  ineffective management by, 154
  and 13th Party Congress, 159
  and U.S. relations, 90
  See also Ministry of Foreign Affairs

Qian Qichen, 13, 50, 52, 59, 63, 107, 164

Index 217

and Foreign Affairs Office, 161
and Ministry of Foreign Affairs, 64, 65
Qiao Guanhua, 54, 55, 56, 59, 137
  accusations against, 61
  as Foreign Minister, 57, 62
  and Gang of Four, 58
  and United Nations, 65
Quemoy, 152–153

Radicalism. *See* Ministry of Foreign Affairs
Reagan, Ronald, 89, 90, 142
  administration of, 109
  and pro-Taiwan stance, 158
Reference Material. See Xinhua News Agency

Secretariat, 12, 76, 79, 93
  and decisionmaking, 150, 154
  function of, 10–11, 157, 160
  and information flow, 30
  and Ministry of Foreign Affairs, 21
  reduction of, 159
Shanghai Institute of International Relations, 16
Situation Room, 30
  daily briefings, 24–25
  structure of, 21
Snow, Edgar, 41, 42, 85
South China Sea, 1, 126–127
Soviet Union, 48, 94, 115, 137, 138, 157, 174
  alliance with, 2, 88, 90
  and Chinese economy, 77
  conflicts with China, 84, 109, 158
  disintegration of, 160
  and expansionism, 140
  and hijacked airliner, 93
  and Korean conflict, 81–83
  and military buildup, 83
  normalization of relations with, 162, 163
  Russian Group, 60
  training in, 45
  See also Mao Zedong, Sino-Soviet relations

Spratly Islands. *See* South China Sea
Stalin, Josef, 77, 78
  and Korean conflict, 80, 82, 83
  talks with Mao, 150, 151
Standing Committee. *See* Politboro Standing Committee
State Science Commission, 13

Taiwan, 2, 80, 81, 89, 114, 120, 124, 140, 152, 153
  U.S. aircraft sales to, 160
Tang Wensheng. *See* Young Mistresses
Third Field Army Group, 60, 61
  and Cultural Revolution, 63
Tiananmen incident, 4
Trade
  with Asia-Pacific region, 1
  in missile and nuclear technologies, 1
  with United States, 1
  with Western Europe, 1
  See also Ministry of Foreign Trade and Economic Cooperation
Treaties, international, 79
Truman, Harry
  and Korean War, 80
  and Marshall mission, 43

United Nations, 49, 56, 57, 65, 87, 129
  and Korean airliner incident, 109
  and Korean conflict, 82
United States, 174
  and international arms market, 123
  intervention in Chinese civil war, 78, 79
  intervention in Korean war, 80–83
  rapprochement with, 83–87, 122, 178
  rivalry with Soviet Union, 109, 136
  tension with, 1, 3, 81
  weapons detection by, 116, 117
  See also Bush, George; Central Intelligence Agency; Deng Xiaoping, relations with the U.S.; Grenada, U.S. invasion; Hua Di; New Zealand; Trade; Zhao Ziyang, relations with the U.S.

University of Foreign Studies, 46

Vietnam, 81, 118, 126–127, 178
  border conflict with, 157
  war in, 5, 83, 88, 136
Voice of America, 24, 25

Wang Bingnan, 41, 43, 45
  and Friendship Association, 52
  and Ministry of Foreign Affairs, 44, 60
  pre-revolution years, 42
  and United Nations, 65
  See also Chongqing Group
Wang Hairong. *See* Young Mistresses
Wang Jiaxiang, 41, 44, 45, 55, 60, 62
  fall of, 61
Wang Shu. *See* Xinhua News Agency
World Affairs Publishing House, 22

Xi'an Incident, 41
Xinhua News Agency, 13, 106, 117, 120, 138
  Hong Kong office, 44
  main functions of, 203
  news analysis and commentaries by, 25
  and *Reference Material*, 24, 25, 29, 30
  role of, 118–119
  and Wang Shu, 138–139

Yang Shangkun, 9, 13
Young Mistresses, 56, 57, 59
  removal from power, 58

Zhang Wentian, 42, 43, 44, 45, 55, 60, 62
  fall of, 61
Zhao Ziyang, 9, 10, 88, 107, 141
  and decisionmaking, 158
  as General Secretary, 159
  meeting with Reagan, 142
  and missile sales, 115, 116
  in nuclear circle, 160
  as Premier of State Council, 157, 166
  and relations with the U.S., 158
  visit to U.S., 89–90
Zhou Enlai, 9, 33, 41, 79, 87, 152, 153
  death of, 58, 87
  and decisionmaking, 94, 150, 154, 155, 177
  and Foreign Affairs Group, 43
  and Japan, 139
  and Korean conflict, 80–83
  and Marshall mission, 43
  and Ministry of Foreign Affairs, 20, 44, 54, 60, 117, 164
  and nuclear weapons, 92
  and party structure, 45, 46
  and pre-revolution years, 42
  and radicals, 55, 59
  and rapprochement with the U.S., 85, 86, 89, 90
  role in training and recruitment, 48, 50
  and Secretariat, 11
  See also Chongqing Group